CW01116570

SERVANTS

SERVANTS

*English Domestics
in the Eighteenth Century*

BRIDGET HILL

CLARENDON PRESS · OXFORD
1996

Oxford University Press, Walton Street, Oxford OX2 6DP
Oxford New York
Athens Auckland Bangkok Bombay
Calcutta Cape Town Dar es Salaam Delhi
Florence Hong Kong Istanbul Karachi
Kuala Lumpur Madras Madrid Melbourne
Mexico City Nairobi Paris Singapore
Taipei Tokyo Toronto
and associated companies in
Berlin Ibadan

Oxford is a trade mark of Oxford University Press

Published in the United States
by Oxford University Press Inc., New York

© Bridget Hill 1996

All rights reserved. No part of this publication may be reproduced, stored in a retrieval system, or transmitted, in any form or by any means, without the prior permission in writing of Oxford University Press. Within the UK, exceptions are allowed in respect of any fair dealing for the purpose of research or private study, or criticism or review, as permitted under the Copyright, Designs and Patents Act, 1988, or in the case of reprographic reproduction in accordance with the terms of the licences issued by the Copyright Licensing Agency. Enquiries concerning reproduction outside these terms and in other countries should be sent to the Rights Department, Oxford University Press, at the address above

British Library Cataloguing in Publication Data
Data available

Library of Congress Cataloging in Publication Data
Hill, Bridget.
Servants: English domestics in the eighteenth century/Bridget Hill.
p. cm.
Includes bibliographical references (p.   ) and index.
1. Domestics—England—History—18th century. 2. England—Social life and customs—18th century. 3. England—Social conditions—18th century. I. Title.
HD8039.D52G7757   1996   331.7′6164046′09420933—dc20   95-50429
ISBN 0-19-820621-6

1 3 5 7 9 10 8 6 4 2

Typeset by Best-set Typesetter Ltd., Hong Kong
Printed in Great Britain
on acid-free paper by
Biddles Ltd., Guildford & King's Lynn

Preface

One thing I have become increasingly aware of in the course of writing this book is the enormous debt that is owed to those pioneers, D. M. Stuart, Dorothy Marshall, and, perhaps more particularly, J. Jean Hecht, who wrote on domestic service long before it was seen as a respectable subject for historians. Hecht's bibliography alone is invaluable for anyone starting to research into domestic service. Without their pioneering work this book would have been far more difficult to write and have taken many more years to complete.

Among the many people contributing to this volume are Mary Prior and Roger Lonsdale, both of whom gave most generously of their time to read sections of the book and made invaluable comments and suggestions. I am indebted to the OUP reader for many stimulating and constructive criticisms. For important references I must thank Joan Thirsk, Bernard Capp, Peter Earle, and Sir Keith Thomas. Maxine Berg kindly lent me her copy of the Julius Hardy diary. Two seminars, one at the University of Belo Horizonte, Brazil, in 1993 and the other at Berkeley in 1994 helped to clarify my thoughts. I benefited greatly from a discussion with Tim Meldrum and others on domestic service, at the London conference on Women's Initiatives in Early Modern England (organized by the Achievement Project) in June 1994, and from the discussion following a paper given at the British Society for Eighteenth-Century Studies Annual Conference in 1995. I would especially like to thank all those at the History Faculty Library in Oxford who have been consistently helpful and tolerant, as well as those at the Bodleian Library. My editor at the Press has been both encouraging and supportive. I would also like to thank Hilary McKee, Sheila Fisher, and Jonathan Ree for valuable injections of adrenalin when it was most needed. As always my greatest debt is to Christopher Hill, whose unfailing encouragement and support have always been generously given, as was his time in reading and re-reading the script and making suggestions for its improvement.

B.H.

Contents

1. Introduction — 1
2. Male and Female Servants — 22
3. The Sexual Vulnerability and Sexuality of Female Domestic Servants — 44
4. Vails, Perquisites, and Allowances: The Moral Economy of Servants — 64
5. Opportunity, Identity, and Servility — 93
6. Kin as Servants — 115
7. Pauper Servants — 128
8. Nicholas Blundell's Servants — 150
9. Serving the Clergy — 172
10. A London Domestic Servant: Mary Ashford — 191
11. Richardson's *Pamela* and Domestic Service — 208
12. Literate and Literary Servants in Eighteenth-century Fact and Fiction — 225
13. Conclusion — 251

Bibliography — 263

Index — 273

1
Introduction

'this situation of the servant is crucial in our own society'
   Raymond Williams, *The Long Revolution*, 88

'Domestic service and farm service give social and economic historians a window into the history of youth and children, the history of women, the history of the family, migration, social mobility, the working classes and population.'
   Franklin Mendels, 'Family Forms in Historic Europe', 84–5

SERVANTS were ubiquitous in eighteenth-century England. In London they swarmed the streets running errands, delivering messages, cleaning windows, scrubbing steps, and—those of grander households—attending on their employers wherever they went and delivering them home when they had finished their business. For much of the century theatre galleries were monopolized by servants. But for all the visibility of many, probably far more remained invisible, only rarely leaving their households and venturing into the outside world. For many of those in isolated country houses away from any village or town, life was very largely confined to the household. It is from the letters, journals, diaries, and memoirs of their employers we learn of their existence, discover their names and sometimes their origins, learn what tasks they performed in the household, and how long they stayed in one place. We also learn what their employers thought of them, why they were valued or why dismissed. Only occasionally, however, is their character revealed, their individual personality acknowledged. On the rare occasions when, aggrieved by the demands made on them, suddenly, and quite spontaneously, they answer back or reveal their individuality in some other way, we discover these are real people. Employers usually recorded such outbursts as insolence. Sometimes where a servant had long remained with a kindly employer and where there was mutual affection, there is an attempt by the keeper of the diary or journal to record the real character of the servant.

The 'servant question', as it came to be called in the course of the nineteenth century, existed long before and loomed large from early in the eighteenth century. Newspapers are full of letters from angry, indignant, or sorrowful employers complaining of the many shortcomings of servants, sometimes puzzled by what had changed in their households to account for the difficulties they were meeting. Why, they asked themselves, could servants not behave as they had in the past? Daniel Defoe, Bernard Mandeville, and Jonas Hanway were among those deploring the extravagance, improvidence, dishonesty, and depravity of servants. Relations between servants and their masters and mistresses in some households were clearly at crisis point.

How right Bruce Robbins is when he comments that if 'not hard to find [servants] . . . to find them . . . was not to see them as they were'.[1] Relatively little of the mass of material written about and for servants from their employers and those concerned to instruct them in how to behave came from servants themselves. Indeed their voices are all too seldom raised. In the public as in the private domain servants were expected to keep silent.

Servants abound in eighteenth-century literature. Only a few hold the centre of the stage as much as the servant in Richardson's *Pamela* which created a new genre in novels. Later I shall look at just how true to life was this portrait of a maidservant. For the most part servants—often unspeaking—lurk in the background, ready when necessary to spring to attention, to open doors, serve tea, deliver messages, and act as go-betweens. When they do speak it is often in exaggeratedly illiterate language. There is nothing new in the way in which the drama of the period represents servants. They are invariably found as comic, ignorant, and dishonest characters—a butt for the wit of their superiors.

Visual representations of servants in the eighteenth century are not much more helpful. The faces of servants are mostly without character. Indeed it is clear it was not from any desire to convey their personality that the majority of artists included them in their work. Nor was this the intention of employers in commissioning

---

[1] *The Servant's Hand* (New York, 1986), p. xi.

family scenes. Sometimes it was in order to display the rich liveries they wore—a reflection of their employers' status and wealth. Sometimes the simple dress of servants is in marked contrast to that of their employers. Often they seem to be present as mere accessories of the household alongside its delicate porcelain and silver dishes. They form part of a carefully contrived background. As in so much of the drama of the period they are frequently caricatured. Sometimes, and more particularly in country scenes, they are romanticized. Of course there are exceptions and perhaps none more startling than Hogarth's painting of the *Heads of Six Servants* (c.1750–1755).[2] Hogarth painted it for his own satisfaction. Before he died, he said, he wanted to record his friends and family. His whole intention, to which other considerations of composition are sacrificed, was to show them as individual personalities. He succeeded brilliantly.

So while servants are present in many aspects of eighteenth-century life and culture, for the most part they remain enigmatic figures. Although there was much written about them in real and fictitious households, although both the literature and art of the period contain many servants, we are left knowing remarkably little. We learn something of their work and the way they functioned in their particular household, we learn something of how they were recruited and dismissed, but very little of their real characters, of how they felt about their work as domestic servants, of their relations with their masters and mistresses, of their ambitions and fears. It is very difficult to get behind the elaborate conventions of so much of servants' conduct and behaviour. For the historians there is the tantalizing feeling that something important is eluding them, for domestic service touches on so many aspects of social life in the eighteenth century.

When Mendels wrote that domestic service offered 'a promising area for future research' he had a point.[3] The history of domestic service does offer a way in to research on a whole host of subjects. It is closely related to the history of internal rural–urban migration and to international migration movements. Of the nineteenth century it is claimed that 'the history of domestic service . . . is the story of urban migration'.[4] But this is equally

---

[2] *Heads of Six Servants* (c.1750–1755), Tate Gallery.
[3] Franklin Mendels, 'Family Forms in Historic Europe: A Review Article', *Social History*, 11 (1986), 81–7 at p. 84.
[4] Theresa McBride, *The Domestic Revolution* (1976), 34.

true of eighteenth-century domestic service. The history of the waves of immigrants to San Francisco or New York that have serviced these cities over the last century would provide a fascinating study, as would the migration of Pakistani and Indian women to become domestic servants in the countries of the Middle East. In England in the eighteenth century the largest concentration of domestic servants was in London. Most of them were almost certainly migrants from the countryside and the majority were women. 'There was a constant stream of young country girls entering into domestic service in urban households', P. J. Corfield writes, many of them in London.[5] It is an assessment confirmed by contemporary accounts. In 1762 there were said to be 'waggon loads of poor servants coming every day from all parts of this kingdom'.[6] In 1771 it was held 'the grand supply of servants' came 'from the country'. So great was employer preference for country girls that London servant-maids found 'it difficult . . . to get a service'.[7] When in 1777 Jonas Hanway estimated the number of annual migrants to London as 5,000, he added 'chiefly for service'.[8] Just what proportion of London domestic servants were rural migrants it is difficult to say. By 1851 it was 60 per cent. Where exactly they came from, their reasons for leaving their homes and villages, and what attracted them to London are all important questions for historians. The same questions have been given fresh urgency by the situation in a large part of the Third World—perhaps most significantly in Latin America—where vast numbers of rural migrants—also mostly women—are pouring into the fast-growing cities, many to become domestic servants. Indeed domestic service in Latin America has been described as 'virtually an exclusive female domain'.[9] In eighteenth-century England, as indeed in the Third World today, the great majority of rural immigrants to the great towns were young, mainly unmarried, girls. So domestic service provides a way in to the history of adolescence and, it would seem, to a fairly representative experience of children and young people in the period before marriage. 'Domestic service', Edward Higgs has written, 'was a job for women between leaving home

[5] *The Impact of English Towns 1700–1800* (1982), 99.
[6] Letter in *London Chronicle*, 12 (1762), 58. [7] *Oxford Magazine*, 6 (1771), 82.
[8] *Virtue in Humble Life*, 2 vols. (1777), vol. i, p. vi.
[9] Nadia Haggag Youssef, *Women and Work in Developing Societies* (1974), 28.

and getting married.'[10] Just because for many women service was an essential preliminary to marriage, service can throw new light on marriage—how marriage was regarded, what were the opportunities for marriage, and why so frequently in the case of domestic servants it was delayed.

In the highly complex and paradoxical relations between employers and servants there is rich material for the study of class that deserves more careful analysis. That relationship was not static. During the eighteenth century—if not before—the old paternalistic relationship between masters and servants was giving way to a stricter contractual one. It happened slowly and at very different times in different areas of the country and different households. Service, it has been argued—but with varying interpretations—was 'a bridging occupation'.[11] Some have seen it as a modernizing influence facilitating the migration of the rural poor into the modern world and the means to other occupations and a higher standard of life. 'Through the acculturation received in middle and upper-class households', we owe, or so it is argued, the 'formation of the modern urban labour movement.' The argument assumes upward social mobility was characteristic of servants. 'Servants used the period of service to acquire either the skills or the working capital or both to launch a small commercial venture.'[12] It is admitted that male servants were more likely to be upwardly mobile than female. Domestic service nevertheless 'provided rural-born women in particular with a useful and respectable occupation before marriage'. It is also claimed that the employment of servants 'initiated the middle class woman into the role of employer/manager and initiated her into certain professional skills'.[13] Service certainly provided a link between the middle and upper classes and the labouring poor. It served to distance the upper classes from contact with the poor and provided the only close contact most of the middle and upper classes had with the labouring class. Perhaps this goes some way to

---

[10] 'Domestic Service and Household Production', in Angela V. John (ed.), *Unequal Opportunities: Women's Employment in England 1800–1918* (1986), 125–50 at p. 137.

[11] L. Broom and J. H. Smith, 'Bridging Occupations', *British Journal of Sociology*, 14 (Dec. 1963), 321–4 at p. 322.

[12] Theresa McBride, 'Social Mobility for the Lower Classes: Domestic Servants in France', *Journal of Social History*, 8 (autumn 1974), 63–78 at pp. 63–4.

[13] McBride, *The Domestic Revolution*, 117, 118.

explaining why in literature domestic servants were for long the only members of the labouring class represented. They were made to stand for the whole of that class. It meant servants occupied an important role in defining class attitudes. This relationship between masters or mistresses and servants was a relationship of 'domestic enemies', as Cissie Fairchilds has so vividly called it, with a 'suggestion of simultaneous closeness and distance, intimacy and enmity' which 'epitomised relationships between mistress and servant'.[14]

Of the supreme importance of domestic service as an occupation there is no longer any doubt. Hecht made the point in 1956 when he wrote that 'the importance of the domestic servant class has long been recognised'.[15] Lawrence Stone claimed in 1977 that 'from the time of the first censuses in the early sixteenth century to the mid-nineteenth century, about one third or more of all households contained living-in servants'.[16] In 1986 Franklin Mendels suggested there was increasing recognition by historians of the 'significance of servants'. They were 'a normal component of all but the poorest households'.[17] It is true that until the first occupational censuses of the nineteenth century we have to rely on individual hunches—some of them no doubt as reliable as the later censuses but lacking their authority. But contemporaries in the second half of the eighteenth century were under no doubt that the number of servants of both sexes was increasing. In 1767 Jonas Hanway estimated that one in thirteen of London's population was a domestic servant. Given the population of London at this time this would have meant a total of just over 50,000. Ten years later he increased the estimate to one in eight, or a total of 80,000 servants.[18] The reforming magistrate Patrick Colquhoun, in 1806, put the total number of servants in England and Wales at 910,000 of which 800,000 were women.[19] Recent estimates have tended to confirm that, though not the conclusions of trained statisticians, such contemporary guesses approximate to the truth. So if Peter Laslett is right in his analysis of 100 communities

[14] *Domestic Enemies: Servants and their Masters in Old Regime France* (1984), p. xi.
[15] J. Jean Hecht, *The Domestic Servant in Eighteenth-Century England* (1956), p. xi.
[16] *The Family, Sex and Marriage* (1977), 27–8.
[17] 'Family Forms in Historic Europe', 84.
[18] *Letters on the Importance of Preserving the Rising Generation of the Labouring Part of our Fellow Subjects*, 2 vols. (1767), ii. 158.
[19] *A Treatise on Indigence* (1806), 253.

between 1574 and 1821, which concluded that servants of all types made up 13.4 per cent of the population, Hanway's second figure might seem nearer the truth.[20] According to the Occupational Census of 1851 domestic service was far and away the most important occupation for women, accounting for 905,000. One in every nine females over the age of 10 and one in every four of all females in employment worked in domestic service. Service accounted for 39,000 of the 115,000 London women of all classes between 15 and 20. Men servants numbered 134,000.[21] After agriculture domestic service was the largest occupation for both men and women.

If domestic service provides a point of entry into a host of interesting questions for the historian, it is one that British historians as yet have scarcely started to probe. Very little has been written on eighteenth-century domestic service in England since Jean J. Hecht's work, *The Domestic Servant in Eighteenth-Century England* (1956)—and that, it should be noted, was written by an American. Olwen Hufton's assessment of 1983 that 'the English domestic service sector is still largely described by reference to Jean Hecht' remains true today.[22] Yet in the last fifteen years at least two excellent books have appeared on domestic service in eighteenth-century France.[23] The recognition of the supreme importance of domestic servants in the eighteenth century is of relatively recent date. When Ivy Pinchbeck wrote her *Women Workers and the Industrial Revolution 1750–1850* (1930) female domestic servants received hardly a mention. Dorothy George's *London Life in the Eighteenth Century* (1925), while devoting some space to pauper apprentices bound out to service, has little to say about domestic servants in general although she recognized they were 'a numerous class'. But both George and Pinchbeck were writing early this century. What are the reasons for British historians' persistence over the last forty years in virtually ignoring domestic service? All female domestic servants, it is assumed,

---

[20] Peter Laslett, 'Mean Household Size in England since the Sixteenth Century', in P. Laslett and R. Wall (eds.), *Household and Family in Past Time* (1972), p. 152: table 4.13.
[21] Census of 1851: Ages and Occupations, 1852–3. vol. lxxxvii, pts. I and II.
[22] 'Women in History: Early Modern Europe', *Past and Present*, 101 (Nov. 1983), 125–41 at p. 126.
[23] Sara C. Maza, *Servants and Masters in Eighteenth-Century France: The Uses of Loyalty* (1983), and Fairchilds, *Domestic Enemies*.

performed housework, and until recently housework has had little appeal for social historians. We all know what housework means, it is argued. Women have performed it since history began. Nothing has changed. To historians concerned with change over time it is of no interest. Moreover the work domestic servants performed, like all women's work in the home, was regarded as essentially unproductive. Although recognition of the sheer numbers of domestic servants can no longer be disputed, it has taken some time, it seems, for social historians of the eighteenth century to adjust to the implications of their existence. Those concerned with the first stage of industrialization in the first nation to industrialize have found it puzzling and a little disconcerting to discover that, despite burgeoning manufacture, the most important occupation remained service. What has domestic service to do with the growth of industry and the rise of factories? As Julia Wrigley has recently written 'servants did not seem central to modern societies'.[24] Another strong reason for continuing to ignore domestic servants is that most, it is argued, were women. And it was women who, on the whole, were the servants in one-servant households about which we know so very little. Ann Kussmaul has emphasized the invisibility of farm servants. The same was true of domestic servants, and perhaps this may be some excuse for historians continuing to ignore them.[25] Further explanation is suggested by Mendels when he writes that domestic service 'just withered away, it left neither the documentary sources nor the motivation for historians and others to study this phenomenon' with the same intensity as, say, they approached the emancipation of serfs or slaves.[26] Later I shall suggest Mendels is wrong and that domestic service is far from 'withering away'. It would pay historians anxious to know more of domestic service to look not merely at the Third World—although in many parts domestic service is by far the most important occupation for women—but also at the United States, where domestic service is very much alive, and even at Britain where, if they are no longer described as domestic servants, there remains a vast body of underpaid, exploited women working as char-

[24] 'Feminists and Domestic Workers', *Feminist Studies*, 17/2 (1991), 317–29 at p. 317.
[25] *Servants in Husbandry in Early Modern England* (1981), 9.
[26] 'Family Forms in Historic Europe', 85.

women, baby-minders, and home helps. And if the number of British female domestic servants living in households is few today there are still large number of young foreign girls from all over the world acting as *au pairs* over whom there is no regulation and for whom no minimum working conditions are laid down. Much of this service remains invisible and almost all of it is female. In consequence the history of service has suffered the fate of all women's history and simply been left out.

Some of these arguments deserve more attention. For instance the argument that housework has always meant the same kind of work and that domestic service has been unchanging cannot go unchallenged. The history of housework has not been a subject particularly favoured by historians, but recently we have begun to learn in how many ways housework is constantly changing as homes change in design, as new standards of building and interior decoration are introduced, and as the expectations of families as to what a home should be are transformed. As the trend towards the division of houses into separate rooms with specialized functions developed the nature of housework changed and the work servants were called on to perform was altered. (See Ch. 2 below for a further discussion of these points.)

What of substance has been written of domestic service in England in the eighteenth and nineteenth centuries has been increasingly criticized by historians for concentrating only on large households whose masters left useful records in diaries and journals. The concentration on such households is understandable. It is from them that by far the greatest amount of information about servants is forthcoming. And Hecht—one of those who has been most criticized—never claimed that the households he used to illustrate points were representative of all servant-owning households. Indeed he made the point that 'there existed a large group of employers who kept but a single maidservant'.[27] It is all very well to accuse him of relying 'entirely on material generated by employers of servants in large establishments', but where is material on smaller households to be found that is half as informative?[28] Peter Earle, in explaining why he uses Pepys's diary so

---

[27] *The Domestic Servant in Eighteenth-Century England*, 8.
[28] D. A. Kent, 'Ubiquitous but Invisible: Female Domestic Servants in Mid-Eighteenth-Century London', *History Workshop Journal*, 28 (autumn 1989), 111–28 at p. 112.

extensively in his study of London between 1660 and 1730, makes the point when he writes 'nowhere else can one get the same detail on the relations between master, mistress and servants in a London household'.[29] As Hecht emphasized, 'relatively little of what servants committed to paper has survived, the bulk of the material derives from the employer class'.[30] Dorothy Marshall has also been criticized for the same omission, but she too was well aware that while some female domestic servants were employed 'as cooks, housemaids, and waiting women by the better households', in other households they were used as 'domestic drudges by . . . craftsmen and artisans'.[31] What is regrettable is not so much that historians have so far tended to concentrate on servants in large and wealthy households, nor that they have failed to say much of one-servant households, but that they have focused so exclusively on male servants and allowed the stereotype of male servants in large wealthy households to dominate all thinking about domestic service.

We need to appreciate that despite the great openings for further local research on domestic service in towns or counties or other areas, the lives of by far the majority of domestic servants in the eighteenth and early nineteenth centuries will continue to remain largely hidden from us. So can we ever know what the life of the average servant was like? Or are we to continue to embrace this myth of service on an upstairs/downstairs model, with highly specialized servants whose work was defined by their occupation labels, living in households in which a strict hierarchy was preserved among servants? Are we to continue to treat such servants as representative? This stereotyped image of domestic service is inadequate. There is evidence—admittedly often highly fragmentary—of the work done, master–servant relations, and of the kind of life led by the servant-of-all-work or kitchen skivvy who represents the majority of all domestic servants in the eighteenth and nineteenth centuries. It is evidence that requires only a little historical imagination to bring to life. Examples are not difficult to find. From Francis Place's autobiography, for instance, we learn that when he was a child his father was a publican in the Strand. Ten minutes only were allowed the family for lunch and

---

[29] *The Making of the English Middle Class* (1989), 229.
[30] *The Domestic Servant in Eighteenth-Century England*, 16.
[31] *Dr. Johnson's London* (1968), 49.

'the servant maid, the only servant kept, sat at the table' with them. In such simple households, it suggests, there was not the separation of servants from family associated with larger households. One could surmise that the work of the servant-maid was as much helping out in the pub and looking after the children as housework. The way in which servants were taken on by hitherto non-servant-employing masters is illustrated by the experience of William Hutton, the historian of Birmingham. When, in 1752, he first opened his bookshop he 'took a female servant' to look after the shop in his absence. He was unlucky in his choice for 'she sold the books for what they would bring and got completely drunk with the money'. For a time he had no servant, but his frequent need to be away on business led him to venture 'upon another female servant' in 1754. Who recommended her to Hutton? It was the 'minister of the congregation', who had assured Hutton she would not cheat him. She did not but, as Hutton recorded, 'she cheated my dumplings one Sunday, by setting them to boil without water'. He makes quite clear his purpose in employing her. It was not only to cook for him and do the housework but also to look after the shop. In Myddle when his wife died 'before her children were brought to maturity', Samuel Dowton 'hired a servant maid to look after his children'. Later he married her, which resulted in his children being 'much troubled'. Were they jealous of their father's affection for her? It can hardly have been because they disapproved of their father marrying a servant girl for they all left home 'as soon as they were able for service'.[32] Such fragments can help us to learn something of the nature of these one-servant households and the work expected of their servants.

The term 'domestic servants' is used here to describe servants who were resident in the households in which they worked. Sometimes they were employed inside the house and sometimes outside, but it is not always possible in studying the eighteenth century to make a sharp distinction between domestic and farm servants, not least because in many cases the work servants performed alternated between the two spheres. Historians anxious to learn something of the history of domestic service are not helped by what appears today as the loose way in which the term 'ser-

[32] *The Autobiography of Francis Place (1771–1854)*, ed. Mary Thale (1972), 89; *The Life of William Hutton, Written by himself* (facs. of 1841 edn.), 27–8; Richard Gough, *The History of Myddle (1701–1706)* (1979), 119.

vant' is used in eighteenth-century England. Modern historians often perpetuate the confusion by continuing to use the term far too arbitrarily. How right Richard Mayo was when in 1693 he wrote 'there is scarce any general Name of a *Calling* that contains under it such different kinds of Persons, as this of a Servant'.[33] Frequently apprentices were referred to as servants and indeed they seem often to have been given household work to do. Peter Earle has noted how in the series of assessments produced for the tax on burials, births, and marriages which came into force on 1 May 1695 'only a few assessments distinguish between apprentices and domestic servants, lumping them together under "servants"'.[34] In small households Hecht has argued 'it was often an apprentice who played the role of footboy dividing his time between the shop and attendance on his mistress'.[35] Julius Hardy, the Birmingham button-maker, in his diary always referred to his apprentices as 'servants' but James Stansfield, who was employed in the button manufactory and whose wife was Hardy's housekeeper, is also referred to as 'servant' although almost certainly not an apprentice.[36] When in 1772 Josiah Wedgwood found widespread 'villainy' among his servants, he described how he had to 'sweep the House of every servant we have in it, Male and Female, some from the field Men, and others from the Works'.[37] In the seventeenth century under-tenants were also embraced by the term 'servants'. Yet according to the meaning of servant—'a person of either sex who is in the service of a master or mistress; one who is under obligation to work for the benefit of a superior, and to obey his (or her) commands' (*OED*)—this was not loose but correct usage. It is we who have chosen to narrow the meaning of the term to those living in the homes of their employers. Contemporaries made no such distinction between living-in servants and day-labourers who lived in their own homes and came in to work for an employer on a part-time and casual basis. Similarly charwomen and washerwomen employed on a casual basis are frequently included under the label of 'servants'.

[33] *A Present for Servants* (1693), 1.
[34] *The Making of the English Middle Class*, 213.
[35] *The Domestic Servant in Eighteenth-Century England*, 8.
[36] *Diary of Julius Hardy (1788–1793) button-maker, of Birmingham*, Birmingham Reference Library, 669002 (BRL, MS 218), transcribed and annotated by A. M. Banks (Apr. 1973), 36.
[37] As quoted in Peter Linebaugh, *The London Hanged* (1991), 329.

Introduction 13

The term 'domestic servant' is a fairly recent invention. It is true that in the fifteenth and sixteenth centuries the term 'domestical' or more rarely 'servant domestical' was occasionally used to describe a household servant. By the early seventeenth century this had sometimes become 'domestics' as in Shakespeare's *Henry VIII* (II. iv. 114): 'When Powres are your Retainers and your Words (Domesticks to you) serve your will.' In the early eighteenth century in Addison's *Spectator* (no. 106) we have 'His Domesticks are all in Years, and grown old with their master' but 'domestic servant' may well have been a term only invented for the first occupational censuses in the nineteenth century.

Not all domestic servants were living-in servants residing in the homes of their employers. Many were employed in inns, taverns, and coffee houses. As Ann Kussmaul stresses, 'early modern England contained many different types of service'.[38] Sir Richard Newdigate even referred to his small army of agents, confidential businessmen, bailiffs, and rent collectors as his 'servants'.[39] Edward Higgs, writing of the nineteenth-century censuses, has deplored the use of 'servant' as 'an umbrella category covering such terms as "general servant", "housekeeper", "nurse", "cook", and so on'.[40] In France it was almost certainly even more difficult than in England to know what kind of worker is being referred to as a 'servant'. In the eighteenth century it was a term covering a very wide range of workers including the female silk workers at Lyons who were referred to as 'servantes', as well as workers in taverns and inns.[41]

There has always been some distinction to be made between servants who worked mainly outside the house and those who worked mainly indoors. In the period discussed here the balance between such servants was changing. There is a period when, while service in husbandry was steadily declining, the frontiers between farm service and domestic service were increasingly blurred in respect of the work involved. Leonore Davidoff, in writing of service in the nineteenth century, sees the early years of

[38] *Servants in Husbandry in Early Modern England*, 3.
[39] Eileen Gooder, *The Squire of Arbury: Sir Richard Newdigate (1644–1710)* (1990), 42.
[40] 'Women, Occupations and Work in the Nineteenth-Century Censuses', *History Workshop Journal*, 23 (spring 1987), 59–80 at p. 68.
[41] Maza, *Servants and Masters in Eighteenth-Century France*, 18–19.

the century as a time when there was a 'merging of farm and domestic service' for both men and women.[42] Only by the end of the century had they become separated. But the merging almost certainly began earlier, in the eighteenth century. For a considerable period—certainly well into the nineteenth century—there were domestic servants who did as much work out of the house as inside and a declining remnant of female servants in husbandry who did as much indoor domestic work as they did work in the fields and dairy. A large number—perhaps even the majority—of male servants were employed for tasks outside the house but, as we shall see, this did not prevent them coming into the house to act as indoor servants when the occasion and need arose. The outlines of tasks to be done by Mrs Purefoy's servants, both male and female, make clear the dual role they were expected to play with tasks both inside and outside the house.[43] Nicholas Blundell's servants, as we shall see, moved freely between the two spheres, with ploughmen and coachmen serving as butlers as occasion demanded.[44] Particularly in households in the country such flexibility in function was often demanded of servants (see Ch. 8). It was a pattern that continued well into the nineteenth century. Of the early occupational censuses Leonore Davidoff and Catherine Hall have written: 'it is probable that young women listed as domestic servants on farms were helping in the yard and dairy as well as doing households chores.'[45] But it was not only on farms that female domestic servants right through the eighteenth and nineteenth centuries are to be found doing the milking and looking after poultry and pigs, as well as performing tasks within the house. What perhaps had fundamentally changed in the course of the eighteenth century—although it is difficult to put an exact date on it—was the background from which both servants in husbandry and domestic servants were recruited. The servant, whether called servant in husbandry or domestic servant, who entered the household of an employer with the intention that when he or she left it it would be to become a master or mistress

---

[42] 'Domestic Service and the Working-Class Life Cycle', *Society for the Study of Labour History*, 26 (spring 1973), 10–13 at p. 10.

[43] *The Purefoy Letters, 1735–53*, ed. G. Eland, 2 vols. (1931).

[44] *The Great Diurnal of Nicholas Blundell of Little Crosby, Lancashire*, ed. J. J. Bagley, Record Society of Lancashire and Cheshire, 3 vols. (1968, 1970, 1972).

[45] *Family Fortunes: Men and Women of the English Middle Classes, 1780–1850* (1987), 388.

employing his or her own servants, was an increasing rarity. There are historians who continue to make little or no sort of differentiation between servants in husbandry and domestic servants at any stage in their development.

Servants in eighteenth-century England were a substantial proportion of the working population. They existed all over the country in towns and countryside, but there were certain concentrations that deserve looking at more closely. The greatest was in London and recent research has tended to focus on service in the metropolis. Unfortunately the lack of occupational census material before 1841 makes the study of domestic service in other towns before the nineteenth century more difficult. Research on service in towns in the nineteenth century has revealed some interesting information about the kind of towns in which the servant population was particularly high. Outside the West End of London the greatest concentration of servants was in non-industrial towns of some wealth. So Alan Armstrong's work on York has uncovered 'an astonishingly high proportion of female domestic servants' in 1841. It was an occupation accounting for 'nearly three-quarters of all female employment in the city'. In summing up the characteristics of York at this period Armstrong highlights its lack of modern industry, its relative wealth, and the high proportion of professional people it embraced.[46] Other non-industrial towns like Exeter and Brighton also had high concentrations of servants. Writing of the nineteenth century, Leonore Davidoff and Catherine Hall have emphasized how 'professional households, in their special concern with domesticity, employed more than the average of servants'.[47] In York a large number of servants were employed by the upper two social classes as defined by the Booth-Armstrong classification, that is those of the professional and intermediate occupations. Households in these two classes employed on average 1.15 servants each as compared with Nottingham where the figure was 0.7.[48] But Nottingham had a thriving industry, and alternative occupations were available for both men and women.

Edward Higgs has looked at the domestic service population of Rochdale in Lancashire in 1851, 1861, and 1871 where the most

[46] Alan Armstrong, *Stability and Change in an English Country Town* (1974), 29.
[47] *Family Fortunes*, 388.
[48] Armstrong, *Stability and Change in an English Country Town*, 179.

important employers of servants were shopkeepers.[49] Those households where the head of the house was a retailer accounted for between one-quarter and one-third of all servants in 1851, 1861, and 1871. The '"typical" servant employer' was most likely to come from 'shopkeepers, butchers, grocers, drapers, innkeepers and restaurant owners'.[50] Rochdale was a rapidly expanding industrial area in this period centring on the textile industry. In sharp contrast to York where many servant-employing households contained two or more servants, three out of every five domestic servants in Rochdale were employed in single-servant households. The 'typical servant in Rochdale was the maid-of-all-work who was the only living-in servant in the household'.[51] Large households employing a body of servants were rare.

Where the number of domestic servants in counties is concerned, Michael Anderson has studied Preston and the surrounding rural area in the nineteenth century. In his sample of households in the countryside, 28 per cent contained at least one servant as compared with 10 per cent of the households in Preston itself.[52] Duncan Bythell has pointed out that in 1851 there were 'ten counties in England (and the three in lowland Scotland) where domestic servants were outnumbered by women working in textiles or clothing'. As might have been anticipated they include Lancashire, Cheshire, the West Riding, Derby, Nottingham, and Leicester but also Northampton, Buckingham, Bedford, and Hertford. In all of them alternative employment to service was available for women. It comes as no surprise that half of all working women in London 'were classed as domestics', but the same was true of 'the counties to the south of it' and 'in some mainly agricultural counties along the border with Wales, in Lincolnshire, and in north and east Yorkshire'. Remarkably it was also apparently true 'in the "coalfield" counties of Durham and Glamorgan'.[53]

One important aim of this book is to establish that service was not—and was never—a monolithic phenomenon unchanging over time. Even at any one moment in the past the experience of servants was extremely diverse. Households varied in size and

---

[49] 'Domestic Service and Household Production', 128.   [50] Ibid. 135.
[51] Ibid. 136.   [52] *Family Structure in Nineteenth-Century Lancashire* (1971), 85.
[53] 'Women in the Work Force', in Patrick O'Brien and Roland Quinault (eds.), *The Industrial Revolution and British Society* (1993), 31–53 at p. 37.

Introduction 17

wealth, but their complement of servants did not always reflect their income. Nor did the occupation of the head of the house necessarily indicate the likely number of servants. 'Very few people', writes Peter Earle, 'can be said not to belong to the servant employing class simply on the grounds of their occupation.'[54] It was not just a question of whether you served in a large, rich household, a more modest but comfortably circumstanced household, or a humble one, a one- or at most two-servant household, of whether it was an urban or rural household, but of what work you were expected to do. Just because an individual was taken on as a domestic servant did not mean that domestic service defined their work role. Many appointed as servants became shop assistants, helping in the family business. Sue Wright, in her work on Salisbury, has stressed how wrong it is in the early modern period 'to see domestic and craft labour as two entirely separate entities . . . there was a good deal of interaction between kitchen and workshop'.[55] In pre-Revolutionary France servants would be taken on by artisans and textile workers 'who might well find another pair of hands useful for tending the counter or working the loom'.[56] Then a family's needs changed with the arrival of children, when the woman of the household often required additional help, and changed again as the children grew up, sometimes helped in the house, and left home to be married. 'Some types of household', Davidoff and Hall claim, 'demanded more servant-labour than others.' They give as an example farm households where 'only half as many . . . were without any servants as the average'.[57] Then what had been a paternalistic relationship with—at least in theory—defined obligations towards, and responsibilities for their servants by masters and mistresses, was in process of changing into a strictly wage relationship, and with this change the class tensions between masters and servants were increased. For all these reasons the experience of service by both employers and servants was diverse and never static.

When I started to work on this book my intention was to limit it to female servants. I soon decided this would not only greatly

---

[54] *The Making of the English Middle Class*, 376 n. 24.
[55] ' "Churmaids, Huswyfes and Hucksters": The Employment of Women in Tudor and Stuart Salisbury', in Lindsey Charles and Lorna Duffin (eds.), *Women and Work in Pre-Industrial England* (1985), 100–21 at p. 103.
[56] Fairchilds, *Domestic Enemies*, 8.   [57] *Family Fortunes*, 388.

narrow the study but would also make it much more difficult to see the relationship between male and female servants, their different work roles in the household, and their relative treatment by employers. I recalled Natalie Zemon Davis's 'plea for a recognition that equal weight should be given to the experience of both genders'.[58] Nevertheless some chapters (Ch. 3 on the Sexual vulnerability and sexuality of female servants, Ch. 10 on Mary Ashford, and Ch. 11 on Richardson's *Pamela*) are inevitably more about women than men. A word about the time-span of the material: almost all the texts used here are from a 'long eighteenth century'. It embraces Pepys's diary at one end and Mary Ashford's autobiography at the other, although the main diaries drawn upon are firmly eighteenth-century. But in the more general chapters on male and female servants, sexual vulnerability and sexuality, and opportunity, identity and servility, I have allowed in other material of the later nineteenth and even early twentieth centuries. In part this is because when it comes to these subjects by far the most stimulating discussions have been carried on by historians of nineteenth-century domestic service. While I stand by my main argument that servants were not one thing but many and that service changed over time, in some few respects there was continuity: first in servants' state of servility and what this meant in terms of master–servant relationships, secondly in their sexual vulnerability and frustration, and thirdly in the very different ways in which male and female servants were viewed by employers. The servants covered here are mainly English but there are also a few Scots, Welsh, and Irish. As far as France is concerned I have deliberately made comparisons between service in France and England. French domestic service is far better documented than English and might suggest new ways of looking at service in England. Apart from the grouping together of the three case studies on servants in households of very different sizes, and the two literary chapters, there is no particular logic to the ordering of the essays, which are largely self-contained. Readers should not feel bound to adhere to the order in which different themes are treated here but must feel free to read chapters in any sequence.

[58] Quoted in Hufton, 'Women in History: Early Modern Europe', 132.

Introduction

The next four chapters (2–5) are on general aspects of domestic service. A number of historians today have argued that, far from service becoming feminized in the course of the eighteenth or early nineteenth centuries, it has always been feminized. I disagree. 'Male and Female Servants' looks at the reasons behind the employment of men or women servants, the sexual division of labour in households of different sizes, the diverse tasks undertaken by men and women in service, the different status of male as against female servants, and how far that difference was reflected in their wages and conditions. In the course of the eighteenth century the number of male servants began to decline in relation to female. By the mid-nineteenth century service was overwhelmingly female. If I am right, how are we to explain this trend?

'Sexual Vulnerability and the Sexuality of Female Servants' is concerned with the long-acknowledged vulnerability of female servants to the sexual advances of their masters, their masters' sons, and their fellow male servants. It probes the causes of that vulnerability. It seeks to explain the attitude of employers to pregnancy in their servants and the lengths they would go to in order to avoid it—all of which only increased the sexual frustration of servants often virtually cut off from contact with the world outside. The chapter looks at the incidence of illegitimate births among servants and asks whether it is evidence of their sexual licence or whether there were real problems in servants achieving marriage even where sincerely meant promises of marriage had been made. 'Vails, Perquisites and Allowances, looks at the customary practices which had developed by the eighteenth century and which determined servant earnings over and above wages. It analyses the way in which such practices operated, their value, and why it was that the eighteenth century saw a concerted attack on them by employers, and an equally firm resistance to attempts to abolish them by servants.

Recently there have been suggestions that far from being a highly exploited, overworked, and underpaid occupational group, domestic servants were in fact relatively well paid in relation to other occupations of the labouring class. It has been claimed that service offered an attractive career prospect offering the acquisition of skills that would be of great benefit to them in their lives after service. It is also suggested that the differential between the wages of male and female servants has been exaggerated and that, in fact there was little between them. 'Opportunity, Identity and Servility' sets out to suggest that such claims are at least questionable.

The next two chapters (6 and 7) focus on two special types of servant largely ignored to date—servants who were near or distant kin of the household head, and pauper servants who were placed out by the parish authorities all too anxious to be rid of the responsibility for their maintenance. In both cases these were servants who were paid very little if anything and so provided a cheap source of labour for those with small incomes—although these were not the only employers to use them. The three chapters that follow (8, 9, and 10) are case studies which concentrate on servant-employing households of very different size. First the rural household of Nicholas Blundell, a substantial and wealthy household just north of Liverpool. Secondly, three households of clergy of comparable income with similar complements of servants. And thirdly the mainly modest households in which Mary Ashford worked during her seventeen years of service.

Given the extraordinary popularity of Richardson's novel *Pamela, or Virtue Rewarded*—not least among female servants and the parents of daughters destined for service—it is pertinent to ask whether this story of a servant-maid who not only succeeds in bettering herself but in marrying her rich aristocratic master has any basis in fact. This is the theme of 'Richardson's *Pamela* and Domestic Service'. Finally 'Literate and Literary Servants in Eighteenth-century Fact and Fiction' looks at the question of literacy among servants and focuses on a group of servants who were not only literate but literary.

A final point that relates not only to the two last chapters but to the entire book is the legitimacy of using literary sources, and more particularly novels, as evidence. Of course when it comes to the part played by servants in the plot we must never forget that this is a fiction with little or no basis in reality. Nor should we take the personality of fictional servants, in so far as they are allowed one, as evidence. But novels are an excellent source for much often unwitting testimony about employers' attitudes to servants, the nature of servant households, of customary practices among servants, and of the ways in which servants were hired and fired. Servants in novels may not be real characters, but many of the assumptions novels make about servants provide invaluable information, and information that it is difficult to get elsewhere.

2
Male and Female Servants

> 'If the employment of servants was a measure of social standing the keeping of men-servants was of much greater significance than the number of women servants.'
>
> Phyllis Cunnington, *Costume of Household Servants*, 104

IF the term 'domestic servants' covers a vast range of experience of very different individuals doing different work in different households, it also lumps together indiscriminately men and women servants. The sexual division in the various tasks for which domestic servants were employed is well known. For men there were places, among many others, as valets, footmen, coachmen, butlers. For women, lady's maids, chambermaids, kitchen maids. But just how important were these occupational labels? We shall see that in some eighteenth-century households—and not just small households—servants moved freely and often between roles. Far from adhering to a strict hierarchy among their servants, some households seem to have regarded the labour of servants as highly flexible, changing their role to fit their employers' needs. In the eighteenth century, it has been argued, 'the duties of butler, valet, footman were not so sharply differentiated as they became in Victorian times', when the increasing need of employers to assert their superiority to their servants led to their attempting to create a strict hierarchy among servants.[1] Writing of the late seventeenth and early eighteenth centuries Dorothy Stuart has made the same point when she writes 'the lines of demarcation between one household department and another must at this time have been irregular and indistinct'.[2] The upstairs/downstairs model of service with a rigid servant hierarchy

---

[1] E. S. Turner, *What the Butler Saw: 250 Years of the Servant Problem* (1962), 28.
[2] *The English Abigail* (1946), 46.

may well have been the invention of the Victorians. In analysing the census figures for 1851 and 1871, John Burnett concludes that in these years 'domestic service was becoming increasingly differentiated, and that the largest increases were among the more skilled and specialised staff like housekeepers and cooks, nursemaids and coachmen'.[3] These increases were far and away larger than the increase in general servants. It was reassuring for new servant-employers to be able to count the rungs of the ladder that separated the footman from the kitchen skivvy and conclude that an equal gulf lay between the footman and themselves. In many modest households where only one or, at most, two servants were employed, whether male or female, it was pretty arbitrary what they were labelled—cook, housemaid, or general servant. Often they were given no label but simply referred to as the 'servant'. As the only servant in the household they performed whatever tasks their employers demanded. Housework did not always have much to do with them. In the mid-nineteenth century, J. H. Walsh made it clear that a 'butler', even in households of incomes of £1,000 a year, was not quite the specialist usually associated with such a label. He was 'really a man-servant-of-all-work, often undertaking an immense number of duties, from cleaning shoes and knives and forks to the cellar management'.[4] In modest households employing just one male servant, he might well be labelled footman but he was 'expected to make himself generally useful'.[5]

A random study of newspaper advertisements for servants reinforces this point. In the *Ipswich Journal* for the year 1755, for example, there appeared an advertisement for 'a Livery Servant who has been used to wait at Table, and knows something of Horses, and if he has any Knowledge of Gardening it will be the more agreeable'. Another asked for 'an honest, sober, and diligent Servant, that understands looking after Horses, Sporting, and waiting at Table'. A third wanted 'a Butler that can shoot and shave well'. One advertisement wanted 'a Sober sprightly LAD, not under 13, or exceeding 15 Years of Age, to look after a Horse,

---

[3] *Useful Toil: Autobiographies of Working People from the 1820s to the 1920s*, ed. John Burnett, 2nd edn. (1994), 130.

[4] *A Manual of Domestic Economy*, 2nd edn. (1857), 224, as quoted in J. Banks, *Prosperity and Parenthood* (1954), 73.

[5] Samuel and Sarah Adams, *The Complete Servant* (1825), 376.

work a little in a Garden, and must be able to write tolerably, which will be his chief Employments'. It was the same where female servants were demanded. 'Wanted immediately. A Cook Maid in a large Family, who must look after two Cows.' Another asked for 'a woman-servant in a Gentleman's Family that can cook plain Roast and Boil'd, and manage three Cows'.[6] It is noticeable that in most cases the work the servant was expected to do is not given a label except that of 'man-servant' or 'woman-servant'. The work demanded of them nearly always included varied tasks both inside and outside the house.

Despite Hecht's salutary warning on 'how hazardous must be any attempt to compare wage data for servants', it is sometimes assumed that meaningful comparisons can be made between their wages, as though they were doing the same kind of tasks or doing different tasks that were in some way equivalent.[7] Or again that equal length of experience was sufficient ground for comparison of male and female wages. In nineteenth-century England and France, it is claimed, 'male servants were the élite of domestic service, earning far more than females with equivalent experience'.[8] But can the work of footmen, coachmen, butlers, and stable boys really be compared with the work of housekeepers, nursery and chamber maids, housemaids and kitchen skivvies? Are butlers to be regarded as the equivalent of housekeepers or cooks? And if the outcome of such a comparison is to conclude that men servants were paid more than women servants what does that tell us that we did not already know? What it does not tell us is why male servants were seen as deserving higher wages than women. Was it because the work of male servants was more valued than that of women, perhaps because the employment of male servants gave a family prestige, or that in general in the eighteenth century all male workers were paid more than female? Boswell posed the same question for Doctor Johnson: 'What is the reason that women servants, though obliged to be at the expense of purchasing their own clothes, have much lower wages than men servants to whom a great proportion of that article is furnished and when in fact our female house servants work much harder than the

---

[6] *Ipswich Journal*, nos. 842, 845, 865, 874 (1755).
[7] J. Jean Hecht, *The Domestic Servant in Eighteenth-Century England* (1956), 152.
[8] Theresa McBride, *The Domestic Revolution* (1976), 60.

male?'⁹ Johnson, remarkably, had no reply. One interesting thing about male and female servants' wages is that, if both tended to be fixed for long periods, the former appear to have been raised more often than the latter. Take the example of the household of the dowager Mrs Senhouse of Netherhall when she moved in 1771. It consisted of a butler–handyman whose yearly wages were increased in 1773 from £9 to £10, and three maidservants, Mary Glaister with an annual wage of £6, Dinah Gait with £5, and Molly Pattinson with £4. Her head maid was still receiving the same wage twenty years later, as were both the other maidservants.[10]

The only real point at which the work of male and female servants coincided was in 'cooks'. Earlier cooks had always been male and there is no doubt that in wealthier households male cooks were preferred to female.[11] Indeed the best recommendation for a female cook was that she had 'lived under a man cook'.[12] In the household of Sir Richard Newdigate there was a man cook employed and a woman as under-cook.[13] Because French cuisine was regarded as the best, French male cooks were often employed by the larger and grander households. It was 'a sign of distinction'.[14] 'English cooks are not very clever folk', wrote Rochefoucauld dismissively of English cooking, 'and even in the best houses one fares very ill. The height of luxury is to have a Frenchman, but few people can afford the expense.'[15] The employment of foreign servants was, as we shall see in Chapter 4, a source of some resentment among English servants. In the model of a household of 'a respectable Country Gentleman with a young family whose Net Income is from £16–18,000 a Year, and whose expenses do not exceed £7,000' given by Samuel and Sarah Adams in 1825, a 'French Man-Cook' earned £80 a year—by far the highest paid of all the male servants and 'twice or thrice the

---

⁹ As quoted in Turner, *What the Butler Saw*, 28.
[10] Edward Hughes, *North Country Life in the Eighteenth Century*, 2 vols. (1952, 1965), ii. 375–6.
[11] Phyllis Cunnington, *Costume of Household Servants* (1974), 2.
[12] Hecht, *The Domestic Servant in Eighteenth-Century England*, 65.
[13] Eileen Gooder, *The Squire of Arbury: Sir Richard Newdigate (1644–1710)* (1990), 37.
[14] Peter Earle, *A City Full of People* (1994), 83.
[15] *A Frenchman in England 1784*, ed. Jean Marchand, trans. with notes by S. C. Roberts (1933), 25.

sum given to the most experienced female English Cook'. By the early nineteenth century, as the Adams's commented, male cooks were kept 'only in about 300–400 great wealthy families'. After the French man-cook the next highest paid in the model household was the butler at £50 per annum. The highest paid female servant was the housekeeper at twenty-four guineas a year.[16]

There were also some exceptional cases where the frontiers of the sexual division of labour between the tasks performed by male and female servants were breached. So when the Revd Sydney Smith could not solve his servant problem he 'caught up a little garden girl, made like a milestone, christened her Bunch, put a napkin in her hand and made her my butler'. According to her master she became 'the best butler in the county'.[17]

In both England and France it has been assumed that great, rich, and aristocratic households tended to employ large numbers of men servants. Peter Earle, writing of London servants in the period 1650–1750, talks of 'huge male staffs maintained by the aristocratic and gentry families in the West End, some of whom employed over twenty men and boys in their town residences'. Indeed he claims that 'only where there was a staff of 3 or 4 or more were there likely to be male servants'.[18] It is suggested that, at the beginning of the eighteenth century, 'in great households the number of male dependents always exceeded the number of female'.[19] Peter Laslett wrote in 1972 that 'males predominated among servants in traditional times', but he went on to speculate that 'they were not simply domestics in our sense of the word, in the Victorian sense, and may have been rather different in their social role'.[20] On the other hand, Earle argues that in the sixteenth and early seventeenth centuries 'many household chores were done by male servants' and that there was not the sexual division of labour among domestic servants that developed later.[21] Daniel Roche, writing of eighteenth-century France, talks of aristocratic households with large bodies of servants where there was 'a predominance of male servants'.[22] On his visit to England in 1784,

[16] Adams, *The Complete Servant*, 7.
[17] As quoted in Turner, *What the Butler Saw*, 96.
[18] *A City Full of People*, 82, 124.   [19] Ibid. 28.
[20] Peter Laslett and Richard Wall (eds.), *Household and Family in Past Time* (1972), 151.
[21] *A City Full of People*, 124.
[22] *Paris and her People*, trans. Marie Evans in association with Gwynne Lewis (1981), 67.

Rochefoucauld held there were 'certain noblemen who have thirty or forty men servants'. Although he did not give any idea of their number he went on to add that 'the cooking and the housework that is not seen are usually done by women'.[23] Jonas Hanway in 1760 certainly thought great houses should, and in fact did, employ women as indoor servants. 'Were I a *Great Man*', he has Thomas Trueman say, 'I should rather be served *within doors*, by Women than by Men; and most of the laborious part of *service within doors* is already performed by *Women*.' On the latter point he was almost certainly right although not all the heads of large households would have agreed with Trueman in his preference for women as indoor servants. Hanway's imaginary servant, Thomas Trueman, goes on to make an interesting prophecy and to give a warning to other male servants. 'I should not be surprised', he says, 'to see women act universally as *Butlers*; indeed they always do so in small families, and their *sprightliness, ingenuity* and *cleanliness*, recommend them; therefore, if we give ourselves *airs* and are not upon our guard, we shall play our *game* into the hands of the *Women*'.[24]

In the case of the London household of the Duke of Bedford in 1753 forty servants of both sexes were employed, and by 1771 forty-two. 'Outside the kitchen the proportion of the female to the male staff remained very much as it had been for the past hundred years or more...female staff were entirely subordinate in number and salaries to male staff.'[25] Unfortunately there is not always evidence that households contained any female servants. As we have seen, frequently they are just not mentioned. It is another indication that it was the number of *male* servants that gave a household status. It does seem, however, that contemporaries assumed large households contained many men servants. In 1814 the author of a manual of instruction for female servants told them they must be particularly circumspect if they lived 'in a considerable family, where there are many men servants'.[26] However a later manual of 1825 directed at both servants and their masters by two former domestic servants, in outlining the household establishment of 'a respectable Country Gentle-

---

[23] *A Frenchman in England 1784*, 25.
[24] *The Sentiments and Advice of Thomas Trueman* (1760), 51.
[25] Gladys Scott Thomson, *The Russells in Bloomsbury 1669–1771* (1940), 226–7, 238.
[26] J. A. Stewart, *The Young Woman's Companion, or Female Instructor* (1814), 619.

man with a young family of Net Income £16–18,000' recommended hiring fourteen females and twelve men.[27]

The household of Sir Richard Newdigate in 1684 consisted of eleven female and sixteen male servants.[28] According to the Revd Joseph Price, Sir Edward Knatchbull of Mersham le Hatch had an impressive body of servants when he moved into his new house. The household had between twenty-two and twenty-four servants, thirteen females and nine to eleven males.[29] Nicholas Blundell in the early years of the eighteenth century certainly employed more male than female servants. In a household consisting of between ten and thirteen servants, the probable ratio of his female to male servants was 5:8 with the number of female servants amounting to about 60 per cent of the male.[30] On the other hand, the Middleton family at Stockeld Park at Wetherby in Yorkshire enjoyed an income of about £4,000 a year and in 1791 employed a large retinue of servants that consisted of 'two to three indoor and three outdoor male servants, making five to six in all, and six to seven female indoor servants'.[31] At Turkey Court near Maidstone, the home of James and Susanna Whatman, the female servants in 1778 numbered six. In addition Whatman 'generally had six or seven men on his payroll'. Two of them were the coachman and gardener but the rest were employed in 'domestic duties'.[32] John Baker, the lawyer, employed five men servants and five female.[33] When John Christian's father died in 1767 he was still a minor. Until he came of age the very young household was run by Bridget, the eldest of the six unmarried daughters, and Charles Udale, who managed the estate. At first and for some years they engaged only four servants—all women. Only later was a man servant, a coachman/handyman, added, together with a gardener and a huntsman. But their decision to employ only women servants may have had something to do with the number of young and orphaned unmarried women in the house.[34] It was usual for Henry Purefoy to employ three women and three men

---

[27] Adams, *The Complete Servant*, 7.   [28] Gooder, *The Squire of Arbury*, 37.

[29] *A Kentish Parson: Selections from the Private Papers of the Revd. Joseph Price Vicar of Brabourne, 1767–1786*, ed. G. M. Ditchfield and Bryan Keith-Lucas (1991), 133.

[30] See Ch. 8 below.   [31] Lawrence Stone, *Broken Lives* (1993), 176.

[32] *The Housekeeping Book of Susanna Whatman 1776–1800*, ed. Thomas Balston (1956), 12–13.

[33] *The Diary of John Baker*, ed. Philip C. Yorke (1931), 53.

[34] Hughes, *North Country Life in the Eighteenth Century*, ii. 115–16.

as servants.[35] In the 1730s the lawyer Francis Sitwell of Sheffield, who at his death was reputed to be worth between £400,000 and £500,000 and was the owner of a substantial property, employed four women and three men.[36] The Revd J. Trusler in 1775 advised a country gentleman with a wife and four children and 'a few acres of land' how many servants he should employ and at what wages. He recommended five servants, three men and two women; one man servant to act as both coachman and farm manager, another to combine the role of footman with that of gardener, a boy servant and two maidservants.[37] It was a pattern followed by the Revd James Woodforde, who had two man servants plus a boy, and two maidservants.[38] The Revd William Cole of Blecheley had almost the same complement of servants except that one of the two women was the gardener's wife who helped out in the house. There was also a cook and three men, a gardener, a man servant and a boy.[39] The Revd George Woodward employed three servants in all, one male and two female.[40] The Revd Gilpin, we are told, though his 'income could not amount to 700 l. per annum, yet, a discreet management, enabled him to support...his two male domestics, and as many female servants'.[41] In more modest households we find the Revd Francis D'Aeth, vicar of Godmersham, whose living was valued at £145 a year and who employed one man servant and a housekeeper.[42] The Revd David Davies of Barkham with a probable income of just over £200 a year employed two servants in the 1780s, a housekeeper and a male servant.[43] On an income of half the size, the Revd Gilpin's aunt, Mrs Appleby, employed 'two maids, an indoors servant, an outservant, and a gardener'.[44] Such households

---

[35] *The Purefoy Letters 1735–53*, ed. George Eland (1931).
[36] George R. Sitwell, *The Hurts of Haldworth* (1930), 251, 257.
[37] J. Trusler, *The Way to be Rich and Respectable* (1775), 14, subtitle, 18–19.
[38] *The Diary of a Country Parson: The Reverend James Woodforde, 1758–1813*, ed. John Beresford, 5 vols. (1924–31).
[39] *The Blecheley Diary of the Rev. William Cole 1765–7*, ed. Francis Griffin Stokes (1931), pp. liii, lv–lvi, and *passim*.
[40] *A Parson in the Vale of White Horse: George Woodward's Letters from East Hendred 1753–61*, ed. Donald Gibson (1982), 153.
[41] Richard Warner, *Literary Recollections*, 2 vols. (1830), i. 362.
[42] *A Kentish Parson*, 152–3.
[43] Pamela Horn, *A Georgian Parson and his Village: The Story of David Davies (1742–1819)* (1981), 16.
[44] Warner, *Literary Recollections*, i. 327.

make Patricia Branca's confident assertion that 'the "normal" middle class servant retinue of cook, parlour-maid and nurse-maid', described by many of those who have written of domestic service, 'would have been totally beyond the the means of most middle class families with an income of £100 and £300 a year' a little suspect.[45] Equally doubtful is the claim made by McBride that 'only after achieving an income of £300 or more could a family afford to introduce a second servant'.[46] But what these examples do suggest is that throughout most of the eighteenth century over the country as a whole there was no overwhelming predominance of female servants in households of this size. If female servants were in the majority they must have been employed in the most modest of servant-employing households about which we know so very little.

The eighteenth century, according to Cunnington, saw a 'great change in the status of men servants who were now mostly drawn from a lower social class than formerly. Even upper servants might be the sons of labourers and artisans'. This was in marked contrast to earlier periods: from medieval times to as late as the sixteenth century 'all the upper class servants were usually "persons of gentle blood and slender fortune"'.[47] If this was still true of some households in the seventeenth century, by the early eighteenth 'very few noblemen still accepted young men of good birth as pages, to educate along with their own sons'.[48]

The employment of male servants—preferably in livery—went with a household's need to display its wealth and status. The point has been made that while the work of most male servants involved confrontation with guests and visitors to their employer's household as well as frequent meetings with both servants and their employers of other households, women's work kept them not only inside the house but often invisible. When Rochefoucauld visited England in 1784 he may have slightly exaggerated when he claimed 'men servants are employed only for such duties as are performed in the presence of guests' but in many instances he was right. He was struck not merely by the

---

[45] *Silent Sisterhood: Middle Class Women in the Victorian Home* (1975), 54.
[46] *The Domestic Revolution*, 19.   [47] *Costume of Household Servants*, 2.
[48] Turner, *What the Butler Saw*, 17.

sheer number of servants but that 'more than half of them are never seen'. Among these he listed 'kitchen-maids' and 'maid servants in large number'.[49] This invisibility may well account for the fact that vails were far more important to male servants, who frequently accompanied their masters and mistresses on visits, than to female. Even inside houses that employed both male and female servants it was likely that the former were far more in evidence than the latter. The number and dress of male servants was a measure of a master's standing. Indeed it could be said that in some instances the employment of male servants was as much to impress neighbours and friends as to benefit from the particular services they provided. Catharine Cappe, at the end of the eighteenth century, commented on 'the crowds of footmen in the metropolis, retained, not for use, but for show, idle themselves, corrupted and corrupting'.[50] 'There is no doubt that a man-servant in the house', explained a mid-Victorian manual, 'is an expensive luxury.' But as it went on to argue, those aspiring to acceptance in high society were 'almost compelled to inflict this nuisance on themselves, as it is considered by many people one of the tests of their position'. If they were able to resist such pressures, however, they would find 'a great saving will be effected, and much more comfort secured by the substitution of a good parlour-maid for the man-servant'.[51] Davidoff and Hawthorn are cautious in their claims. In the eighteenth century 'wealthy households employed almost as many men as women for work indoors', but this does not tell us how many men it employed outside the house nor of those who divided their time between outdoor and indoor tasks.[52] In the nineteenth century the proportion declined as new jobs for men opened up, until by the end of the century men were 'only employed as footmen and butlers by very rich households.'[53]

Of eighteenth-century France, Sara Maza has estimated that while up to the middle of the century one-third to one-half of the

---

[49] *A Frenchman in England 1784*, 25.
[50] *Observations on Charity Schools* (1805), 132.
[51] Walsh, *A Manual of Domestic Economy*, 224.
[52] Leonore Davidoff and Ruth Hawthorn, *A Day in the Life of a Victorian Domestic Servant* (1976), 73–4.
[53] Ibid.

servant population in most towns was male, by the 1790s eight or nine servants in every ten were female.[54] She sees this change as closely related to the growth in the number of single-servant households. Where a household employed only one servant, more often than not it tended to be a female. This analysis is confirmed by Roche in respect of 'the middle-class world of shopkeepers and artisans' in Paris where only one servant was employed.[55] Apparently relatively little of the work they did involved what we now call housework. 'Much of the servants' time', writes Cissie Fairchilds of French domestic service, 'was taken up with tasks very different from the cooking and cleaning which the nineteenth-century has taught us to think of as servants' work.' They could be employed at running errands, delivering messages, helping in their employer's shop or workshop, cutting their master's hair, gathering apples, weeding in the garden. By the 1780s, Fairchilds argues, far fewer households in France were employing servants. Those who did 'tended increasingly to forgo the expensive male domestics in favour of the cheaper, if less prestigious, female servants'.[56]

Much the same was true of England. The further down the social scale one descended and the simpler the household, 'the fewer the number of servants and the more likely it was that all the servants would be women'.[57] The lowest ranks of domestic service were quite simply not filled by men. In such one- or two-servant households servants were nearly always general servants—and women. As *The Complete Servant* informed its readers, 'in small households where only one female servant is kept, the servant-of-all-work will be expected to do all the work of the house'. The authors, in an attempt to make this picture of a skivvy more attractive, added that 'no servant has it in her power to render herself and her employers more comfortable, than the maid of all work'.[58]

---

[54] *Servants and Masters in Eighteenth-Century France: The Uses of Loyalty* (1983), 277.

[55] *Paris and her People*, 68.

[56] Cissie Fairchilds, 'Masters and Servants in Eighteenth-Century Toulouse', *Journal of Social History*, 12 (1979), 367–93 at p. 378; id., *Domestic Enemies: Servants and their Masters in Old Regime France* (1984), 22.

[57] Olwen Hufton, 'Women, Work and Family', in Natalie Zemon Davis and Arlette Farge (eds.), *A History of Women*, iii (1993), 20.

[58] Adams, *The Complete Servant*, 285, 293.

Let us take one such modest household—that of Thomas Turner, the shopkeeper in East Hoathly, Sussex—as an example. When his diary starts in 1754 he was 24 and newly married. In March of that year a Mary Martin 'came to live with me' as servant. Her annual wages were to be 30s. Although she remained his servant for four years there is very little mention of her in the diary. But when Turner does mention her it is always as 'my servant'. It might be assumed this indicated she was his only servant, although at times when the family goes to church he refers to the 'two boys' accompanying them. They seem to have lived in, but there is no record of what they did. And after a few months, from March 1757 to February 1758, nothing more is heard of them. Whether Turner paid them anything we do not know. As with many young boys so employed they may have been given only bed and board with sometimes a little pocket-money. Turner certainly never refers to them as his 'servants'. Of the work Mary Martin did from day to day we hear very little. On 30 July 1754 she helped Turner, his wife, and mother-in-law make 'bolster and pillow-ticks and a bed bottom for Jos. Fuller'. If, as seems likely, she cooked for the Turners, there is no reference to it. There is an interesting reference to her wages. They were first paid on 30 July 1755, fifteen months after she started her service, and were paid 'in goods'.[59]

Most of the references to her as a servant were visits she made on behalf of Turner to Framfield, a village about four miles away. Once 'she was gone all day'. Twice she goes 'to buy some lump sugar'. On one occasion she is sent 'for a shroud for Mr. Adam's daughter'. Such references suggest the wide range of tasks general servants in small households were called on to do. In October 1757 Mary Martin goes 'to Blackboys Fair and stayed all night'. The only other references to her in his diary are made when she accompanies Turner and his wife to church—which she habitually did, often twice on Sundays. When the Bishop of Chichester confirms the parish in July 1757 Mary Martin attends. Then in December 1757, suddenly, without any explanation, Turner's wife gives her 'warning to provide herself with other service at new Lady Day next'. Why she was given notice we never learn. For the next three months Mary Martin continues to live with

[59] *The Diary of Thomas Turner 1754–1765*, ed. David Vaisey (1985), 2, 127, 3, 9.

them and to attend church regularly, but on 28 March Turner's wife 'paid Mary Martin . . . in cash and goods 40s. for one year's wages and she accordingly went away'. Her wages it would seem had been increased by 10s. a year. This was far from being the end of Mary Martin, as we shall see. But having, for whatever reason, dismissed Mary Martin, what did the Turners do? She had served out her notice but no mention is made of any attempt to find her successor. For six months they appear to have had no servant. It is only in June 1758 that Turner records 'Molly Hook came today as a servant during our pleasure'. Two weeks later Turner described her as only 'a poor, wild girl to take care of the household affairs' when his wife was away. But even for this she seems to have proved incapable for on 6 July, exactly one month after starting her services she 'went away'. The next time we hear of any resident servant in the Turner household is February 1759— over six months later. She was Hannah Marchant.[60]

Meanwhile Mary Martin had been visiting the Turners regularly—apparently as a friend. But in April 1759 she came 'to assist my wife tomorrow in my absence'. She stayed three nights and when she went home the Turners gave her 'a present of a handkerchief, value 13½d. for her trouble of coming over'. Two weeks later she is back and goes to church with Turner, his wife and the newly appointed maid. The visits continue until in April 1761, not long before the death of Turner's wife, Mary Martin 'came to assist me in the shop' and stayed to dine with Turner 'on the remains of yesterday's dinner with the addition of a veal pudding and green salad'. Three weeks later she came again 'to stand the shop for me while I went to serve Mr. Piper's funeral'. Just after the death of Turner's wife she came again to visit him and stayed to dinner.[61]

The death of Turner's wife in June 1761 called for some reorganization of his household. Some time the following August he acquired a second servant. Only in August 1762 do we learn her name. She was Sally Waller who was described by Turner as his housekeeper. Her wage was £4 a year, which Turner paid in August 1762 when she left to keep her uncle's house. There is no evidence that when she went he replaced her with another

---

[60] *The Diary of Thomas Turner 1754–1765*, ed. David Vaisey (1985), 12, 17, 79, 23, 113, 11, 128, 144, 154, 158.
[61] Ibid. 180, 181, 223, 231.

servant. Indeed when she regretted moving to keep house for her uncle she had begged Turner to let her return to his employ 'in the spring' if he was still without a servant. When the next spring came she was in love and to be married the following year. There is no evidence that Turner ever replaced her. The following 3 February Mary Martin came to visit Turner and stayed the night. Next day she aired all Turner's wife's clothes. She was still with him on the 7th when he acted as father in the marriage of James Marchant, his servant's brother, and Elizabeth Mepham. Mary Martin 'stood the shop for me during my absence'. She finally went home on 9 February. Mary Martin was clearly Turner's favourite servant. She seems to have been devoted to him. Such a relationship between master and servant was sufficiently rare to be worth remarking. But as Turner's sole servant for a period she is probably representative of many other servants in single-servant households. The work they were called on to do was pretty arbitrary and could cover a great range of tasks. Whether or not such households employed any servants, or replaced servants when they left, depended on their changing needs. When Turner's wife died Mary Martin came back to help him out and keep him company. It is an example of the use of casual local labour—often as in this case former domestic servants—to cope with crises. But Turner's experience of regular servants after the death of his wife was not to be an entirely happy one. He complained that 'to keep house with servants in the business I am situated in is not either agreeable to my natural inclination, or advantageous to my interest'.[62] Remarriage proved the answer.

It has been estimated that in the nineteenth century two-thirds of all female servants were 'general servants' with 'broad and unspecified' responsibilities.[63] It is difficult to avoid the conclusion that the expansion in the numbers of single-servant-employing households greatly increased the ratio of female to male servants and contributed to the 'feminization' of domestic service. The real question is when exactly that expansion took place. Hanway in 1760 was looking to the future when he argued that 'if *Women* serve for less Wages than *Men*, or if *Men* should continue to be wanted for *war*, in order not to distress *Agriculture*,

---

[62] Ibid. 255–6, 270–1, 265–6.   [63] McBride, *The Domestic Revolution*, 12.

or *Manufactories*, women will be more courted, for *domestic service*'.[64]

Whether or not the feminization of domestic service started in the eighteenth century and continued throughout the nineteenth, women were always in a minority in service in husbandry. But if there were always more men than women the balance of the sexes was more even than became the case in domestic service by the late eighteenth century. 'Many women', writes Ann Kussmaul, 'were at some time in their lives productive farm servants.' She has estimated the ratio of male to female servants in husbandry in 1851 as 213:100 but by then service in husbandry was already well in decline.[65] In rural areas servants in husbandry of both sexes probably made up almost 60 per cent of the population. In 1770 Arthur Young arrived at figures which would have made the ratio between female and male 3:4—not so very different from Kussmaul's figures.[66] But by 1770 the decline in service in husbandry had already started so the ratio may not be truly representative. In the records of the Spalding Statute Sessions in Lincolnshire which give lists of farm servants hired between 1767 and 1785 there were 844 males to 722 females.[67] Whatever the relationship between male and female domestic servants' wages, there is little doubt of how they related in service in husbandry. At the same Spalding Hiring Sessions between 1763 and 1785 the mean annual male wage was £6. 5s. 0d. compared to £2. 15s. 0d. for a female. 'Women systematically received only a fraction of mens' wages'.[68] It is very difficult to estimate exactly how many servants in husbandry there were for, as Kussmaul emphasizes, there was no distinction made between them and personal servants. It makes it difficult to arrive at any exact proportion of females in relation to males in service in husbandry. It might suggest that at least a little caution is needed in making assumptions about the predominance of female domestic servants before say the middle of the eighteenth century.

Until recently the generally accepted view of what was happen-

[64] *The Sentiments and Advice of Thomas Trueman*, 52.
[65] *Servants in Husbandry in Early Modern England* (1981), 4, 15.
[66] *A Six Months' Tour through the North of England*, 4 vols. (1770), iv. 317.
[67] Ann Kussmaul. 'The Ambiguous Mobility of Farm Servants', *Economic History Review*, 34/2 (May 1981), 222–35 at p. 228.
[68] Kussmaul, *Servants in Husbandry in Early Modern England*, 37.

ing to domestic service from the second half of the eighteenth into and through the nineteenth century is that it was steadily becoming 'feminized' just as some occupations, such as midwifery, were fast becoming the monopoly of men. What this meant was not that women suddenly stopped being midwives but that the trend was for men to replace women. But, of course, there is a profound difference between the two cases. Male midwives deliberately set about excluding women from midwifery. Female servants had neither the power nor the intention of excluding men from service. Lower wages for female servants may well have had their influence on employers' choice of females rather than males, but this was a factor outside women's control. With domestic service it was rather a case of men opting out of service. In the second half of the eighteenth century, with little choice of alternative occupations, more and more women were entering domestic service, it is argued, so that the proportion of male servants fell steadily. On when exactly this happened there is less agreement. Some historians of the nineteenth century are convinced it occurred in this period. Theresa McBride, for example, claims that 'one of the characteristic aspects of domestic service after 1800 was the feminization of service—the balance between males and females in service was increasingly tipped toward the women so that by the first world war service was substantially a female occupation'.[69] Leonore Davidoff and Catherine Hall write of how 'in the early nineteenth century, domestic service began to be seen as a separate category marked by a gradual preponderance of females as men moved into day labour or white collar positions'.[70]

There is a suggestion that the employment of women rather than men by employers was a calculated economic strategy. There was 'a growing feeling that indoor men servants were a luxury not many people could afford'.[71] It is worth noting that it was in 1777 that Lord North first imposed a tax on male servants. His estimate of the number of male servants at the time was 100,000.[72] In 1806 Patrick Colquhoun estimated there were 110,000

[69] *The Domestic Revolution*, 15.
[70] Leonore Davidoff and Catherine Hall, *Family Fortunes* (1987), 388.
[71] Leonore Davidoff and Catherine Hall, *A Day in the Life of a Victorian Domestic Servant* (1970), 74.
[72] Hecht, *The Domestic Servant in Eighteenth-Century England*, 34.

men servants.[73] In other words, the number of male servants had increased by 10,000 in nearly thirty years. The tax was fixed at one guinea per servant, with bachelors required to pay double that sum and families with children given special dispensation from the full burden of the tax. Eight years later Pitt increased the tax imposed by Lord North to £1. 5s. 0d. when only one male servant was kept, with a progressive scale according to the number of servants in a household up to £3 per head. Bachelors were still made to pay double tax. At the same time Pitt introduced a tax on maidservants. It was far less than the tax on male servants but it too varied according to the number of servants kept. It ranged from 2s. 6d. for one servant up to 10s. Again bachelors were taxed at a double rate.[74] Had these taxes been rigorously applied and measures taken to deal with offenders it might have been a valuable source of information about servants in the final decades of the eighteenth century. The evidence, however, suggests there was widespread evasion or under-assessment. Nevertheless it may have been a contributory factor in households' decision to employ fewer men servants in relation to female.

There is also a suspicion that men were resenting more and more the 'close personal supervision' by employers of their indoor staff. Work outside distanced them from their employers and enabled them to live 'in their own homes'.[75] Male servants in London in the period 1650–1750, Earle has suggested, left service before they were 40. In explanation he writes, 'the need for constant deference and servility may ... have palled after a while'.[76] Among other reasons given for this feminization process, McBride thinks wars and shortage of manpower helped, but that 'basically ... the decline in male servants marked the change from aristocratic employment to middle-class employment'.[77] Davidoff 'sees men resisting the nature of the master/servant relationship as other occupations became available'.[78] The deterioration in servant–employer relations that is so noticeable in contemporary comment at the end of the seventeenth century and throughout the eighteenth may have been more about employers'

[73] *A Treatise on Indigence* (1806), 253.
[74] Turner, *What the Butler Saw*, 79–80; *The Diary of a Country Parson*, ii. 207–8.
[75] Davidoff and Hawthorn, *A Day in the Life of a Victorian Domestic Servant*, 75.
[76] *A City Full of People*, 85.   [77] *The Domestic Revolution*, 15.
[78] 'Domestic Service and the Working Class Life Cycle', 10.

difficulties in keeping their male servants under control than about vails and perquisites. It is also suggested that 'working class definitions of masculinity and independence made domestic service less and less palatable to young men'.[79] In commenting on the increasing reluctance of young men in eighteenth-century Toulouse to enter domestic service 'which they were coming to consider demeaning', Cissie Fairchilds echoes such views.[80] In England by 1851, it is estimated, 85 per cent of the country's domestic servants were women.[81] By the 1880s, Davidoff believes, domestic service was completely feminized.[82]

But the rural–urban migration in which women were to play an increasing and—ultimately—dominant role had started earlier, in the seventeenth and eighteenth centuries. It seems probable that by the second half of the eighteenth century—if not before—this great influx of female migrants into towns contributed to making cheap servants available to households that had never previously employed them. On the other hand women in modest households that had become a little better off were anxious to shift some of the burden of the drudgery of housework—perhaps more particularly the drudgery of washdays—on to other shoulders. Olwen Hufton has argued that 'since female labour was cheap and abundant, it [the employment of a maidservant] was one of the first luxuries even a modest family permitted itself'.[83] So both supply and demand played a role in the increase in female domestic servants.

Another reason why it seems plausible to assume that a great increase in the demand for female domestic servants occurred in the eighteenth century—particularly in the second half—is that new demands were being made by the changing lifestyle of the urban middle class in houses where the family and the servants were now physically separated, where wooden floors had replaced stone or brick ones, where there were far more curtains and hangings, upholstered furniture, ornaments, and pictures

---

[79] Davidoff, 'Class and Gender in Victorian England: The Diaries of Arthur J. Munby and Hannah Cullwick', *Feminist Studies*, 5/1 (spring 1979), 86–141 at p. 94.
[80] 'Masters and Servants in Eighteenth-Century Toulouse', 377.
[81] Duncan Bythell, 'Women in the Work Force', in Patrick O'Brien and Roland Quinault (eds.), *The Industrial Revolution and British Society* (1993), 31–53 at p. 36.
[82] 'Domestic Service and the Working Class Life Cycle', 10.
[83] 'Women, Work and Family', 20.

than formerly. It was a development that had started much earlier, but only in the homes of the wealthy. By the end of the eighteenth century some of these changes were affecting not merely the homes of farmers and merchants but even those of artisans and retailers. And what these changes involved was more washing, sweeping, dusting, and polishing—work that was almost always exclusively women's work. For middle-class wives of modest income who had never employed servants before, a young female maid-of-all-work who could do all the work of the house must have seemed the ideal.

Technological change in the household before the nineteenth century may not seem of great importance but in terms of the changes it brought to the work of servants and housewives it was dramatic. In the eighteenth century only the large houses of the rich, and relatively few of those, had a piped water supply, a water-closet, and a bathroom but the effect of these on the kind of labour demanded of their servants was considerable. The drawing and fetching of water from well or stream had been a major part of a household's labour needs which, while not exclusively confined to women, was normally performed by them. It was not just a question of servants providing enough fresh clean water for the household, but of disposing of the dirty. Both were time-consuming and onerous tasks. Once there was a ready supply of water it was far easier to clean clothes and floors, curtains and bed-linen, and to wash up kitchen pots and pans as well as china. Standards of cleanliness immediately rose and, almost certainly as a result, so did the frequency of washdays and the regularity with which floors and steps were scoured. It also made it possible for bedrooms to be provided with water morning and night—an increasingly important part of a chambermaid's or housemaid's duties.

The arrival of the kitchen stove involved the new task of blackleading it. It made possible more elaborate cooking. The gargantuan meals eaten by many of the gentry in the eighteenth century could not easily have been cooked over an open fire. It also necessitated more pots and pans and kitchen implements. All this almost certainly led to much more work in the kitchen and the need for more kitchen staff. More furniture, more silver and brass ornaments, more knick-knacks made for more polishing and dusting. The move towards greater privacy for the family and

Male and Female Servants

the multiplication of rooms with servants' quarters separated from those of the family also made more work and work that was customarily regarded as women's work.

Recent views of historians tend to refute such arguments in support of nineteenth- or eighteenth-century feminization. It is claimed by some that domestic service has always been feminized. The majority of such arguments have been based on work done on London parishes. Of domestic service in London in two wealthy parishes in 1695, for example, Peter Earle, on the basis of a series of assessments produced for the tax on burials, births, and marriages, has shown how female servants predominated. They 'represent four out of every five domestics and were the only domestics in over three quarters of the households'.[84] Earle claims that in London, 'domestic service accounted for 25.4 per cent of the total number of women employed'.[85] In half the households covered by the survey only one servant was employed and that almost always a woman. The 'normal domestic staff' was one or two servants—nearly always female.[86] Earle analyses closely only thirty-six households and, as he acknowledges, there was widespread evasion of the tax, but perhaps the most vulnerable of his arguments is that of assuming that most examples of 'male servants' in the assessments were in fact apprentices, journeymen, clerks, and bookkeepers. Without such an assumption his figures for male and female 'servants' in the thirty-six households are remarkably even. More recently he has written of 'a very visible minority of male servants' in London.[87]

Tim Meldrum in 1993 echoed Earle's conclusions when he argued that in the metropolis domestic service 'either side of 1700 was already a female occupation; just over 80 per cent of current servants (in service or out of a place) were women, while male domestic servants form a clear minority in a segmented labour market'.[88] He concludes that domestic service in London was an overwhelmingly female occupation. But can we take London as representative of the whole country? Gregory King, whose estimates of population are generally regarded as remarkably accu-

---

[84] *The Making of the English Middle Class* (1989), 218.
[85] Ibid.   [86] Ibid.   [87] *A City Full of People*, 82.
[88] 'Ubiquity and Visibility: Domestic Service in London, 1660–1750', paper given at the Economic History Society Conference (Apr. 1993), 6.

rate, in 1695—the same year as that on which Earle bases his conclusions—estimated that in England there were 300,000 female servants to 260,000 male, a ratio of 15:13, somewhat different from the ratio of 4:1 arrived at for London by Earle.[89] How can the difference be explained? It suggests that migration to London in search of places was already predominantly female. It in part explains the sex ratio in London in 1695, based on forty parishes, of 87:100.[90] Gregory King's estimate of 230,000 males to 300,000 females would have made the ratio 77:100.[91] It is perhaps significant that the ratio of male to female servants in London relates to an abnormally low sex ratio, although the number of female servants exceeds that suggested by the ratio. There are other reasons for thinking London was far from representative in its servant population. The kind of technological changes which we have seen as having a marked influence on the sex of servants required had almost certainly gone much further in London than elsewhere. One would also expect rural households to employ more men servants whose work was outside the house on the land or in the garden. In 1806 Colquhoun estimated that for the country as a whole there were 110,000 male household servants and 800,000 female or a ratio of 1:7.[92] By the time of the 1851 Occupational Census the ratio of male to female servants in England and Wales was approximately 1:8, and the ratio of female general servants to male indoor general servants was almost the same. Twenty years later the ratio was 1:11 when the number of female domestic servants had increased by over 56.6 per cent while the number of male servants had risen by only 9.5 per cent.[93] Such figures suggest a considerable expansion in the number of female servants at the expense of male over these twenty years but a steady expansion from the late seventeenth century.

We come back to the question of what exactly is meant by 'feminization' of service. There is a difference between the claim that women servants have always existed and constituted a sig-

---

[89] Gregory King, *Natural and Political Observations and Conclusions upon the State and Condition of England*, ed. George E. Barnett (1936), 22.
[90] Peter Clark and Paul Slack, *English Towns in Transition 1500–1700* (1976), 88.
[91] King, *Natural and Political Observations*, 12.
[92] *A Treatise on Indigence*, 253.
[93] Census figures of 1851 and 1871 analysed by John Burnett in *Useful Toil* ed. John, p. 130.

nificant proportion—even perhaps the preponderance—of all domestic servants and what happened in the eighteenth and nineteenth centuries when as we have seen, men started to withdraw from service and the number of women servants increased, to a point some time in the nineteenth century when domestic service was an almost exclusively 'female' occupation. The description of what happened some time between the early eighteenth and the end of the nineteenth century as a 'feminization' of service appears still to be a valid one.

3

The Sexual Vulnerability and Sexuality of Female Domestic Servants

> 'So profligate and abandoned is the world become, that you had better turn your daughter into the street at once, than place her out to service. For ten to one her master shall seduce her.'
>
> John Moir, *Female Tuition; or an Address to Mothers on the Education of Daughters* (1786)

THE vulnerability of female domestic servants to the sexual advances of their masters, their masters' sons, or their male fellow servants and others, has long been acknowledged. The very characteristics which distinguished female domestic servants made them particularly prone to sexual exploitation. The fact that by far the overwhelming majority were young, single girls, away from their family, their friends, and relations meant that just when they needed protection from such exploitation they were taken away from those best able to give it. In a strange household miles away from their own village and family the young female domestic servant must have been both lonely and isolated. The very nature of servants' quarters contributed to their vulnerability. Often they were mere spaces on landings or virtual cupboards without windows or, sometimes, even doors. As late as the second half of the nineteenth century, when she was a scullery maid in a large household, Hannah Cullwick lived 'in a rough outhouse next the kitchen'. Without windows, it could only be reached via the coal hole. In France, according to Olwen Hufton, a maidservant was 'even expected to sleep on the kitchen floor' where 'she was a prey for both master and apprentice'.[1] It seems probable that among those single-servant households in England about which we have so little evidence the same conditions may well have been those of at least some female servants. When servants were given rooms they were usually small attics. But wherever their quarters were, something that was common to them all was that they could rarely be locked. When, in 1760, John Macdonald returned to Bargeny as Mr Hamilton's body servant there were rumours of a liaison between him and the lady's maid. The housekeeper responded by locking the rooms 'as she thought thereby', Macdonald wrote, 'to keep us from meeting'.[2] It is significant that the housekeeper kept the keys—no doubt on the instruction of her mistress and to prevent servants locking their rooms against intruders. Servants had to be accessible at all times. Privacy was not for them. In Pepys's household some of the maidservants seem to have occupied rooms very close to that of their master. In 1668 Mrs Pepys accused Pepys of being 'false to her with Jane', their servant. Jane, it was held, never got up in the morning until Pepys himself had risen and left his room, so, as he recorded, 'her letting me thereby see her dressing herself'.[3] In 1764, when hired by two bachelors at Aldermanbury, John Macdonald described his experience one night on 'going to bed, the maid's room and bed facing the stairs as I came up, she in bed and the candle burning, I could see her at different times uncovered'. As he commented it was 'very tempting to a man, for she was a pretty young girl'.[4] According to him the only action he took was to give her a lecture on the danger of going to sleep with the candle still alight.

There were other ways in which female servants were particularly vulnerable to sexual advances from members of the household. The organization of servants' day-to-day work routine was known to everyone in the house. Often housemaids and chamber-

---

[1] As quoted in Leonore Davidoff, 'Class and Gender in Victorian England: the Diaries of Arthur J. Munby and Hannah Cullwick', *Feminist Studies*, 5/1 (spring 1979), 86–141 at p. 107; Olwen Hufton, 'Women in Eighteenth-Century France', in R. B. Outhwaite (ed.), *Marriage and Society: Studies in the Social History of Marriage* (1981), 186–203 at p. 194.

[2] *Memoirs of an Eighteenth-Century Footman, John Macdonald*, ed. John Beresford (1927), 50.

[3] *The Diary of Samuel Pepys*, ed. Henry B. Wheatley, 3 vols. (1946), vol. iii (vol. viii of the diary), p. 207.

[4] *Memoirs of an Eighteenth-Century Footman*, 72.

maids worked alone cleaning rooms far from the kitchen and the rest of the household's servants. Any predatory male in the house would know where they could be found at any time of the day—and night. Given the intimate services maidservants often performed for their masters, even undressing and putting them to bed, there was, as Pepys found, ample opportunity for sexual advances. Sometimes a single maid servant was expected to stay up waiting for her master to come home. So in that most ordered household of Susanna Whatman the housemaid was expected to sit up for the master's return home, and to warm his bed. Where a female servant was the only servant employed in a household there was no resort to the kitchen and the safety of numbers. So female domestic servants were easily accessible to the other inmates of the household.

Servants at inns were probably even more vulnerable. Henry Fielding certainly thought so. A chambermaid at an inn was 'daily liable to the Solicitations of Lovers of all Complexions, to the dangerous Addresses of fine Gentlemen of the Army...and above all exposed to the Caresses of Footmen, Stage-coachmen and Drawers'.[5] If Dudley Ryder was typical, male clients expected the servants of such inns to be available to them. 'At the George', Ryder recorded, 'I met with a pretty girl for a maid. I did not know how at first to introduce a kiss but at last did and kissed her twice with a great deal of zest.' He had hopes of other such servant maids at inns: 'Pleased myself as I came along with the hope of meeting with a pretty girl to kiss at the inn at Newbury.' He was to be disappointed: 'There was such a one as I could kiss but not extraordinary.'[6] Knowing Ryder, it did not stop at kissing.

The very division of labour between servants meant that their duties often involved them working alone in rooms in the house, sweeping and dusting, making beds, emptying the slops. This can only have increased their accessibility to male members of the household. As we have seen, some of the duties servants were called on to perform could involve great intimacy with their masters and mistresses. Pepys not only regularly had his maidservants help to dress him, but also to comb his hair and even, on occasion, to wash his feet or ears. When John Macdonald became

---

[5] As quoted in Dorothy Margaret Stuart, *The English Abigail* (1946), 115.
[6] *The Diary of Dudley Ryder 1715–16*, ed. William Matthews (1939), 238.

butler and hair-dresser to a gentleman in Kent he was responsible for dressing his master—and his mistress. The man servant to John Skinner's mother 'slept in her room'.[7]

Writing of eighteenth-century France, Sara Maza has said that 'the most abiding threat that a female servant faced was sexual', and 'the women most likely to be sexually abused and exploited were domestic workers'.[8] One aspect of their vulnerability was their total dependence on their masters. The insistence by most employers on the unmarried status of their servants, Maza has convincingly argued of France, is comparable to the vows of chastity extracted from those entering monasteries and convents. In place of God was the servant's master to whom the same commitment was made. In their day-to-day existence, in which total obedience to the demands of their master and mistress was expected, they became morally, economically, financially, and, as we shall see, even sexually, dependent on their masters and wholly confined in the isolated and tight little world of one household. Steven Marcus in *The Other Victorians: A Study of Sexuality and Pornography in Mid-Nineteenth-Century England*, discusses the scandalous life of the anonymous author of *My Secret Life*. In a comment on the 'assumptions that governed the relations of masters and servants' he writes: 'it is assumed by everyone, including the servants that the author has a right to be doing what he is doing'.[9] If their master or a fellow servant made sexual advances what were female servants to do? If such advances came from their masters they were well aware that their whole future—both economic and marital—lay in their employer's hands. The *déclarations de grossesses* in France are an important source of evidence giving far more detail than English records. Marguerite Angellin, for instance, told the court that she slept with her master although he was married and a grandfather, because 'he said that if she didn't he couldn't pay her wages'.[10] In Nantes in 1748, Marie Toutescotes yielded to a Monsieur de Kernoel. She explained the

---

[7] *Journal of a Somerset Rector, 1803–34*, ed. Howard and Peter Coombs (1930), 237.

[8] *Servants and Masters in Eighteenth-Century France: The Uses of Loyalty* (1983), 89.

[9] *The Other Victorians: A Study of Sexuality and Pornography in Mid-Nineteenth-Century England* (1966), 131.

[10] Cissie Fairchilds, 'Female Sexual Attitudes and the Rise of Illegitimacy: A Case Study', *Journal of Interdisciplinary History*, 8/4 (spring 1978), 627–67 at p. 639.

circumstances. De Kernoel was a friend of her master who had come to stay when her master was away on a military campaign. 'She felt', she said, 'that she should not refuse him, being afraid that her master would be angry with her.'[11]

Servants could be dismissed on the slightest of excuses. With a master refusing to give them a character another place might be difficult if not impossible to find. With an insistent master the life of a servant must have been made impossible. Little wonder then that in such circumstances some voluntarily succumbed. 'The majority', writes Cissie Fairchilds, 'accepted their master's advances because they had no choice.'[12]

But what positive evidence is there that female servants were sexually exploited by their masters or their sons? In eighteenth-century France affairs between masters and servants were frequent. 'Most female servants', we are told. 'experienced some form of sexual harassment by their masters at one point or another.'[13] Just how widespread such affairs were is indicated by the number of wives in eighteenth-century France petitioning the church for legal separation. If physical abuse was the first reason given, their husbands' adultery with a servant maid was a close second. There is no reason for thinking the situation in England was different. Evidence there is, but often the fact was concealed—from the master's wife and fellow servants—for fear of instant dismissal. When a domestic servant became pregnant and was hauled before the local JP and the identity of the father demanded, many lied under pressure from their masters. Dudley Ryder recorded how his 'sister's maid, Mrs Jane was discovered this week to be with child and was examined by brother and sister about [it]. She was very unwilling at first to make any confession, but at last by threatenings was brought to give them satisfaction'.[14] When Mary Hubbard, servant to Thomas Osborne, was reputed to be pregnant in July 1757, Thomas Turner, as overseer of the poor, went to interview her. She persuaded him she was not in fact pregnant. By September she could no longer conceal her

---

[11] Jacques Depauw, 'Illicit Sexual Activity in Society in Eighteenth-Century Nantes', in Robert Forster and Orest A. Ranum (eds.), *Family and Society* (1976), 145–91 at p. 161.

[12] *Domestic Enemies: Servants and their Masters in Old Regime France* (1984), 88.

[13] Maza, *Servants and Masters in Eighteenth-Century France*, 165.

[14] *The Diary of Dudley Ryder, 1715–16*, 355.

condition and Turner once again visited her with the object of ascertaining the name of the father of the child. But, Turner recorded, 'she would give us no satisfactory, answer'. Even as late as the end of October she 'could not be persuaded to swear her great belly'. By late November she had yielded enought to promise that if the father of her child 'did not come and give this parish proper security to their liking', she would reveal his identity. One can only imagine the nature of the exchanges between master and servant which finally persuaded Osborne to come forward and offer 'his bond to indemnify and save harmless this parish from any charge that shall ever arise touching or concerning his servant now being pregnant, and from all charges that may arise therefrom'.[15] A warrant was issued the following February, after her child was born, to bring Mary Hubbard before a justice in order to swear the father of the child. She had had prior notice of their coming and had gone, but they finally caught up with her and she swore the father of the child was Thomas Osborne, her late employer. In the early nineteenth century the Revd Skinner was accused, but with what justification we are not told, of intrigues with his nursemaid.[16] Frequently the man concerned would exert pressure on the girl to refuse to disclose his identity, to put the blame on somebody else, or even to sign a disclaimer. In 1701, after accusing the powerful laird of Cockpen of fathering her child, Isobel Hall was summoned to appear before the presbytery where a paper was produced, apparently signed by her, retracting the charge. Asked to explain she said that when she had signed the paper 'she was made to believe it was a quit ither thing'. The laird had told her he would give her 'a testimonial that would carry me through all the world'.[17]

Almost certainly the threat offered to female servants from their employers was much greater than might appear from the evidence that exists. And, of course, for many in the eighteenth century it seemed very natural that masters—and their sons—should regard their servants as sexually available. Female servants existed, it was held by many, for their masters' convenience.

---

[15] *The Diary of Thomas Turner 1754–1765*, ed. David Vaisey (1985), 104, 110, 120, 124, 125.
[16] *Journal of a Somerset Rector 1803–34*, 95.
[17] R. A. Houston, *Scottish Literacy and the Scottish Identity* (1985), 239–40.

Sexual encounters with servants seemed 'natural' and were 'socially acceptable'—at least to the upper class.[18]

In the early years of the eighteenth century in Myddle 'Richard [Guest] ... had ... a daughter named Mary (Moll), who was a servant to Sir Henry Vernon of Hodnett'. The son of the household, Thomas, 'was over familiar with her, and had a child or more by her'.[19] When he married 'a beautiful and well accomplished lady', Moll Guest announced she was his wife and that they had had several children. The case came before Lichfield Consistory Court where it soon became clear the evidence for the marriage was conclusive. Sir Henry, much grieved by events, soon after died. His son then came to an agreement with Moll by which she received 'a yearly salary or annuity'.[20] Masters did not confine their sexual advances to their own servants. In a letter of 1765 to George Selwyn, from the Rt. Hon. Richard Rigby, it was suggested that Lord Abergavenny had been 'making love to my lady's maid and that her ladyship is gone out of town sulky'.[21] In 1783 Woodforde recorded in his diary that 'Charlotte Dunnell is reported to be with Child by old Page ... She lately lived with him as Housekeeper'.[22] The relationship was not always severed on the servant's leaving the household. John Skinner, the Somerset rector, writes of a Lavinia Purnell who 'when young lived as servant with Farmer Emery'. He 'seduced her, and a discovery being made by his wife of the connection, she got into service at Bath, where he still kept up the intercourse, and got her two or three times from good situations pretending that he was her uncle and had need of her services at home'. So, we are told, she was prevented from 'gaining an honest living'.[23]

It has been suggested that there was a particular sexual attraction for middle- and upper-class men in women of the lower classes—an 'eroticism of inequality'.[24] The author of *My Secret Life* as a young boy in a wealthy household had discovered at a young age 'that servants were fair game'. 'Soon', he tells us, 'there was not one in the house whom I had not kissed.' His mother ordered

---

[18] Maza, *Servants and Masters in Eighteenth-Century France*, 165.
[19] Richard Gough, *The History of Myddle (1701–1706)* (1979), 108.
[20] Ibid.
[21] J. H. Jesse, *George Selwyn and his Contemporaries*, 4 vols. (1846), i. 365.
[22] *The Diary of a Country Parson: The Reverend James Woodforde, 1758–1813*, ed. John Beresford, 5 vols. (1924–31), ii. 107.
[23] *Journal of a Somerset Rector 1803–34*, 68–9.
[24] Maza, *Servants and Masters in Eighteenth-Century France*, 166.

him 'to cease speaking to the servants'. The great majority of the author's experiences which were numerous—were with domestic servants. Of one, Kitty, he wrote 'there was a frankness, openness, and freshness . . . which delighted me'. On another occasion he talks of 'the relatively free sexuality' of these servant girls.[25] The very nature of their work, Leonore Davidoff has suggested, 'made them more intimate and earthy than middle-class adults . . . debarred from many activities because of taboos, manners and etiquette'. Despite the emphasis of Victorians on cleanliness, and indeed almost as a reaction against it, 'the naturalness, even "rankness" of working class people could have a subtle attraction'. The attraction is closely related to the attitude to prostitution of Mandeville and many others, as something necessary to keep middle-class women pure. Whether prostitutes or household servants, working-class girls existed to satisfy the inordinate lusts of men. Men had 'need for a debased object since the sexual act is seen as something degrading which defiles and pollutes not only the body'.[26]

If the mistress of a house got to hear of a relationship between a maidservant and her husband or son regardless of whether or not the girl was pregnant she was instantly dismissed. Directly she learnt of a servant's pregnancy, no matter who was the father of the child, the servant was sent away. Cissie Fairchilds has suggested it was the reaction of women always fearful that their husbands or sons might be responsible.[27] The evidence suggests they were right to be suspicious. The wife wanted all reminder of such a possibility removed at once. Such fear was a potent factor in the tense relationship between wives and female servants. Some indication of the real threat posed to female servants by the men of the household can be seen in the lengths mistresses would go to to avoid hiring a pretty maidservant. The assumption was that pretty servants were bound to be seduced by their masters. Novels of the period abound with examples. In Richardson's *Pamela, or Virtue Rewarded*, Lady Towers makes the point to Pamela.[28] In Fielding's *Tom Jones*, there is the schoolmaster's wife who 'in order to guard herself against matrimonial Injuries in her

---

[25] Marcus, *The Other Victorians*, 129.
[26] Leonore Davidoff, 'Class and Gender in Victorian England', 95–6, 99.
[27] *Domestic Enemies*, 90.
[28] *The Shakespeare Head Edition of the Novels of Samuel Richardson*, 18 vols. (1929), i: *Pamela, or Virtue Rewarded*, 64, 112.

own House, as she kept one Maid Servant, she always took care to chuse her out of that Order of Females whose Faces are taken as a Kind of Security for their Virtue'.[29] In Sarah Scott's *Millenium Hall*, a beautiful young girl of 15, Louisa Mancel, is suddenly left with no means of support. She starts to look for a place as a domestic servant, but is told by her counsellor 'she must not expect, while her person continued such as it then was, that a married woman would receive her in any capacity that fixed her in the same house with her husband.'[30] The only place she could hope for was with some widow.

But it is not only in fiction that such cases are found. In February 1669 Mrs Pepys was looking for a chambermaid. Pepys thought she had found one much to his liking—'she pleasing me, though I dare not own it'. But his wife told him that 'she had one great fault, and that was, that she was very handsome . . . many times . . . she took occasion to discourse on her handsomeness, and the danger she was in by taking her'. When Pepys assured her of his resolution 'to have nothing to do with her maids' she clearly did not believe him. She was right to doubt his word. She had second thoughts and decided not to employ the 'handsome maid' but to Pepys's fury took on 'another that was full of the smallpox'.[31] Elizabeth Purefoy may have harboured some hopes that her son would ultimately marry. She seems to have thought him susceptible to a maidservant's charms. When looking for a new maid in February 1749 she wrote to Mary Harris outlining her needs. Her final point was that she would 'like her never y worse if she was forty years old'.[32]

Of course there was another side of the coin—but one far more rarely met with. John Macdonald, who according to his own accounts was a lady's man, in his *Memoirs* relates how one of his employers, Colonel Dalrymple, tells him 'no family will have you for fear of their women' and when finally hired by a Major Joass he was told 'I shall take you for my servant, for you must live with a single gentleman: no family will admit you into their house'.[33] In

---

[29] *The Wesleyan Edition of the Works of Henry Fielding*, 9 vols. (1972–88), *The History of Tom Jones*, 2 vols. (1974), i. 83.
[30] *Millenium Hall* (1762), 66.
[31] *The Diary of Samuel Pepys*, iii (vol. viii of the diary), 242, 244.
[32] *The Purefoy Letters 1735–53*, ed. G. Eland, 2 vols. (1931), i. 154.
[33] *Memoirs of an Eighteenth-Century Footman*, 57, 59.

1793, writing of the treatment of servants by their mistresses, Richard Graves hinted at more than a mistress–servant relationship. 'Their footmen', he claimed, 'sometimes experience more than a fraternal affection.'[34]

Both masters and mistresses seem to have been acutely aware of the consequences for themselves of their servants becoming pregnant. It was very inconvenient and upset the household for an uncertain period of time. It is linked to the insistence on celibacy by most masters and mistresses. But it was not just the threat of illegitimate children that worried them. Even when a pregnant servant had a suitor willing and anxious to marry her the result was the same—an interruption to the household. In the Earl of Crauford's household, when John Macdonald was servant, there was a young maidservant, Kitty Cochran, to whom Macdonald felt drawn. But Macdonald tells us 'Ross the waiter got her with child and married her'. When it was discovered they were married, both were turned away. It was a story that had a sad ending: 'She bore a child that was blind, and she herself broke her heart and died.'[35] To guard against servants marrying or getting pregnant employers tried to keep them immured in their houses and did everything to prevent them going outside the house, visiting the village, or making contacts with those not of the household. If 'marriage was the goal of nearly every woman servant' as Rosina Harrison has suggested of a later and, almost certainly, somewhat less restricted service, 'it wasn't easy for them . . . the maids' limited and irregular time off was an added disadvantage. Then there was the having to be back by ten o'clock which made every date like Cinderella's ball, only you didn't lose your slipper, you could lose your job.'[36] Both masters and mistresses seem to have been always on the look-out for pregnancy in their servants. In November 1778 the Revd James Woodforde was certain one of his maidservants, Nanny, was pregnant as 'she looked so big about the Waist'. He discussed the matter with Betty, another of his servants, who convinced him he was mistaken. In June 1800 Woodforde wrote in his diary that his maid Betty was 'poorly and weak still. Nancy thinks it is owing to a Love Affair with my farming man & servant Ben Leggatt who hath for a long time

[34] *The Reveries of Solitude* (1793), 37.
[35] *Memoirs of an Eighteenth-Century Footman*, 41.
[36] *Rose: My Life in Service* (1975), 24.

taken notice of her. They have for a long time been talked of. Whether he now slights her or not, I cannot say.' His real concern is revealed when he adds 'I hope he hath not been too intimate with her'.[37] In April 1787 John Gabriel Stedman recorded 'Our maid Betty casts her stomach, *I suspect*.'[38] He seems to have been wrong. Some employers went so far as to impose a 'no followers' ban or to insist that female servants in their employ had visits from only family and relations. In 1717 the Revd John Thomlinson was cautioned 'against Mr. Brown's wife's sister' coming as housekeeper—'she is a confident, tatling woman, and for all the good opinion he has of her, she will wast and destroy things by entertaining sparks etc.'[39] In 1777 an advertisement for a cook in the *Morning Post* read 'No person need apply who has followers'. Alcock cautioned employers that 'no male guests should be admitted except relatives, viz., father and brothers, or *authorised* suitors'. If this rule was adhered to it might prevent 'many of these clandestine nocturnal assemblies which are so detrimental, if not ruinous, to the character of female servants'.[40] Such efforts to keep servants from contact with others outside the household also reflect a dislike by many employers of servants entertaining their friends at their expense, as well as a fear of what servants said about them when outside the household. But the most important reason for imposing such rules was fear of losing their female servants by their marriage or illegitimate pregnancy.

Female servants were often very resentful and unhappy about such a ban. In Claver Morris's household, for example, Betty Biggs, a new servant, when told by another that her master 'would allow of no Sweet-hart to come to a Maid-Servant in my House, cam to me & said Though she could very easily do the Work of my House; Yet she could [not] take the Care of it, nor Buy Things proper to be spent in it; And she could not be settled in it & therefore desired she might be at liberty to return to Somerton . . . which she did'.[41] Every effort was taken by masters

[37] *The Diary of a Country Parson*, i. 238, v. 261.
[38] *The Journal of John Gabriel Stedman 1744–97*, ed. Stanbury Thompson (1962), 313.
[39] *The Diary of the Rev. John Thomlinson*, in *Six North Country Diaries*, Surtees Society, cxviii (1910), 64–167 at p. 73.
[40] Thomas Alcock, *Observations on the Defects of the Poor Laws and on the Causes and Consequences of the Great Increase and Burden of the Poor* (1752), 7.
[41] *The Diary of a West Country Physician 1684–1726*, ed. Edmund Hobhouse (1934), 126.

and mistresses to keep their servants at home, and to keep would-be suitors away. 'Be not fond of increasing your acquaintance', servants were advised, 'for visiting leads you out of your business, robs your master of your time, and puts you to an expense you cannot afford.'[42] When in 1821 John Skinner heard of his maidservant's 'entanglement' with a man from the village who had 'no intention of marrying her', she was warned to drop the association or leave. Skinner repeated his warning to servants about 'forming any acquaintance with people around me'. Apparently, when he took a new servant on he 'made it a rule . . . to state my dislike of them going into the village'. In some compensation he promised them permission to 'go home to their friends, or occasionally see them here'. He expressed his dislike of young servants being 'left to their own machinations more than we can help'.[43]

When, on 22 May 1828, after knocking at his kitchen door 'till I was tired' Skinner ventured to go in 'to inquire what was become of two female servants'. George, a fellow servant, tried desperately to cover up for the two, claiming they 'had gone to the orchard about three minutes'. But Skinner was not deceived and set off towards the village 'where I met them coming from thence'. They were under orders 'not to leave the premises or have any communication with the village'. They pleaded that they 'had been visiting people—but only for 10 minutes'. Skinner threatened to dismiss them if they were caught leaving the house again for 'it was disgraceful to see girls like street walkers stealing out by twilight'. As a warning he gives them a month to mend their ways. A few months later he catches them 'standing before the door to gape at everyone passing by'. He told them 'it was discredit to any modest woman to do so'.[44] The two servants responded by reminding Morris that the month's warning he had given them was more than up and they wished to leave the next day. Not always did servants observe the ban on callers. The wife of Francis Place was servant in a household where 'her fellow-servants had their sweethearts in the house unbeknown to their master and mistress'.[45]

---

[42] Anon., *The Servants' Friend*, (c.1780), 22.
[43] *Journal of a Somerset Rector 1803–34*, 174–5, 319.
[44] Ibid. 335, 344.
[45] *The Autobiography of Francis Place (1771–1854)*, ed. Mary Thale (1972), 102.

So great was the desire of some masters to keep their servants at home that they locked them in when they went out. So when Mr Goodwin, the minister at Tankersley, went to church, he locked his maid and two children in the house.[46] The lives of servants, particularly female servants, were subjected to an intense, and unhealthy, scrutiny by their masters and mistresses. Claver Morris in June 1723 thought it worth recording in his diary that 'last night I saw my Man George Champion Hugging and Kissing my Wife's Maid Molly Mitchell'. Later he was to dismiss his servant, Charles Cook, 'because he was too much in favour with my Servant Hannah Beal, & was bolted into his Chamber with her Sunday Oct. 3 for a considerable time'.[47] In October 1787 John Gabriel Stedman's curiosity about his servants' private lives was momentarily satisfied when he recorded in his journal 'I discover the new maid's lover, William A-gue'.[48] In 1803 John Skinner, the Somerset rector, noted in his diary that his cook, Rebecca, had 'formed an acquaintance with West the Collier'. He found out she 'used to entertain him whenever she could without fear of detection'. When one night he hears a man's voice he hastens to investigate. The poor man, West, only escaped by 'getting over the hedge' at the end of the orchard. Rebecca was later to marry West.[49]

But it was not only from their masters or their masters' sons that the threat to female domestic servants came. There were also their fellow servants in or outside the household. Sara Maza has talked of 'the hothouse atmosphere of the world below stairs'. All we know of the restrictions on some servants and the denial by their employers of contact with their friends, their suitors, or those of the locality confirms such a view. In such an atmosphere 'relations between male and female servants in the same household could easily turn into sentimental or sexual involvements'.[50] When his friend and neighbour, Mr Du Quesne, dined with James Woodforde in March 1789, he was in low spirits owing to 'the disagreeable things happening in his Family with regard to Ser-

---

[46] *The Journal of Mr. John Hobson*, Surtees Society, LXV *Yorkshire Diaries and Autobiographies*, 2 vols. i (1877), 245–329 at p. 245.
[47] *The Diary of a West Country Physician*, 97, 123.
[48] *The Journal of John Gabriel Stedman 1744–97*, 321–2.
[49] *The Journal of a Somerset Rector, 1803–34*, 13.
[50] Maza, *Servants and Masters in Eighteenth-Century France*, 140–2.

vants'. Two of his maidservants were pregnant by his man servant, James Atherton. Atherton had married one of them—a fact just discovered by the other pregnant maidservant.[51] Six weeks after hiring Deborah Coleman as her servant Elizabeth Purefoy realized her maid was pregnant. She wrote at once to the girl's father telling him of the urgent need to come and take his daughter home to avoid 'farther inconvenience'. The girl was 'very forward with child'. When the maid denied her pregnancy Elizabeth Purefoy had a midwife 'to search her upon which she confessed it was so, and by Mr. Launder's man servant whom she lived with'. Later Elizabeth Purefoy's coachman ran away from her house 'pretending a wench followed him with a great Belly'.[52]

Apart from voluntary liaisons with fellow servants there was also a degree of sexual harassment of female domestics in some households. So the wife of Francis Place was in service where 'there was a brute of a fellow a porter in the house, who used to annoy her'.[53] A. J. Munby, writing of Hannah Cullwick's experience as a servant, talked of households where 'visiting gentlemen, as well as men servants tried to "make a pass" at her'.[54]

Was illegitimacy among servants a proof of sexual licence? It could take many years before they had accumulated enough savings on which to marry. For most servants marriage was delayed and occurred late. Their very isolation in service, it has been argued, 'put them at a disadvantage in the marriage market'.[55] In the time they were waiting to accumulate enough savings to marry anything could happen—and often did. It has been argued that 'many servants... were disaster-bound precisely because they aspired to marriage, because perfectly reasonable courtships happened to go awry'.[56] It was often a promise of marriage that 'enticed a maid to sleep with a footman'.[57] There is the story told by Philip Thicknesse of Betty, 'an innocent country wench' who had recommended her sweetheart John as man servant to

---

[51] *The Diary of a Country Parson*, iii. 86.
[52] *The Purefoy Letters*, i. 137–8, 156.
[53] *The Autobiography of Francis Place*, 102.
[54] As quoted in Davidoff, 'Class and Gender in Victorian England', 107.
[55] Leonore Davidoff, 'Mastered for Life', in Pat Thane and Anthony Sutcliffe (eds.), *Essays in Social History*, ii (1986), 126–50 at p. 139.
[56] Maza, *Servants and Masters in Eighteenth-Century France*, 89; see also J. A. Sharpe, *Crime in Seventeenth-Century England: A County Study* (1983), 62–3.
[57] Fairchilds, 'Female Sexual Attitudes and the Rise of Illegitimacy', 641.

Thicknesse: 'John *had given* Betty *a note of word only*, that he would marry her, but having found out *the riddle* without the assistance of the parson of the parish, he would not *sign it.*'[58] Marriages between fellow servants were fraught with difficulties. On the whole few masters seem to have employed married couples as servants. If two servants within the same household wanted to marry custom dictated they ask for the permission of their master—and such permission could be withheld—or leave the household. Even if permission was granted they were expected to serve out their time. Mary Leadbeater wrote of a servant, Nicholas Cannon, who 'thought of marrying, and consulted his master whose approbation did not sanction the proposal; the woman being much his senior, besides other objections'.[59] Employers were apprehensive that a married couple, particularly if they had children, would be as much concerned with their own family as their master's. But if marriage between two servants was to have any chance of success the married couple needed to be employed in one household. The result was that many sincerely made promises of marriage were thwarted by absence of opportunity. In these circumstances some female servants may well have concluded that if marriage was unlikely their 'only chance of companionship and sexual fulfilment lay in an illicit relationship'.[60] So, writing of Victorian London, John Gillis has concluded 'it was servants who were most at risk of unwed motherhood, largely because there were so many obstacles to their nuptiality'.[61] The same seems to have been true of France. In Nantes in the period 1725–88, according to the *déclarations de grossesses*, there were 8,000 cases of unmarried motherhood, of which 40 per cent were definitely domestic servants.[62] Since many failed to give information about their occupation, the percentage is almost certainly considerably understated. The majority of cases were likely to be domestic servants.

When John Macdonald was in service at Kilburnie an Amelia Burn, the daughter of the groom, came as chambermaid. She was

[58] Philip Thicknesse, *Memoirs and Anecdotes* (1790), 359.
[59] Mary Leadbeater, *Cottage Biography* (1822), 32.
[60] Fairchilds, 'Female Sexual Attitudes and the Rise of Illegitimacy', 644.
[61] *For Better for Worse* (1985), 165.
[62] Depauw, 'Illicit Sexual Activity in Eighteenth-Century Nantes', 147, 159.

a pretty girl and Macdonald fell in love with her. When in 1759 he was discharged from the service, he tells us, 'Amelia came away with child at the same time'. Macdonald took a room for her near her mother, he gave her six guineas 'and other things necessary'. We cannot doubt Macdonald's sincerity when he confessed he 'thought to marry her when I got a place'. When he left for Edinburgh Amelia told him 'she would wait twenty years and then beg her bread with me for life'. Two years passed before, with his master's permission, he sent for her and his son to come and spend two weeks at the local public house. He records how he managed to get away from his master late at night and would spend 'three or four hours' with Amelia. After this we hear no more of her.[63] Mariann Noddle was in service 'in different Places and when she lived at Mrs Turner's at Barbon near Kirby Lonsdale she came Home with Child by one Thomas Bains'. We do not know whether he was a fellow servant. The child was born and left for her mother to look after and she 'went to service again'.[64] Like Amelia she was fortunate. Few servants can have had Mariann's options. Many were afraid of how their parents would respond and avoided returning home at all costs. Others went home and were thrown out, either because there was not the means of supporting them or from parents' shame at their daughter's predicament. Some committed suicide. When Lucy Mott, 'servant to Mr. French' disappeared in March 1760, when there was 'the greatest reason imaginable' for thinking her pregnant, Thomas Turner immediately jumped to the conclusion she had committed suicide.[65] In fact he was wrong for, although she was pregnant, a few days later she reappeared with a would-be husband, James Trill.

If rumours of liaisons between their male and female servants reached the ears of their employers it was usually the woman who was dismissed. So the result of John Macdonald's reputed liaison with Mrs Manderson, the lady's maid, was that three months after she was hired she was dismissed. At Colonel

[63] *Memoirs of an Eighteenth-Century Footman*, 44, 49, 52.
[64] *The Family Records of Benjamin Shaw Mechanic of Dent, Dolphinholme and Preston 1772–1841*, ed. Alan G. Crosby, Record Society of Lancashire and Cheshire, cxxx (1991), 20.
[65] *The Diary of Thomas Turner*, 203.

Skeene's, Macdonald boasted, 'the French governess was turned away on my account, and afterwards the housekeeper'.[66] When a servant became pregnant with no hope of immediate marriage the outlook was grim.

When the maidservant of Julius Hardy, the Methodist button-maker of Birmingham, became pregnant, her master remained ignorant of her condition. It was a visiting friend who told him. He was 'sadly thunderstruck'. The servant had been in his employment ever since he started to keep house. At the time she was almost certainly his only servant. 'Her condition, abominable past practices, and the probable consequences', he recorded in his diary, 'were uppermost and well-nigh constantly in my thoughts.' He immediately 'resolved to have her off the premises directly'. The only thing that prevented him turning her out that night—despite a thick fall of snow—was that his old housekeeper could not come immediately to help him out. The following night he was only restrained from putting her out of the house by others advising him that someone might 'impute it as a piece of cruelty'. Finally she left after Hardy had accused her of deceiving him and rendering 'herself infamous and detestable'. We are not told what happened to the servant but there is some hope her story had a happy ending as she left 'in company with the man who is reported to have had this criminal commerce with her', the son of Hardy's neighbour. Hardy's chief concern from the moment he learnt of his servant's condition was his own reputation. Had his friend not detected her pregnant state it 'might have involved my reputation in *supposed* guilt beyond the power of remedy'. He wanted to get her out of the house at once because it was 'absolutely necessary . . . to the establishment of my own innocence'. Even after she had gone he was still concerned that 'some bitter tongues may utter reproachful insinuations'. To prevent such a thing ever happening again he decided he must marry.[67]

What alternatives had female servants if they did get pregnant? Many attempted to abort the child—often with disastrous results. Frequently there was an attempt to conceal their condition for as long as posssible in the forlorn hope that some solution would

---

[66] *The Family Records of Benjamin Shaw*, 53, 57.

[67] *Diary of Julius Hardy (1788–1793) Button-Maker of Birmingham*, Birmingham Reference Library, 669002 (BRL MS 218), transcribed and annotated by A. M. Banks (Apr. 1973), 53–5.

present itself. But it was also of vital importance to the pregnant woman to continue to be able to support herself as far into her pregnancy as possible. Once dismissed and pregnant—or with a young child—there was little or no chance of finding another place. For some unable to contemplate the shame of dismissal, returning to their homes, and having to confess their condition to their parents, infanticide seemed the only way out. The 'typical infanticidal mother', J. A. Sharpe has written, 'was an unmarried servant girl, and her motives were usually a desire to avoid the shame and the consequent loss of position which unmarried motherhood would bring'. He estimates that over half of those accused of infanticide were unmarried mothers.[68]

Masters were not always prepared to act in cases of their maleservants' sexual assaults on women. John Skinner recorded the 'violent assault' of one 'Lowe, the gardener of Mr. Stephens, one of his neighbours' on Lizzie Cottle. He had 'carried her into the thickest part of the coppice wood with the intent to ravish her' but was interrupted by a passer-by. Skinner called on his neighbour, expecting some action on his part against his servant. But Mr Stephens was not prepared to believe the account as 'he had an excellent opinion of Lowe, who was a married man, and seemed to be going on very steady in his business'. When Lowe was summoned he claimed the attack was caused by being drunk but that he 'had only meant to kiss the girl' and 'had not the most distant idea of offering her any violence'. He confessed to being afraid he would lose his place. Stephens as a magistrate took no further action 'saying it was a delicate situation for him to act in, it being his own servant etc.'. The matter was settled out of court with Lowe giving five guineas to the girl and offering an apology. Later, when another of his servants—a footman—'got Heal, the Washerwoman's daughter, with child', Mr Stephens refused to act against him. 'If he was obliged to attend the private conduct of his servants, he should have enough to do', and he added, 'he could not well reprove his servants for a conduct which his example taught them to pursue'.[69]

The question of the effect of what often amounted to virtual imprisonment of female servants in a house has never been suffi-

---

[68] *Crime in Early Modern England 1550–1750* (1984), 110.
[69] *Journal of a Somerset Rector 1803–34*, 21–2, 33–4.

ciently addressed. When Dudley Ryder in October 1718 was travelling to London by coach he got into conversation with a servant-maid of an 'eminent merchant of Hackney'. She complained of her mistress 'and their manner of living'. She told Ryder 'they had no company at all, and lived in a kind of nunnery'.[70] Quite apart from the loneliness such isolation from the outside world must have induced, for young adolescent girls the sexual frustration that resulted from being barred from contact with members of the opposite sex outside the household must have been extreme. Many came from country villages where pre-marital sexuality was customary. Little wonder that when sexual advances were made to them they reacted over-enthusiastically. The surprising thing is that so many female servants managed to preserve their chastity. It is difficult to get evidnece of sexual repression among servants in the eighteenth century. It is hinted at in the accounts of the wildness and abandon of some servants on the relatively rare occasions they entertained other servants and were allowed to dance. The American Quaker J. P. Malcolm, engraver and topographer, was clearly shocked by the scene he was taken to witness 'at a three-penny hop' in Piccadilly in a room over a stable. 'We found near one hundred people of both sexes, some masked, others not, a great part of which were dancing to the musick of two sorry fiddles.' Footmen and servant-maids were prominent as well as 'butchers, apprentices, oyster and orange women' and, according to Malcolm, 'common w——s, and sharpers'.[71] Such opportunities to meet the opposite sex were not given to many servants, even in London. Outside the metropolis they were rare unless your master was particularly liberal. In the mid-nineteenth century when Arthur Munby 'comes across a group of women—mainly shop girls and servants—playing Kiss-in-the-Ring at Crystal Palace' he is fascinated by 'one tall buxom wench, a servant maid from Islington, who played with great vigour and abandon, and was immensely in demand. For greater freedom she had taken off her shawl. She evidently enjoyed the game intensely: it was the satisfaction, in a rude and sensuous kind, of a long repressed and half-unconscious desire to be let loose, from the solitude of her kitchen where no followers are allowed, into a

[70] *The Diary of Dudley Ryder 1715–16*, 352.
[71] *Anecdotes of the Manners and Customs of London during the Eighteenth Century*, 2 vols. (1811), i. 291.

Sexual Vulnerability of Female Servants

circle of young men prepared for unlimited kissing.'[72] Munby's is a perceptive comment. But such delight in the rare chances of sexual freedom was surely not confined to nineteenth-century female domestic servants. It was a manifestation of the kind of sexual repression suffered by female domestic servants from their deliberately restricted and confined lives. 'Sex', writes Cissie Fairchilds, 'was probably the one available escape from the constricting disciplines of their lives.' It would be foolish to try to claim that all women servants were victims of men's seduction. Many voluntarily entered into sexual liaisons. As compared with 'other lower-class women', in eighteenth-century France, it is argued, 'maid-servants . . . were more likely to enter into illicit relationships purely for sexual pleasure'.[73] The same was almost certainly true of servant-maids in England.

[72] Derek Hudson, *Munby: Man of Two Worlds: The Life and Diaries of Arthur J. Munby 1828–1910* (1972), 104.
[73] Fairchilds, 'Female Sexual Attitudes and the Rise of Illegitimacy', 644.

4

Vails, Perquisites, and Allowances: The Moral Economy of Servants

> Of vails: 'There is no Grievance more complain'd of than the giving Money to Servants. . . . This custom is a National Reproach.'
>
> *Gentleman's Magazine*, 4 (1734), 131
>
> 'Tis too much Money, excessive Wages, and unreasonable Vails that spoil Servants in England.'
>
> Bernard Mandeville, *Fable of the Bees*, i. 349.

THIS chapter looks at the customary practices which, in the eighteenth century, determined what, over and above annual wages, domestic servants might expect in allowances in both money and kind, perquisites and tips. Whatever the origin of such practices it is clear that by the eighteenth century they had become so established that servants regarded them as their right. As the relationship between servants and their masters and mistresses was in process of changing from a paternalistic to an increasingly contractual one, such practices came under attack from employers. Servants reacted angrily to attempts to abolish such practices and fought for their retention.

My devotion of a whole chapter to a theme which, in ten pages or so, Hecht opened up so effectively may be queried. It is because I see it as playing a vital role in the generally acknowledged deterioration in master–servant relations that most probably began in the seventeenth century but the full manifestation of which only emerged in the eighteenth. As I make clear below, opposition to vails concealed far more fundamental issues and was symptomatic of much deeper tensions in the relations between servants and their masters and mistresses. It is also because, despite the view of servants as on the whole passively accepting their servility, it reveals, in the little-recorded riots of footmen against all attempts to abolish vails, the ability of at least some servants to resist—and to resist effectively—their employers' demands. It is only the most visible sign of such resistance. One suspects that, if less publicly, some servants in individual households up and down the country, were in more subtle ways making a silent protest against the whole nature of the servant–master relationship.

In retreading some of the ground covered by Hecht I want to bring out just how strongly entrenched such customary practices were among domestic servants and how the threat to abolish them was a threat to what they had come to understand as their rights—and essential to their livelihood. When the footmen of London rioted against attempts to do away with vails they were just as convinced they were defending traditional rights as the crowds that rioted against high bread prices. It is these rights and customs that Edward Thompson called the moral economy of the poor.

Apart from annual wages it was normal for a servant to receive food and lodging. Sometimes an employer would make an allowance or provision for servants' washing, indeed it could be a built-in part of their wages, as in one of John Meller's staff at Erddig in 1725, John Jones, the butler, who was paid £10 a year plus a guinea 'allow'd him for washing whilst in Town'. Or there could be a special arrangement for dealing with it. On 19 January 1767 the Revd William Cole recorded in his diary that he 'had Sarah Tansley to wash a few things for the servants'.[1] Susanna Whatman in her instructions for her housemaid included the setting aside of early Tuesday morning (at 7 o'clock) 'to wash her own things and the dusters, and help wash stockings. To iron her own things of an evening.'[2] In May 1786 Woodforde records in his diary the payment of 10s. 6d. 'To Norton's wife for washing my boy's shirts etc. for a whole

---

[1] Merlin Waterson, *The Servants' Hall: A Domestic History of Erddig* (1980), 26; *The Blecheley Diary of the Rev. William Cole 1765–7*, ed. Francis Griffin Stokes (1931), 176.
[2] *The Housekeeping book of Susanna Whatman 1776–1800*, ed. Thomas Balston (1956), 18.

year'.[3] Normally servants had to cope with their washing themselves. Anne Cook tells of a housekeeper who, having distributed the cast-off gowns of her mistress among all the maidservants, limited their wearing them to Sunday attendance at church 'for no Maid in the Family she allows above one Gown washed in a Quarter of the Year'.[4] Was it the time such washing took or the demands on the soap supply that worried her? Daniel Defoe complained of the amount of soap used by maidservants who wore 'printed linen, cotton, and other things of that nature, which require frequent washing'.[5] He provoked an angry response from Robert Dodsley, the footman poet: 'Allowing a Servant to have a Gown wash'd amongst the rest of the Cloaths every Week, which is more than most of them have, that five shillings extraordinary in a whole twelvemonth is the outside of this mighty Expence'.[6]

'The most lucrative perquisites', argues Hecht, 'were the used clothes that upper servants received by agreement and the liveries that generally fell to lower servants after they had worn them "*long enough to have New*"'. But it was not just upper servants that received the cast-off clothes of their employers. According to Hecht, 'when servants were engaged, they were frequently granted the right to the "cast clothes" of the master or mistress as a regular perquisite'.[7] Often the clothes would be sold, but sometimes they were worn by the servants. This would explain the sense of outrage expressed in Smollett's *Humphry Clinker* when 'the Squire gave away an ould coat to a poor man; and', we are told by Winefred Jenkins, 'John says as how 'tis robbing him of his parquisites'. At this John was firmly told by Winefred Jenkins that his agreement specified 'no vails', but as John replied 'there's a difference betwixt vails and perquisites'.[8] He had a point, for perquisites were normally in kind not money. Jonas Hanway wrote of an 'upper Servant to a great personage' who stole his

[3] *The Diary of a Country Parson: The Reverend James Woodforde 1758–1813*, ed. John Beresford, 5 vols (1924–31), ii. 247.
[4] Anne Buck, *Dress in Eighteenth-Century England* (1979), 112.
[5] *Everybody's Business is Nobody's Business* (1725), 10–11.
[6] *Servitude: A Poem: to which is prefix'd an Introduction, humbly submitted to the Consideration of all Noblemen, Gentlemen, and Ladies, who keep many Servants* (1729), 29.
[7] *The Domestic Servant in Eighteenth-Century England* (1956), 157, 115.
[8] *The Works of Tobias Smollett*, ed. George Saintsbury, 12 vols. (1895), xi. 8.

master's watch. When asked why he had done so he said that 'he had taken it in lieu of the vails of the Suit of Clothes, which in point of time HIS HONOUR should have left off, but chose to continue to wear'. This, we are told, 'was not esteemed *Robbery*, but... was acquiesced in as warrantable'.[9] Often on the death of their mistress, servant-maids, as in Richardson's *Pamela*, were left their clothes.[10] When Mrs Willis, neighbour and friend of the Revd William Cole, died in 1767, she left '£10 to her Maid Jane Browne & her Clothes'.[11] When the wife of Joseph Nollekens died in 1817 'his handsome maid... became possessed of her mistress's wardrobe, which she quickly sold and cut up to her advantage'. When Joseph died six years later, he bequeathed 'to Mary Fearey, my late servant, all my wearing apparel, clothes and body linen'.[12] Thomas Alcock thought the practice of mistresses allowing their servants 'the disposal of *left off clothes*' a mistake. Either the clothes were 'never taken as much care of as they ought to be' or they were sold. It was infinitely better, he argued, to give them 'a few pounds more per annum' and give cast-off clothes to charity.[13]

Gifts of clothing were on occasion made by employers to other people's servants. In July 1766, when Jem Wood, Cole's boy servant, was sent over to Loughton with some cucumbers for Mrs Holt, he was rewarded by the gift of 'a very good Great Coat of her Son Edmund's, which had become too small for him'.[14] Sometimes outright gifts of new clothing were given to servants. A few servants seem to have been wholly provided with clothes. Sometimes the particular garments to be given to servants could be stipulated in the annual contract when they were seen as a supplement to wages. So dresses for maidservants were often provided as 'an agreed allowance'. When in 1756 Mrs Philip Powys was visiting the Jacksons at Wesenham Hall she found all the maidservants 'in green-stuff gowns'. On enquiring of the daughter of the house she was told 'a green camblet for a gown

[9] Jonas Hanway, *Eight Letters to his Grace Duke of—— on the Custom of Vails-giving in England* (1760), 38.
[10] See Ch. 11 on *Pamela*.
[11] *The Blecheley Diary of the Rev. William Cole*, 221.
[12] John Thomas Smith, *Nollekens and his Times*, 2 vols. (1828), i. 347, ii. 21.
[13] M. A. Baines, *Domestic Servants as they are and as they ought to be by a practical mistress of a household* (1859), 12.
[14] *The Blecheley Diary of the Rev. William Cole*, 70.

used for many years to be an annual present of her mother's to those servants who behaved well, and had been so many years in her family'.[15] When the wife of Jerediah Strutt, the Derbyshire hosier, died in 1774, his two young daughters were left to cope with his household while he was in London. Without any experience they soon confronted difficulties in dealing with servants. One, Alice, insisted that 'besides her wages' there were 'two new Gowns owing to her'. As Eliza Strutt explained to her father 'when her wages were raised which is four years since my Mother promised her a new gown every year that she took no veils [*sic*.: vails], & she has only had two of them'. We should note the condition attached to the new gown. It suggests allowances of clothing were seen as a far preferable means to supplement wages than vails—and one that remained firmly in the hands of the employers. A year later another maidservant, Molly, was persuaded to stay until the return home of Jerediah. But, as she tells Eliza, 'she thinks her place is not profitable enough, she has had two old petticoats (one I gave her today) & a bed gown but I suppose she thinks she deserves a new gown'. Molly clearly did think so and had dropped heavy hints to Eliza of her 'Mamma's rules'.[16]

There are cases of some resentment by employers at the cost of clothing servants. When Samuel Pepys hired a new maid in October 1666 he recorded that 'we fain to lay out seven or eight pounds worth of clothes upon her back, which methinks, do go against my heart'.[17] It was quite usual for boy servants, 'livery boys', particularly when they were paid no wages, to be clothed by their masters. Sir Richard Newdigate had two or three boy servants who were 'regularly kept in clothes'.[18] The ever-economical Elizabeth Purefoy gets her son to 'buy cloath enough for two servants frocks' adding 'her price is about 4 shillings a yard & if it be worth ye money & will wear well she don't care what country cloth it is, but it must be sure not to shrink'. Another time

[15] *Passages from the Diaries of Mrs. Philip Lybbe Powys of Hardwick House, Oxon, 1756–1806*, ed. Emily J. Climenson (1899), 222–3.

[16] R. S. Fitton and A. P. Wadsworth, *The Strutts and the Arkwrights 1758–1830* (1958), 149, 162.

[17] *The Diary of Samuel Pepys*. ed. Henry B. Wheatley, 3 vols. (1946), ii (vol. vi of diary), 16.

[18] Eileen Gooder, *The Squire of Arbury: Sir Richard Newdigate (1644–1710)* (1990), 37.

she refers to some cloth she had ordered 'for the servants wastcoats'.[19] But such clothes were usually regarded as the servants' during the time of their service. It was when they left that difficulties could arise and, as Fielding claimed, 'the Property of their Livery frequently begets very disagreeable Disputes, from the mistaken Opinion that a Servant having worn his Livery a Year intitles him to it'.[20] Anthony Stapley of Hickstead Place recorded taking on Will Gates as footman in 1704 at 50s. 'He is to have a hat, coat, and breeches once in two years. If I turn him away the first year, I am to give him 5s. more, and take his livery.'[21] The footman, John Macdonald, recorded that he was 'hired for twenty guineas a year and two suits of clothes'. His employers told him 'they did not want me to wear a livery'. He was sent to their tailor where he was measured for two suits: 'one of fustian to do my work in, and another of blue cloth'. As Macdonald explained 'I did not want to be fine. I wanted to be like a servant'.[22] Elizabeth Purefoy was clearly annoyed when she discovers that her footman had gone off and 'took his frock & wastcoat with him.' When she employed a new footman in June 1745, her son wrote to their tailor to 'take measure of him as well as ye coachman'. The following month the tailor was asked to bring the clothes soon and at the same time to 'bring the coachman a linnen frock to put over his cloaths when hee rubs his horses down'.[23] Woodforde in May 1783 gave both his maids 'a Gown apiece'. Six years later on returning from a three-month stay at Cole he again gave them 'a cotton gown apiece' that he had bought in London and to Ben 'a Waistcoat Piece'. In 1791 he sent his maid, Betty, to Norwich 'to buy my two old Washer-women Mary Heavers and Nanny Gooch a New Gown apiece which I intend giving to them'. When in March, 1800, a Mr Aldridge came round 'selling cottons' Woodforde brought from him '2 Coloured Handkerchiefs' for his two washerwomen, and '2 waistcoat pieces for my two Men'. In 1786 his diary records 'My Man Briton

[19] *The Purefoy Letters 1735–53*, ed. G. Eland, 2 vols. (1931), ii. 302.
[20] Sir John Fielding, *Extracts from such of the Penal Laws as particularly relate to the Peace and Good Order of the Metropolis* (1762) 141.
[21] *Extracts from the Journal and Account Book of Timothy Burrell, Esq., Barrister at Law 1683–1700*, Sussex Archaeological Collections, iii (1850), 117–72 at p. 147.
[22] *Memoirs of an Eighteenth-Century Footman, John Macdonald*, ed. John Beresford (1927), 71.
[23] *The Purefoy Letters*, ii. 308, 315, 318.

had a new suit of Livery ... with a very good new great Coat of Brown Cloth and red cape to it.' But, as Woodforde told Briton, 'I gave neither to him, but only to wear them during his service with me'. In 1801 he paid a tailor £1. 1s. 6d. 'for a new Pair of brown striped Velveret Breeches for Briton'.[24] The Revd Moyle Breton, a friend of Joseph Price, was said to give his servant 'leather breeches yearly and a thick-set frock and waistcoat. A suit of livery once in a year and a half or two years. Hat, boots, great-coat when wanted.'[25]

'It is now usual with many Female Servants', wrote Thomas Alcock in 1752, 'to insist on Tea in their Agreement, and to refuse serving where this is not allowed.'[26] But Trusler, in his advice to masters and mistresses of 1786, recommended that women servants provide their own tea and sugar.[27] In March 1788 James Woodforde recorded in his diary 'gave my 2 Maids a pd of Suchong Tea between them'.[28] But such generosity was rare among employers. A letter in the *London Chronicle* wrote of 'the unaccountable passion for tea ... coveted by the poor with a degree of madness and folly'. It held that no mistress of whatever status could hire 'a menial servant ... that does not require this regular beverage'.[29] Secretly mistresses were concerned that their servants were developing tastes considered unsuitable to their station. In November 1784 Woodforde engaged 'a new Servant Maid ... as Cook, Molly Peachman, she is to have 5 Guineas Per Annum, Tea included'.[30] 'Two washerwomen run off in a most impertinent manner', recorded John Gabriel Stedman in October 1785, 'because they could have no sugar to their tea.' When he complained of 'the two bitches' to the mayor they were put in Bridewell and brought to Stedman by the keeper of the prison 'to beg forgiveness'.[31]

The other allowance made by some employers was board wages—that is cash—in lieu of meals. These were often a tempor-

---

[24] *The Diary of a Country Parson*, ii. 72, 143, iii. 299, v. 304, 389, ii. 212.
[25] *A Kentish Parson: Selection from the Private Papers of the Revd. Joseph Price Vicar of Brabourne 1767–1786*, ed. G. M. Ditchfield and Bryan Keith-Lucas (1991), 153.
[26] *Observations on the Defects of the Poor Laws* (1752), 48.
[27] John Trusler, *The London Adviser and Guide* (1786), 48.
[28] *The Diary of a Country Parson*, iii. 10.
[29] *London Chronicle*, 21 (1767), 103.
[30] *The Diary of a Country Parson*, i. 236, ii. 161.
[31] *The Journal of John Gabriel Stedman*, ed. Stanbury Thompson (1962), 267–8.

ary expedient when employers were away from home or when servants accompanied their masters and mistresses on journeys. But it was possible for a servant to be permanently on board wages—usually with the object of economy. When Joseph Nollekens was still single he kept only one servant. Nollekens 'always applied to him for money to purchase every description of article *fresh*, as it was wanted for the approaching meal: and by that mode of living, he concluded, as he kept his servant upon board-wages, he was not so much exposed to her pilfering inclinations, particularly as she was entrusted with no more money than would enable her to purchase just enough for his own eating'. Later Mrs Nollekens was reputed to be particularly mean and continued her husband's practice. 'Poor Bronze', it was said of their maidservant, 'had to support herself upon what were called board-wages, had barely a change [of clothes], and looked more like the wife of a chimney sweeper than any other kind of human being.'[32] Others also seem to have found board wages a convenience. Frank Filmer, a lawyer, for instance 'gives his servant £40 per annum and he keeps himself. Has no trouble with him.'[33] The amount of board wages paid varied. According to the *London Adviser* an upper servant was paid more than a lower, and male servants were always paid more than female. Board wages for an upper servant were quoted as '10s. 6d. a week with fire and candle', and '7s. for an under-servant'.[34] A foreign visitor to England complained they had risen. 'Foreigners without exception', he claimed, 'have to give their servants half a guinea board wages per week, instead of, as formerly, a third of a guinea (seven shillings), which was the usual sum.'[35] In 1725 *The Complete Servant* quoted board wages of 10s. per week for females and 12s. for males. 'In a large establishment' they could be reckoned at 'an average of 10s. per head, per week, expense'. In addition 'Men were allowed a pot of Ale per day and Women a pint, besides table beer'.[36] In her *Housekeeping Book* Susanna Whatman detailed the allowances to be given to servants. 'Ale, 1 pint to the men, and ½ a pint to the maids per day. Small beer. As much as they

[32] Smith, *Nollekens and his Times*, i. 78, ii. 8.   [33] *A Kentish Parson*, 30.
[34] Trusler, *The London Adviser and Guide*, 48.
[35] Count Frederick Kielmansegge, *Diary of a Journey to England in the Years 1761–2*, trans. Countess Kielmansegge (1902), 20.
[36] Samuel and Sarah Adams, *The Complete Servant* (1825), 8.

chuse.'[37] But often, and increasingly, employers preferred giving beer money in lieu of beer. When the Revd Moyle Breton went on his travels and servants accompanied him he allowed them board wages of '1s. 6d a day [= 10s. 6d. a week], some allow 2s, others 2s. 6d.'[38] What employers who opposed board wages objected to was the independence such wages gave their servants. On the other hand, to many employers they seemed infinitely preferable to leaving servants the freedom of their kitchens. It was a convenience that many employers resorted to when away from home. They may have felt that on balance it was more economical than having servants fed in the house when there was no one to supervise the catering. But at the same time it was resented as it gave 'a constant excuse to loiter at public houses' where they squandered their money 'in gaming, drunkenness, and extravagance', and where, it was suspected, they discussed the idiosyncrasies and private lives of their employers.[39] 'It was to be wished', wrote one correspondent to the *London Chronicle* in 1762, 'a method could be devised for having servants fed without suffering them to finger the money.'[40]

'Many Things are committed to the Custody of Servants', wrote the author of an early eighteenth-century manual of advice to servants, 'with respect to which if they prove false, 'tis not easy to detect them; as in the Stores and Provisions for a large Family.'[41] The custom lent itself to abuse and there is no doubt many servants of both sexes exploited it. But there is also no doubt that the extent of the abuse was exaggerated by those critical of the whole custom of perquisites. So Daniel Defoe accused maidservants of being 'light of finger'. 'Tea, sugar, wine, etc., or any such trifling commodities, are reckoned no thefts', he wrote, and 'some of these maids are mighty charitable, and can make a shift to maintain a small family with what they can purloin from their masters and mistresses.'[42] 'All broken victuals are to be at the disposal only of the housekeeper', Susanna Whatman dictated, 'and no liberty is allowed of any other servant giving anything away that is left.'[43] According to Alcock 'anything ... convertible or transferable' was taken by

[37] *The Housekeeping Book of Susanna Whatman*, 18.
[38] *A Kentish Parson*, 153. [39] *The Gentleman's Magazine*, 26 (1756), 14.
[40] *London Chronicle*, 21 (1762), 165.
[41] Anon., *The Servant's Calling* (1725), 35–6.
[42] *Everybody's Business is Nobody's Business*, 8.
[43] *The Housekeeping Book of Susanna Whatman*, 28.

servants, *'torn-up* damask clothes and *broken* silver, to rugs, old brass, and metal of every description'. According to him there were 'receiving houses' carrying on 'the most nefarious traffic with' servants.[44] In Fielding's *Grub Street Opera* two servants, Will and Robin, quarrel. Will starts to threaten Robin with disclosure of his 'tricks' to his master: 'your selling of glasses and pretending the frost broke them and making master brew more beer than he needed, and then giving it away to your own family.' The cook, Susan, was not excluded from the deceit, as another servant John makes clear: 'Who basted away dozens of butter more than she need, that she may sell the grease?—Who brings in false bills of fare, and puts the forg'd articles in her own pocket?—Who wants wine and brandy for sauces and sweetmeats and drinks it herself?'[45] Henry Mayhew in 1874 saw cooks as being in a special position in relation to perquisites, having 'much in their power and much they can legitimately dispose of'.[46] The distinction between legitimate perquisites and theft was anything but clear, but the consequences of being caught 'thieving' were often drastic. In 1786 the maidservant of a near neighbour of John Gabriel Stedman was 'whipt for stealing'.[47] In 1790 the *Gentleman's Magazine* reviewed Huntingford's *The Laws of Masters and Servants considered* (1790) in which he had claimed that 'near one-third of the prisoners tried during the last twelve months at the Old Bailey, were servants for robbing their master'.[48] As late as 1801 Sarah Lloyd, a servant, was executed for robbing her mistress.[49] In April 1737 Elizabeth Purefoy went as far as getting a warrant issued for 'the apprehension of Mary Dawes . . . upon oath for her taking and conveying away strong beer out of the cellar', and offering a reward for information on her whereabouts.[50] In Smollett's *Humphry Clinker* a charwoman is caught leaving the house 'with her whole cargo . . . Her buckets were foaming full of our best beer, and her lap was stuffed with a cold tongue, part of a buttock of beef, half a turkey, and a swinging lump of butter, and the matter of ten moulded kandles, that had scarce ever been lit.' When the cook is called to account she 'brazened it out,

[44] Baines, *Domestic Servants as they are, and as they ought to be*, 11.
[45] Henry Fielding, *The Grub Street Opera* (1731), act II, scenes iv and xiv.
[46] *London Characters* (1874), 317.
[47] *The Journal of John Gabriel Stedman*, 274.
[48] *Gentleman's Magazine*, 60/1 (1790), 429.
[49] As quoted in E. S. Turner, *What the Butler Saw* (1962), 98.
[50] *The Purefoy Letters*, i. 128.

and said it was her rite to rummage the pantry, and she was ready for to go before the mare'.[51] When in 1803 John Skinner the Somerset rector was trying to find a 'good servant' he 'engaged a middle-aged man' but he proved 'as bad as the rest—receiving his friends in my house when I was absent, and never going to Bath without taking something to his children who resided there'.[52] 'The allowance of perquisites', wrote a correspondent to the *London Chronicle* in 1760, 'has introduced great vices among men servants', and, he warned, 'dressing, tea-drinking, and pleasure-hunting females make dangerous and unhappy wives to poor men'.[53] Not surprisingly Trusler was totally opposed to the practice whereby 'women cooks and servants of all work, when they hire themselves, will endeavour to get the kitchen-stuff allowed them as a perquisite'.[54] Thieving was certainly regarded as one of the main drawbacks to having servants, though they were not always guilty of the accusations made against them. If something went missing in a household servants were always blamed. In Sunderland in May 1731, 'the parson's maid . . . poysoned herself, occasioned by her mistress charging her with conveighing some linnens out of the house'.[55] In Sarah Trimmer's *Teacher's Assistant*, children in charity schools who were intended for service were made to learn the following questions and answers:

Q. Who do victuals and drink properly belong to in a family?
A. The Master or Mistress.
Q. Is not robbing them of those things the same as taking their money?
A. Yes.
Q. Who sees people when they are pilfering tea and sugar and such things?
A. God.
Q. Does God approve of such actions?
A. No.
Q. What will God do to thieves of all kinds?
A. Punish them.[56]

[51] *The Works of Tobias Smollett*, i. 91–2.
[52] *The Journal of a Somerset Rector 1803–34*, ed. Howard and Peter Coombs (1930), 14.
[53] London Chronicle, 7 (1760), 164.   [54] *The London Adviser and Guide*, 49.
[55] *The Journal of Mr. John Hobson*, Surtees Society, lxv, *Yorkshire Diaries and Autobiographies*, 2 vols., i (1877), 305.
[56] Sarah Trimmer, *Teacher's Assistant*, 2 vols. (1836), i. 232–3.

In 1764 Lord Harrington was robbed. Closely implicated was John Wesket, his footman. At the court case brought in 1765 it emerged that Wesket had been told by the steward that money had been received to pay tradesmen's bills. When asked why he had passed on this information to Wesket, he replied 'it was to apprize him of tradesmen receiving their money, that he might get from them what these people have long exacted, by the tyranny of custom, under the name of *perquisite*'. He went on to add that he took care that the tradesmen came 'to the house to be paid, to ensure the levying of this tax by the porter'.[57] A large household's custom would have been worth a great deal to tradesmen. Those servants responsible for ordering and paying them were rewarded by generous tips and Christmas boxes. Cooks were the main gainers. 'The fact is your custom is large', explained Henry Mayhew to masters in the nineteenth century, 'and the tradesman makes it worth the while of your cook to have him retained'. Butlers who often paid bills also benefited from 'the odd pence' which by the end of a year amounted 'to a pretty handsome sum'.[58] If the tradesman 'refuses to comply with what they call the established custom', wrote one correspondent in the *London Chronicle*, 'he is almost sure of losing that family'. He went on to insist that such tips were passed on by tradesmen to the master of the household.[59]

Many employers imposed their own system of deductions from wages for breakages and 'misdemeanours'. As Mary Ashford related of one of her places: 'my mistress deducted from my wages for every little thing I had broken during the seven months I had been with her.'[60] Some, like Anthony Stapley, gave wages conditional on his servants staying an allotted time. On 1 May 1730 Mary White began her service. She was to receive £1. 5s. 0d. if she stayed until the following May. Hannah Morley was 'to have £2 if she stay to Lady Day next'. In 1740, when a Sarah Charman left his service after two months having been promised £2. 10s. 0d. if she stayed a year, she was given only 1s.[61] In 1809 a Suffolk farmer deducted 2s. from his maidservant's

---

[57] *The Gentleman's Magazine*, 35 (1765), 16.
[58] Mayhew, *London Characters*, 327.   [59] *London Chronicle*, 7 (1760), 196.
[60] *Life of a Licensed Victualler's Daughter, Written by Herself* (1844), 33.
[61] *On the Domestic Habits and Mode of Life of a Sussex Gentleman*, ed. the Revd Edward Turner, Sussex Archaeological Collections, xxiii (1871), 36–72 at p. 49.

annual wages because she had gone home for three days for Christmas and Easter. As she earned three and a half guineas a year the deduction represented over three times the daily wage.[62] Sir Richard Newdigate imposed forfeits for misdemeanours. When two of his servants, Betty Air and Sarah Hazeldene, went to Coton (presumably the church) 'when I ordered them to go to Astley, this [money] Hester shall have because she obeyed' they forfeited half a crown each. Later Sarah Hazeldene, a dairy maid, was fined again and forfeited 1s. for 'naughty butter and sour cream'. Ned Bryan, the waggoner, was fined 10s. (a quarter of his annual wage) for 'tempting James Morris and old Ri Nash to the alehouse and making them drunk'. His male cook, described as 'good if less given to drink', forfeited the same amount when found 'dead drunk'.[63] When, in 1704, Sir Walter Calverley engaged Joseph Mawde as stableman and coachman, he outlined his duties and warned that 'if he does not his best, but neglects these things, to have no wages'.[64] Wages were frequently not paid on time. Indeed, in order that servants could pay 'for anything missing' it was recommended that employers 'keep part of their wages in hand', and that 'they should always be paid one half year under another, reserving half-a-year in hand'.[65] A correspondent in the *London Magazine* of 1779 admitted that if there was to be better order among servants they must have the security of 'an easy and ready method of coming at the payment of their wages'.[66]

Quite apart from the wages paid to servants there were other ways in which their income could be augmented. The most important was vails. The *Oxford English Dictionary* defines vails as 'a gratuity given to a servant or attendant; a tip; specially one . . . given by a visitor on his departure to the servants of the house in which he has been a guest'. How and when exactly the practice of giving vails began we do not know. It was an ancient custom and certainly well established by the beginning of the seventeenth century. The practice was the subject of a furious

[62] Ann Kussmaul, *Servants in Husbandry in Early Modern England* (1981), 47.
[63] Gooder, *The Squire of Arbury*, 38.
[64] *Memorandum Book of Sir Walter Calverley*, Surtees Society, lxxix, *Yorkshire Diaries and Autobiographies*, 2 vols., ii (1886), 43–148 at p. 103.
[65] Trusler, *The London Adviser and Guide*, 49.
[66] *London Magazine*, 48 (1779), 165.

debate in the course of the eighteenth century. As early as 1725 Defoe was fulminating against what he called an 'unnecessary and burthensome piece of generosity unknown to our forefathers'. Vails, he argued, were 'intended as an encouragement to such as were willing and handy, but by custom and corruption', they had become 'a thorn in our sides . . . for now they make it a perquisite, a material part of their wages'.[67] In the light of such hostility towards vails, it is important to remember that whether or not they came into existence on their initiative, employers must have given them their tacit agreement. It was a point made by a footman who joined in the debate: 'Did not you first allow the taking of Vails?'[68] One can only speculate about employers' motives. Was it an ostentatious method for the aristocracy to demonstrate their wealth? Or a way of assuaging a conscience at the lowness of servants' wages? It could have been the response of servants themselves to the inadequacy of their wages, but how that response was first articulated remains a mystery. Was it recognition of the low level of servants' wages that accounts for the *OED* concluding that 'in the 17th and 18th centuries servants were largely paid by these gratuities'? Wages were, according to Dorothy George, 'a very small proportion of the payment of the servants of the well-to-do'; the greater part came from vails.[69]

In 1748 a foreign contributor to the *Gentleman's Magazine* talked of servants having 'too much interest in preserving' the custom of vails, adding 'it often supplies the place of wages'.[70] The lowness—or sometimes absence—of wages was recognized even by those who most opposed the giving of vails. 'Masters in England', a correspondent in the *London Chronicle* wrote in 1762, 'seldom pay their servants but in lieu of wages suffer them to prey upon their guests.'[71] Many urged that successfully to abolish vails would necessitate some increase in servants' wages. Jonas Hanway, for instance, urged the master 'to encrease the wages of his servants, in lieu of the *vails* they used to receive'. It was, he said, 'only giving money to his own servants, instead of bestow-

---

[67] *Everybody's Business is Nobody's Business*, 10.
[68] *London Chronicle*, 11 (1762), 380.
[69] 'The Early History of Registry Offices', *Economic History*, 1 (1926–9), 570–90 at p. 584.
[70] *Gentleman's Magazine*, 18 (1748), 456.   [71] *London Chronicle*, 11 (1762), 164.

ing his liberality on the servants of other people'. 'It is natural to expect upon a change of a custom so long in use', he wrote, 'that the generality of Servants will require an *augmentation* of wages.' Hanway argued—not entirely logically—that 'the general part of Servants hardly receive so much advantage by *twenty* shillings in Vails, as by *ten* uniformly paid in wages.'[72] Some of those who took part in the debate on vails, while opposing them, committed themselves to raising the wages of their servants. 'A Country Gentleman' who wanted legislation introduced to abolish vails, wrote how he was 'resolv'd speedily to advance the wages of all' his servants. But it was a promise made on certain conditions: servants were on no account to accept vails offered on his premises. If they were discovered doing so he would 'turn them adrift to the mercy of a press gang'.[73] And if some employers expressed their willingness to increase the wages of servants if vails were abolished it was unlikely that all would have followed suit. One correspondent to the *London Chronicle*—a footman—expressed his doubt as to whether once vails were abolished many would 'advance in wages in lieu of it', and, as he went on to add, 'what benefit will a servant gain for all the years he has lived with you, if this should take place?'[74]

It was the absence of a clear definition of vails that alarmed critics. 'Wages are pretty much a stated thing, but vails are altogether imaginary.' It was this, it was held, that explained servants 'frequently changing places' and becoming 'heedless, saucy and expensive'. According to the same correspondent vails 'distributed in England amounted to 2 million a year'.[75] Another correspondent, 'a Foreigner', claimed they amounted to 'enormous sums'.[76] Whether or not this was an exaggeration, for some servants vails could substantially affect their yearly earnings. Defoe claimed that a maidservant in the household of a gentleman or merchant could double her wages of £8 by the vails she received.[77] A gentleman's servant, Piggot Horton, who was hanged in 1741 for stealing a watch, claimed that although in his place the wages were only £4 a year, in two years he could earn more than £100 in

[72] *Eight Letters to his Grace the Duke of* ——, 5, 9.
[73] *London Chronicle*, 7 (1760), 260. [74] *London Chronicle*, 11 (1762), 380.
[75] Ibid. 164. [76] *London Magazine*, 48 (1779), 16.
[77] *Everybody's Business is Nobody's Business*, 10.

vails.[78] A letter purporting to come from a servant who had been in service fifteen years spelt out how his wages and vails related. The total of his wages for nine years with one master had been £59. Over the same period his vails and other perquisites amounted to £25. 7s. 6d., making a total of £84. 7s. 6d. He went on to detail his expenses over the nine years:

4 prs. of shoes at 6s. per pair	£1. 4. 0
For mending same at 2s. per pair	8. 0
For 3 shirts, the making, mending etc.	0. 15. 9
For 3 neckcloths at 2s. each	0. 6. 0
For 2 prs stockings, at 4s. a pair	0. 8. 0
For washing the whole year	1. 10. 0
For one wig in 2 years, is per year	0. 10. 6
For spending money when out late nights, etc.	0. 5. 6
	5. 7. 3
In nine years amounts to the sum of	£48. 5. 3
Which being deducted from gains leaves	£36. 2. 3

As he argued 'if I had no vails . . . I should have had no more than £10.14.9. a great sum indeed to keep me when out of place, in sickness, or other casualties.'[79] Whether or not the letter came from a real servant the figures (apart from a minor error in the sum) seem reasonable and his argument is convincing. It was one echoed by a correspondent opposed to vails but conceding that the servants had a case. 'The plea they have for keeping up their vails must be allowed both plausible and reasonable', he wrote, 'it cannot be expected they can save out of their common wages, wherewithal to maintain them when they are old and incapable of service.'[80] Jonas Hanway's fictitious footman, Thomas Trueman, claimed that he was not 'in what they call *a great place*, for I have received but 5 l. *in Vails* all the *blessed year* past. My wages are but 10 l.'[81] With the move after 1760 to abolish vails in Scotland, many servants left for England, but of those that remained it was said their wages had been 'moderately raised'.[82]

What sort of sums were paid in vails and just how important were they as a supplement to wages? When in July 1709 Claver Morris and his wife attend a ball at a neighbour's, 'My wife

[78] Peter Linebaugh, *The London Hanged* (1991), 251.
[79] *London Chronicle*, 7 (1760), 187. [80] *London Chronicle*, 11 (1762), 300.
[81] *The Sentiments and Advice of Thomas Trueman* (1760), 7–8. [82] Ibid. 164.

gave ye Cook-maids 1s. & I gave the 2 Men 2s. & the Boy 6d.'[83] Diaries and journals of the second half of the eighteenth century bear witness to the passionate feelings generated by vails. So when in March 1780 James Woodforde 'dined and spent afternoon with Mr Custance', the local squire, he recorded 'we did not give any vails to Servants'. The squire must have made his views on vails clear. When he goes to dine with Mr Hoare he notes that the 'servants wear Ruffels, but not suffered to take Vails'. But when Woodforde gave vails they tended to be a shilling for each servant. In January 1770 when he dined with Mr Creed he 'gave Mrs Creed's maids, Sarah and Unity 0.2.0.' After dining with Mr Robert White, Woodforde recorded in his diary 'gave maid coming away 0.1.0.' When in June 1782 he called on Taylor Wilmo 'and drank some of his ale', Woodforde 'gave his comical maid Nan 0.1.0.'[84] The same was given to Mrs Figges's maid when he dined with her mistress. It seems to have been a fairly standard rate. 'Even among middling people', it was held, such a level of vails was common. It was 'this small change' that had 'driven them' to refuse invitations to dine.[85] Thomas Turner had a very modest income as compared with Woodforde, but when with his wife he dined with Joseph Fuller 'my wife and I gave their servant 12d'. Not always was he so generous. After dining with Mr French they gave his maidservants '6d. each', and the same was given to the maids when they supped with Mr Atkins. And Turner makes clear he found the payment of vails an unwelcome expense. On Monday 26 January at Mr Porter's, 'being in liquor' he and his wife 'lost at brag between us near or quite 5s. We also gave the servants 2s.6d.' A few days later when they supped with Master Piper, Turner and his wife 'won 3s.6d. and gave the maid 12d.' As he went on to add, 'this brings back some part of Monday night's expenses'. Yet he expressed his disgust for those who never gave servants vails. Dr Snelling, Turner's doctor, 'never gave my servants anything, no, not even the meanest trifle that could be. Notwithstanding they always waited on him like as if they were his own servants.'[86]

[83] *The Diary of a West Country Physician, 1684–1726*, ed. Edmund Hobhouse (1934), 54.
[84] *The Diary of a Country Parson*, i. 276, 97, 31, 34.
[85] *London Chronicle*, 11 (1762), 300.
[86] *The Diary of Thomas Turner*, ed. David Vaisey (1985), 131.

Sometimes much higher vails were given. Nicholas Blundell, when negotiating his marriage to Frances Langdale in 1703, stayed with her grandmother at Heythrop where he went hunting. According to his Disbursement Book, when he left he was generous in the vails he distributed. 'To ye Houskeeper one dubble Pistole [one pistole = about 16s.], to the Maid one Pistole and ½ Guinney, Cook one Broad Peece [a 20s. piece], Groome one Guinney, under Cook, under Butler and under Chamber Maid each half a Guinney, my wives Chamber Maid 10s, under Gardiner 5s, Dary Maid 5s., in all £9. 10. 9d.'[87] He was clearly anxious to impress, but he could afford to be generous on this occasion for part of his wife's dowry was already 'lying at London' for his use.[88]

It was common practice to give vails to servants at inns and to the coachmen who drove them from town to town. When in February 1774 Woodforde stayed at an inn in Cirencester he gave the chambermaid and waiter 1s. 6d. At the George at Shepton the hostler was given 6d.; at the Petty France at Bath he gave the coachman 1s. Occasionally much higher vails were given, as when Woodforde 'breakfasted, dined and spent the afternoon at the Angel' in London in 1786. He recorded in his diary 'to the servant at the Inn very civil People gave 0.12.6', but whether this was really given to one servant seems questionable. The entire bill at the inn came to £3. 4s. 5d., so by any standards and irrespective of the number of servants involved it was a generous tip. The same year when travelling from Norwich to London by coach he gave the 'coachman that drove us half way' 3s.[89]

Vails were also paid to servants or friends or neighbours who came bearing an 'express'—or presents—of value. Blundell on these occasions rarely paid less than 2s. 6d. His Disbursement Book records 'To Mr. Hurst's Servant for bringing a Present 2s. 6d', or again 'To Coz. Scarisbrick's servant for bringing a Present 2s. 6d.'[90] In 1709 Claver Morris was sent by the Bishop 'a large, Fat Hanch of Venison'. Morris gave the Bishop's cook, who brought it, 5s.[91] But when the local squire, M. Custance, sent the Revd

---

[87] *The Great Diurnal of Nicholas Blundell*, ed. J. J. Bagley, 3 vols. (1968, 1970, 1972), vol. i, appendix B, p. 316.
[88] Ibid. [89] *The Diary of a Country Parson*, i. 123–4, ii. 276–7, 251.
[90] *The Great Diurnal of Nicholas Blundell*, vol. i, appendix B, p. 316.
[91] *The Diary of a West Country Physician 1684–1726*, 54.

Woodforde 'a fine Pike' the bearer, Don Breeze, was given only 1s.[92]

In the exchange of letters on the subject of vails there were many graphic descriptions of the behaviour of servants waiting to be paid their vails at the end of an evening. The hosts at such dinners wrote of the embarrassment of waiting with a guest for his horse or carriage to be brought to the door. 'His guest's right hand lock'd in his, and the other fumbling in his pocket for half crowns and shillings' as he passes through 'a parcel of trim, lazy, pamper'd serving men.'[93] Guests were obliged, it was said, 'to ransome their bodies as they pass'.[94] Another account suggested guests had to make their way 'thro' a lane of harping cringing harpies'.[95] Yet others compared them to 'a Row of complaisant Duns'.[96] If guests refused to pay they were 'heartily abused'.

'Strangers', it was held, were 'put to catch their death in damp beds, because they did not sufficiently see the housemaids.'[97] It was the custom for families to rent houses in Bath during the season, and sometimes they were fully provided with servants. In *Humphry Clinker*, Winefred Jenkin is horrified by the way these built-in servants behaved to the Squire. They are not allowed, she writes, 'to stay any longer, because they have been already above three weeks in the house, and they look for a couple of ginneys a piece at our going away.' This perquisite was expected 'every month of the season, being as how no family has a right to stay longer than four weeks in the same lodgings'.[98]

It was held that a guest of 'a person of condition. who has a file of servants . . . must pay much dearer than if he had dined at a publick house'.[99] In some cases it made the host spend more on the dinner than he otherwise would have done. So, it was held, 'a middling citizen, who keeps only one servant . . . cannot for shame do less than add something from the larder, or the market, to a cold joint, if he means to make you pay his man or maid one shilling . . . for your dinner'.[100] Only occasionally was some sympathy expressed for the ignominy of servants queuing up for their

---

[92] *The Diary of a Country Parson*, v. 207. [93] *London Chronicle*, 7 (1760), 260.
[94] *London Chronicle*, 48 (1779), 15. [95] *London Chronicle*, 21 (1767), 239.
[96] *The Gentleman's Magazine*, 4 (1734), 131.
[97] *London Chronicle*, 21 (1767), 239. [98] Smollett, *Humphry Clinker*, i. 91–2.
[99] *London Magazine*, 47 (1790), 15. [100] Ibid. 16.

tips. 'How pitiful', it was to see employers 'permit their servants to stand like beggars at the door with open palm ready to receive whatever is put there.'[101] Another kind of vails that was paid by guests was card money. When invited out to dinner and cards, guests were expected to contribute to the cost of the cards which was always borne by a servant. In fact more than their value was subscribed so that the servant involved stood to gain considerably. In the 1790s the poet John Jones was an 'upper servant' in a household that played cards. 'As I received a little card money at times', he wrote, 'I soon was enabled to procure me some books.'[102] Along with the opposition to vails there was an attempt to do away with card money in the 1760s, but without much success.

Vails had become an established custom by the eighteenth century, one on which servants relied and which they saw as their right. Among servants, it was perhaps footmen who gained most from vails. When the first opposition to them was voiced by employers it was, as we have seen, footmen who responded both in the press and in action. But even before vails had become an issue, there were the first hints of revolt by footmen against their masters. In 1701 *The Gazette* recorded that 'many mischiefs and dangerous accidents' had occurred as a result of 'Footmen's wearing of swords'. Henceforth the wearing of swords when 'attending any of the nobility or gentry of his Majesty's realm' was forbidden.[103] Mandeville wrote in 1724 that 'a parcel of Footmen are arrived at the height of Insolence as to have enter'd into a Society together, and made Laws by which they oblige themselves not to serve for less than such a Sum, nor carry Burdens or any Bundle or Parcel above a certain Weight, not exceeding Two or Three Pounds'.[104] If Mandeville's informant was right it was not surprising that employers were worried. An organized opposition from footmen was a serious matter. Unlike many servants their duties brought them into contact with other households and other footmen. Conditions could be discussed, assemblies planned, and action plotted. And, Mandeville suggested, their

[101] *London Chronicle*, 47 (1790), 342.
[102] Robert Southey, *The Lives and Works of the Uneducated Poets* (1831), 176.
[103] As quoted in J. P. Malcolm, *Anecdotes of the Manners and Customs of London during the Eighteenth Century*, 2 vols. (1811), 314.
[104] Bernard Mandeville, *The Fable of the Bees*, 2 vols. (1724), i. 350.

ideas were spreading to other servants who were 'daily encroaching upon Masters and Mistresses, and endeavour to be more upon the Level with them'. They seemed 'solicitous to abolish the low dignity of their Condition' and had already succeeded in raising it 'from the Original Meanness which the Publick Welfare requires it should always remain in'.[105]

Symptomatic of the footmen's mood was their reaction to being denied entrance to the gallery of the Drury Lane Playhouse in 1737. Ever since the Restoration the Playhouse had granted free entrance to the footmen of those attending the theatre. Other theatres had soon followed suit so that by the 1730s it had become an established right and one much prized. The cause of their exclusion is not entirely clear, but it was 'on account of their Rudeness'. Their reaction was immediate. 'A Body of them to the Number of 300, arm'd with offensive Weapons, broke open the Doors ... They fought their Way to the Stage Door, forc'd it open, and wounded 25 Persons'. Colonel de Veil, who happened to be in the audience, 'attempted to read the Proclamation, but such was their Violence ... he was obstructed in the Execution of his Duty'. Nevertheless he was responsible for sending three of the ringleaders to Newgate. The footmen thereupon sent a threatening letter to the master of the theatre. The wording is of interest. Provided, they wrote, they were treated 'Civil and Admitted into *our* Gallery, which is *our Property according to Formalities*' (my emphasis) they would hear no more from them.[106] Otherwise the Playhouse would be destroyed. Soldiers were brought in to protect the theatre, but no action was taken by the footmen. Perhaps they had already received word that the prohibition was about to be lifted. Just over twenty years later they were banned permanently from the gallery when Townley's play *High Life Below Stairs* was being staged—a satire 'intended to shame the class [of servants] out of its misconduct' and which pandered to the current opposition to vails-giving.[107]

In 1744 the footmen staged another demonstration against 'their bread being taken from them by Frenchmen and other foreigners'. They called a meeting—openly advertised—of all footmen. The meeting was prevented, we are told, by the same

---

[105] Bernard Mandeville, *The Fable of the Bees*, 2 vols. (1724), i. 351.
[106] *The Gentleman's Magazine*, 7 (1737), 186.
[107] Hecht, *The Domestic Servant in Eighteenth-Century England*, 87.

Colonel de Veil who 'at the desire of some great people' shut up the room.[108] What is remarkable is the apparent strength of the body of footmen who made their way to Colonel de Veil's house and tried to force him to open the room for their meeting. Mandeville claimed of a footman that 'everything in the House is his Perquisite and he won't stay with you unless his Vails are sufficient to maintain a middling Family'.[109] In February 1716 the Revd Edward Turner 'bargained with Edward Morley at 35s. until Michs., and if his vailes be not 5s., I have promised to make them so'.[110] In October 1775 John Baker gave his maid, Molly Mant, five shillings, to make up for the absence of a tip from 'his late guests, Mr. Barton and his sister Mrs. Coyly'.[111] Such accounts suggest something of the strength of servants' feeling about vails and its recognition by at least some employers. The main organized campaign against vails was only to begin after the middle of the century. Earlier, it is true, there had been some who rejected the practice. Joseph Nollekens sat for William Hogarth some time in the first half of the eighteenth century (Nollekens described him as a young man) when, as he put it, 'the custom was not introduced of not giving vails to servants'. When, on his leaving, a servant opened the door for him, Nollekens 'offered him a small gratuity'. The servant 'very politely refused it, telling me that it would be the loss of his place, if his master knew it'. As Nollekens commented, 'this was uncommon, and so liberal in a man of Mr. Hogarth's profession, at that time of day', it made a deep impression on him.[112] When at a county meeting in Norfolk the duke proposed abolishing vails, it was the father of the radical leader, Major John Cartwright, who was the first to attempt to implement the idea 'though it was expected that the attempt would be attended with very unpleasant consequences'.[113] He was right.

The organized opposition to vails started in Scotland. At a meeting 'of gentlemen, freeholders and commissioners of the

---

[108] *The Gentleman's Magazine*, 17 (1747), 563 and 562–3 n.

[109] Mandeville, *Fable of the Bees*, i. 347.

[110] *The Marchant Diary*, ed. the Revd Edward Turner, Sussex Archaeological Collections, xxv (1873), 163–99 at p. 175.

[111] *The Diary of John Baker*, ed. Philip C. Yorke (1931), 53.

[112] Smith, *Nollekens and his Times*, i. 48.

[113] *The Life and Correspondence of Major Cartwright*, ed. F. D. Cartwright, 2 vols. (1826), i. 3.

land tax' at Aberdeen in December 1759 it was resolved 'to discourage the practice and [they] agreed among themselves to give no vails nor allow their servants to receive them'.[114] The Honourable Company of Scots Hunters of Edinburgh at its annual meeting in January 1760 also agreed to abolish vails. Several other organizations followed their lead. The abolition led, it was claimed by the *London Chronicle*, to a 'general mutiny of servants'. In Edinburgh many left their service and went 'to London in quest of new places and vails'. Any servant who remained and was found accepting vails was to be 'automatically empressed into H. M. navy or army'. The fate of those coming to London was no different: 'most of them were impressed in the Thames and sent on board the fleet before they had an opportunity of setting foot on shore'.[115] In May of the same year 'the English servants to the officers in the army in Germany, to the amount of fifty or more, agreed amongst themselves to leave their masters, if their wages and perquisites were not advanced'. Their demands were found 'exorbitant' and 'their officers were obliged to discharge them'.[116] As they landed at Sheerness they were impressed.

From Scotland the move against vails spread southwards. By 1767 it was confidently claimed that vails had been abolished 'all over Scotland' and in 'several counties in England'.[117] But here the movement made but slow progress despite the frequent claims that vails were a thing of the past. Even Hecht claims vails were 'eliminated as a source of income during the last quarter of the century'.[118] In fact vails in many households persisted well into the nineteenth century and, even after private families had given them up, in inns and taverns all over the country. By no means were all employers agreed on the abolition. Ironically those opposing vails accused 'vulgar families' of being responsible for its persistence, for vails-giving was 'not suffered in any genteel families'.[119] The facts belie such theories. But what above all delayed the movement in England was the strength of the reaction of servants. Dorothy George saw London footmen as 'a formidable body' and servant riots as frequent.[120] Gladys Scott Thomson in

[114] *London Chronicle*, 7 (1760), 62.   [115] Ibid. 164.   [116] Ibid. 441.
[117] *London Chronicle*, 21 (1767), 239.
[118] *The Domestic Servant in Eighteenth-Century England*, 168.
[119] *Oxford Magazine*, 6 (1771), 84.
[120] 'The Early History of Registry Offices', 584.

her study of the Russell family was intrigued to discover that, whereas most of the male servants in the household were receiving exactly the same wages in the late 1760s as they had received in the early 1750s, there was one notable exception—footmen. Despite the absence of any general rise in wages the £6–£8 paid to footmen earlier had risen by 1771 to £14–£17. In explanation she argues that they were 'highly privileged members of the staff' and that they, above all other servants, 'could count on extra income in the shape of gratuities'. But it is possible that the main reason for their wage rise lay in masters' fear of their power.[121] In May 1768, in a proclamation from the Court of St James, came a warning to masters to keep their apprentices and servants 'from assembling themselves together in the public streets'.[122] If masters threatened abolition male servants moved to other households or, as seems to have been happening increasingly in the last half of the eighteenth century, abandoned domestic service. There were threats made against masters who opposed vails-giving. In 1764 there were 'great riots at Ranelagh among those *beings*, the footmen'. It was said they 'assaulted several gentlemen who had declared against giving Vails. Four of them were secured and dealt with according to law.'[123] In 1771, the *London Chronicle* reported that 'a person of distinction in Charles Street, St. James's, has had a threatening letter sent him on account of his ordering his servants to take no perquisites'. The letter, it was said, was sent by 'some of the servants that were discharged for disobeying his injunction'.[124] Even in Scotland as late as 1787 there occurred 'a meeting and riot at Glasgow by the servants against their employers with respect to their wages'. Several were reported killed or wounded. 'The military' were 'obliged to assist'.[125]

But what were the real causes of the opposition to vails? It was recognized to be an ancient practice but one 'propp'd and supported by nothing but custom grown blind with

[121] Gladys Scott Thomson, *The Russells in Bloomsbury 1669–1771* (1940), 228.
[122] As quoted in Malcolm, *Anecdotes of the Manners and Customs of London during the Eighteenth Century*, ii. 87.
[123] Quoted in Hecht, *The Domestic Servant in Eighteenth-Century England*, 165, 167 (from *Letters of the First Earl of Malmesbury*, i. 108); *London Magazine*, 33 (1764).
[124] *London Chronicle*, 30 (1771), 230.
[125] *The Diary of Nicholas Brown 1722–27*, in *Six North Country Diaries*, Surtees Society, cxviii (1910), 230–323 at p. 290.

age'.[126] It was said to be 'destructive of the morals of servants'. It provided them, it was held, with the 'means of indulging continual luxury and vice'.[127] Vails were seen as perverting 'all order and subordination'.[128] They bred 'an independence amongst servants contrary to all good order'.[129] As one master, George Meanwell, complained, although one of the best of masters and giving good wages, he could not 'establish a proper subordination amongst them'.[130] A writer explained that 'those born in servitude' had 'no right to aim at high stations; and much less to think, while in a state of servitude, that they have any claim to the indulging of themselves in the follies and pleasure of their superiors'.[131] But vails had existed for a long time before this opposition surfaced. The opposition increasingly expressed from the late seventeenth century onwards but, more particularly, from the middle of the eighteenth century, reflects the often unresolved tension between the old paternalistic relationship between masters and servants (in which if servants had clearly defined duties and responsibilities towards their employers, their masters had equally clear duties and responsibilities towards their servants), and a strictly wage contract relationship. Earlier it had been a relationship in which wages were neither central nor considerable. Servants were rewarded for their services when they performed them well and—not necessarily on a regular basis—by hand-outs, often in kind. If employers exercised supreme control over their servants, it was recognized that servants, although unquestionably inferior in status, also had rights. These were never recorded, were not legitimized, and were not always clearly defined from either the masters' or the servants' point of view. Over the years such customary rights of servants were acknowledged—and depended on by servants as a vital supplement to their wages. When opposition to them mounted it must have seemed to servants, particularly male servants who stood to benefit most from vails, that the whole basis of their livelihood was under threat.

The reaction of servants to attempts to abolish vails was not so very different from that of the rural population to the erosion of

[126] *London Chronicle*, 7 (1760), 260.   [127] Ibid. 164.
[128] Ibid. 260.   [129] *London Chronicle*, 11 (1762), 164.
[130] *The Gentleman's Magazine*, 26 (1756), 573.
[131] *London Chronicle*, 7 (1760), 164.

common land and the many perquisites that went with it from the right to graze their stock on the common fields to the right to glean after the harvest. When extra labour was taken on for the harvest the allowances of beer at regular intervals was understood as the labourers' due. At sheep shearings allowances of food and drink were an understood part of the agreement between sheep farmer and labourer. When there was increasing criticism of cooks' and other servants' perquisites, and of the Christmas boxes some servants received from tradesmen, the reaction of those involved was similar to the response of dockers' wives at Portsmouth to being refused further access to the yards where they had been accustomed to glean wood scraps and waste produced in the course of ship-building. More than 2,000 of the women rioted in 1767. It was perhaps easier to employ the law to enforce such restrictions than in the case of vails and perquisites, although as we have seen it was not for want of demands for legislation to ban them. The severe punishments for stealing wood, poaching, trespass, and unlawful gleaning were paralleled by the increasing severity of punishments for petty theft for which so many servants in the eighteenth century were had up before the law.

The opposition to vails came at a time of transition between paternalism and a contractual wage relationship. It is an opposition that deserves far more probing than it has received to date. In looking for the reason why servant–master relations no longer functioned as in the old days some employers fixed on vails as the culprit. The conclusion most came to was that servants were to blame for the breakdown in master–servant relations. It was their increasing greed, insolence, and lack of loyalty to their masters that was the cause. Servants had indeed changed, but not perhaps so much as those employing servants—those newly arrived in the middle class and those artisans, tradesmen, and shopkeepers, all aspiring to middle-class status, who, with a little more money in their pockets, were able to employ one servant as a general help. Many of these new arrivals in the servant-employing class had no time for old-fashioned paternalism. Their aim in employing a servant was to get value for money, to extract as much work as possible for as low a wage as possible. Few would have understood master–servant relations as involving reciprocal duties and responsibilities. 'From the new viewpoint of political economy', writes Bruce Robbins, 'relations between classes were ruled not by mutual rights and duties within a hierarchical family but by the impersonal workings of the market.'[132] Some of these new employers of servants were in manufacturing industry, where workers' perquisites were already under attack. They saw the employment of servants as a straightforward wage contract. In such a contractual relationship there was no place for customary rights.

On the other hand many of those who had long employed servants saw factory hands as enjoying a dangerous freedom. No longer were they completely under their employer's control. They did not live in but at the end of the working day went home to their own houses and families. Their working day was no longer defined by tasks to be done but by hours which, while long, had a clearly defined beginning and an end. Working alongside large numbers of other workers, employers' demands were not only freely discussed but on occasion resisted. The reaction of such employers to their domestic servants was to attempt to reimpose control over them and to regulate their lives in every aspect. They found it was no longer so easily done. Their servants were also aware of the greater freedom enjoyed by factory hands. Some of them were abandoning domestic service and becoming factory workers.

The feelings employers had about living-in servants were often paradoxical and contradictory. This can be seen in the changed attitude to servants in husbandry—living-in farm servants. In the early eighteenth century households were beginning to resent the demands made on them by such servants. Not only had they to be housed and fed, but they mixed freely with the family, eating with them and often sharing the same beds. To a middle class that was becoming very privacy-conscious such unwanted intimacy was intolerable. The result was a rapid decline in the number of servants in husbandry. More and more of such farm labour was hired not by the year but by the month, and lived out. The same resentment of the invasion of their privacy was felt about domestic servants but, by the very nature of the demands made upon them and the tasks they were expected to carry out, it was impossible to banish them from the household. There is an attempt by

[132] *The Servant's Hand* (1986), 111.

employers, nevertheless, to distance themselves from their domestic servants. Where possible they slept in separate servant quarters away from those of the family. It was a development that dated from the sixteenth century. By the early seventeenth century in houses of the richer gentry in the Durham region, for example, there was a move towards 'the provision of defined accomodation for servants which set the latter apart from the family'.[133] By the eighteenth century houses were being built for the gentry in which the strict segregation of servants from family was assumed. Indeed, there was a gradual change in the way in which the term 'family' was used. If earlier it had embraced, as well as blood relations, all apprentices and servants in the household, it was increasingly restricted to only the former. If earlier there had been a careful surveillance of the lives of servants, that surveillance was now intensified. If earlier employers had resented servants telling tales about the family to the outside world, now their concern about servants spying on them and gossiping became almost paranoid. Linda Pollock has talked of the desire of families 'above all to escape the prying eyes' of their servants. 'In this desire for privacy', she writes, 'servants were a perennial hindrance'.[134] There was far less intimacy and exchange with servants. Employers were now warned of the dangerous influence of servants over their children. They were probably right in thinking there was far less servant loyalty to masters in this changed atmosphere. Servants felt fewer qualms about gossiping about their employers than formerly. It was not only in the Victorian household that, as Bruce Robbins suggests, there was 'an impression of increased silence, of a repression of master/servant dialogue motivated ... by fear of its subversive consequences'.[135]

There was often ambivalence in the attitude of employers to servants, perhaps nowhere so well illustrated as in the custom of giving departing servants 'characters'. There seems to have been great reluctance on the part of employers, however bad they felt servants were, and even when they had been dismissed, to give

[133] Mervyn James, *Family, Lineage and Civil Society* (1974), 14.
[134] 'Living on the Stage of the World: The Concept of Privacy among the Elite of Early Modern England', in Adrian Wilson (ed.), *Rethinking Social History* (1993), 78–96 at pp. 79, 86.
[135] *The Servant's Hand*, 78.

them a thoroughly bad character. It came 'from an imperfect accomodation of the impersonality of the market. The old pre-industrial ideology weighed heavily on masters and mistresses whose allegiance to industrial modernity remained fragile.'[136]

Although there was a very vocal opposition to vails, there were also employers who were against any such abolition, arguing that the system had worked satisfactorily for years, so why disturb it? Other employers were caught between a rejection of paternalism with the wish to abolish vails and perquisites, and a reluctance to accept a purely wage relationship. Strong though their desire to get rid of vails was, the majority of masters were not so anxious to increase wages in compensation as so many of the more objective writers on the subject proposed. If they demanded that perquisites be abolished they were unwilling to listen to those who suggested it was better to give servants a little more in wages than cast-off clothes. The same advice was given to servants. 'Do not covet to have the Kitchen Stuff for your Vales', advised *The Compleat Servant Maid* in 1677. 'but rather ask for more wages.'[137] Asking was one thing, getting another. One reason why the opposition to vails failed was that the masters concerned were unwilling to consider the alternative to vails and perquisites. It is surely no coincidence that today we continue to give tips to the worst paid—waiters, porters, hairdressers, and hotel servants. The opposition to vails must be seen as symptomatic of the 'contradictions between familial forms and market relations', but for many those contradictions remained unresolved.[138]

[136] *The Servant's Hand*, 111–12.
[137] Hannah Wolley, *The Compleat Servant-maid, or the Young Maiden's Tutor*, 4th edn. (1685), 107.
[138] Leonore Davidoff and Catherine Hall, *Family Fortunes* (1987), 390.

5
Opportunity, Identity, and Servility

'There was no status in being in service, you were a nobody; marriage was the way out of it.'

Rosina Harrison, *Rose: My Life in Service*, 24

'the employment of servants was a way of defining oneself socially as not being working class'

Eric Hobsbawn in a discussion, 1973

'What was most irksome about domestic service was almost certainly the continuous and all-pervading degree of subordination which the job involved, far more than in virtually any other type of occupation in the city'.

Peter Earle, *A City Full of People*, 127

ONE of the recent tendencies in new work on domestic service in early modern England has been the desire to improve its image. Far from servants being overworked, underpaid, exploited, restricted, and, above all, servile members of the labouring class, it has been argued that service—for women and men—compared favourably with other occupations of the labouring poor. Indeed, where women were concerned, it has been suggested that service in the eighteenth century offered a real career. It is not surprising therefore—or so it is argued—that so many were attracted into it.

In this chapter I want to look more closely at these arguments and to explore some of the disadvantages service held for the labouring class—disadvantages not just measured in terms of financial reward, security, or the chances of promotion and social betterment it offered, but in what was sacrificed in independence, a sense of identity, and self-respect.

Perhaps above all else it is security and opportunity for social advancement which, it has been argued, service provided. 'The principal motives' of those entering service, it has been said, 'were the desire for security and the desire to rise in the economic and social scale.' Service was, it is held, 'the occupation offering the greatest degree of security and protection'.[1] 'The security of servants' food and lodging', it is claimed, 'was one of the great advantages of service.'[2] John Burnett, writing of London female domestic service in the early nineteenth century, qualified such a view by adding that provided it involved 'employment in a good household ... It was a secure and regular occupation'.[3] Some appearance of security domestic service certainly seemed to offer. It is difficult to overestimate the importance for parents—and their daughters—of what appeared a stable occupation that provided bed and board, and often clothing, that involved entering not a factory or alien workplace but another household to become members of the family in its widest sense. For many anxious parents it must have seemed like the next best thing to their daughters staying at home but with the great advantage that they no longer had to feed them, and entry into domestic service, unlike apprenticeship, did not involve the payment of a premium. But real security and stability depended on servants' ability to keep a place and, judging by eighteenth-century experience, dismissal could be so arbitrary and on such slim grounds that every servant was constantly in danger of losing his or her employment. As a correspondent of the *London Chronicle* wrote in 1791, 'a *servant*, though never so attentive and industrious, lives in a continual dread of their [employer's] displeasure upon every trivial offence, and lives in *fear* of not only being discarded from their service, but also of being deprived of that which is the only recommendation to his future subsistence, which recommendation consists in a good *character*'.[4]

In 1776 James Woodforde paid his servant, Molly Salmon, and she left his service. He commented in his diary: 'I should have been glad to have kept her as she is good-tempered, but she never once asked to stay after I had given her notice, therefore I dismissed her.' But why had he given her notice in the first place?

[1] J. Jean Hecht, *The Domestic Servant in Eighteenth-Century England* (1956), 19.
[2] Theresa McBride, *The Domestic Revolution* (1976), 55.
[3] *Useful Toil: Autobiographies of Working People from the 1820s to the 1920s*, ed. John Burnett, 2nd edn. (1994), 137.
[4] *The London Chronicle*, 61 (1791), 1172–3.

Her fault had been putting eggs into some rice-milk prepared for Woodforde's servants who had just been inoculated against smallpox. It had made Woodforde 'very angry, so angry that I gave her warning to go away at Christmas'.[5] How was the girl expected to know what was and was not good for those newly inoculated? None of the servants seems to have come to any harm, but Woodforde's pride prevented him asking her to stay. In consequence he lost a good servant. In May 1785 John Gabriel Stedman turned away his 'workmaid, whose only fault was her humour'.[6] Mary Davis, laundry maid to the Dormer family, 'was turned out by her mistress because she refused to take mouldy starch unfit for her business from one of her trades people'. But this was only the pretext for her dismissal. The real reason was that the footman who was her mistress's lover invaded her laundry room 'and there pretended to pry into matters which in no wise belong to him'.[7] When she asked him to leave he became aggressive, but Mary managed to lock him out. She was dismissed.

Even if they were not dismissed, servants' security could be totally jeopardized by chronic illness. There are frequent examples of female servants being dismissed because of repeated illness and, if they were not able to return to their families, their fate was precarious. When Molly Dade, one of Woodforde's maidservants fell ill in September 1784, 'very bad in a Cough and am afraid it is rather consumptive', her master expressed his sorrow. She was 'one of the best Maids that ever we had and very much liked by us both', but while they wanted to keep her Woodforde recorded in his diary his fear that it would not be possible because of her illness. By November it was clear Molly 'could not recover'. She was replaced. In April 1791 a Nanny Golding came to be Woodforde's servant. By the following month she was 'very ill'. By August she was suffering from regular fits. Woodforde records 'I must part with her at Michaelmas'.[8] What happened to such servants we do not know, but that they must have rapidly

[5] *The Diary of a Country Parson: The Reverend James Woodforde 1758–1813*, ed. John Beresford, 5 vols. (1924–31), i. 190, 196, ii. 154, 157–8, 160, iii. 274, 290.
[6] *Journal of John Gabriel Stedman 1744–97*, ed. Stanbury Thompson (1962), 259.
[7] As quoted in Tim Meldrum, 'Domestic Service in London, 1660–1750: Training for Life or Simply "Getting a Living"', paper given at a conference on Women's Initiatives in Early Modern England, 1500–1750 (4 June 1994), 7.
[8] *The Diary of a Country Parson*, ii. 154, 157–8, 160.

used up any savings is clear. If they had homes to return to family resources would have been put under great strain. Liberal employers had their servants inoculated at their own expense. But woe to a servant who was unfortunate enough to get smallpox in Elizabeth Purefoy's household. She made her servants enter into an agreement which would come into force in the event of their getting the disease. So Priscilla Matthews, who was hired for a year, was first called on to agree that if she was 'at any time of her... service... visited with the Distemper of the Small-Pox', after her mistress had paid her what was due to her, 'the aforesaid Hire to be void'.[9]

There was also old age to provide for. If in the early years of service a servant's wages tended to rise, this trend failed to continue after middle age. The need to provide for their old age must have been an ever-present concern of servants, particularly of women who remained single or who had been widowed. 'Certainly', wrote Jonas Hanway, 'we should lay up something for a rainy day.'[10] Mary Collier, the washerwoman poet, continued to work at washing and brewing until she was 63 but she did not retire. Instead she became housekeeper to a farmer. It is notable how many of those who were forced on the parish in their old age were women who, formerly, had been servants. In his collection of epitaphs and obituaries of servants, Arthur Munby has many examples of servants who continued working right up to their deaths. So Mary Banks of Croydon was a single woman who had been a most 'faithful and trusty Servant in two Families in this Town in the first for ten and in the second for twenty-four years'. She died in the service of the latter family in August 1791 aged 62. Or there is Mary Whitty, 'a faithful Servant that lived in Mrs. Winford's Family Sixty-three years', who died in 1795 aged 82. She must have continued working well past the age of 70. Nor was this lengthy working life confined to female servants. John Philips, who died in 1735, is described as 'sometimes Housekeeper at Chatsworth'.[11] He was 73 when he died and in the sixtieth year of his service with the Duke of Devonshire. Among the more liberal of employers there is some recognition of the financial dilemma of old servants whether present or past. Some

[9] *The Purefoy Letters 1735–53*, ed. G. Eland, 2 vols. (1931), ii. 444, appendix D.
[10] *The Sentiments and Advice of Thomas Trueman* (1760), 13.
[11] Arthur J. Munby (ed.), *Faithful Servants: Epitaphs and Obituaries* (1891), 210.

left bequests to their servants in their wills. Others remembered old servants and gave them financial help from time to time. In June 1782 Woodforde met 'an old Servant of mine (by name Luke Barnard) whom I saw at Ansford to day gave 0.2.6.'[12] On the other hand there is the horrifying story told by the Revd John Skinner of an elderly couple, both of whom had been servants. 'The woman is the granddaughter of a clergyman, is upwards of 80, the husband I believe is older; they have no one to assist them, both being so infirm they cannot assist themselves. They lived as servants to that wretched miser and magistrate, Purnell of Woodborough, who . . . instructed the parish to reduce their allowance of 5s. a week by 1s.'[13]

Defoe accused servants of making inadequate reserves against sickness or loss of their place so that 'if they fall sick the parish must keep them, if they are out of a place, they must prostitute their bodies or starve'. Looking at the level of female servants' wages it cannot have been easy to set aside anything for sickness or periods between places, let alone save up for marriage or old age. Many servants, Defoe continued, 'rove from place to place, from bawdy house to service, and from service to bawdy house again, ever unsettled and never easy, nothing being more common than to find these creatures one week in a good family, and the next in a brothel'.[14] In fact Defoe's description may well have been true of some servants who experienced sudden dismissal. Short of returning home, an option not open to all, female servants out of a place had little choice if they were not to starve. On the basis of those servant witnesses before the Church Courts in the period 1660–1750 who disclosed what if anything they were worth, two-thirds 'answered "little", "nothing", or "their wages"'.[15] It makes it difficult to accept Theresa McBride's confident assertion that 'a servant had almost no need and little opportunity to spend his salary, so servants were able to amass considerable savings'. They were, she argues, thus enabled 'to return to the country or to marry in relative comfort'.[16] Many servants, as we have seen, had to supply themselves with clothes.

[12] *The Diary of a Country Parson*, ii. 31.
[13] *The Journal of a Somerset Rector 1803–34*, ed. Howard and Peter Coombs (1930), 428.
[14] *Everybody's Business is Nobody's Business* (1725), 7, 8.
[15] Meldrum, 'Domestic Service in London 1660–1750: Training for Life', 10.
[16] *The Domestic Revolution*, 50.

Deductions from their wages could be made for breakages or misdemeanours. Some were forced to borrow their wages in advance from their employers. When Molly Peachman left Woodforde's service in October 1796 to get married, he paid her '11 Months Wages at 5.5.0. pr Ann. 4.16.6. She paid me out of it, what I lent her being 1.1.0.'[17] A Yorkshire family at the end of the eighteenth century kept two maids who were paid 'about four guineas a year'. To one of them, Betty, her mistress 'notes more than once that she had to "lend Betty money against the next half-year".'[18] The amount a servant could save, writes Olwen Hufton, 'depended upon her ability to accumulate without cutting into her wages to help her family or to cope with periods of illness or unemployment'.[19] Many servants, like Richardson's Pamela, aimed to send back to their families some part of their earnings.

When in 1763 'three dead women, near naked, and all appearing as if starved' were found in Stonecutter Street in London there were also in the house three other women who had survived. One of them was a domestic servant 'out of a place'.[20] And the experience of being out of a place was one which almost all servants suffered at some time in their years of service. For most it was a frequent occurrence. Jonas Hanway, writing in 1760 of servants leaving their places because of their loss of vails, wrote that there were 'above Two Thousand in a kind of rotation, always out of place and in search of good Services' in London at any time.[21] By 1796 Colquhoun thought there were 'seldom less than *Ten Thousand Servants*, of both sexes, at all times, out of place in the Metropolis'.[22]

If servants were dismissed and their master or mistress refused them a character, obtaining another place might be difficult if not impossible. Even when they left voluntarily they were entirely at the mercy of their employers for any recommendation and, as Sir John Fielding observed, unjust characters could be

---

[17] *The Diary of a Country Parson*, ii. 211.

[18] Anne Vernon, *Three Generations: The Fortunes of a Yorkshire Family* (1966), 37.

[19] 'Women, Work and Family', in Natalie Zemon Davis and Arlette Farge (eds.), *A History of Women* iii. (1993), 15–45 at p. 22.

[20] J. P. Malcolm, *Anecdotes of the Manners and Customs of London during the Eighteenth Century* (1811), 60.

[21] *The Sentiments and Advice of Thomas Trueman*, 50.

[22] Patrick Colquhoun, *A Treatise on the Police in the Metropolis*, 3rd edn. (1796), 423 n.

given 'either from false good nature or undeserved resentment'.[23] Tim Meldrum, in his work on London servants, has outlined 'three common strategies taken by servants who had left or lose their place'. Either they 'left London for a time, or even for good', or 'they went into lodgings, or where it was possible they returned to former employers if they had a place to be filled'.[24] But often not one of these strategies was open to them. For some, prostitution was the only answer. In the late seventeenth and early eighteenth centuries London women were 'more than twice as likely as men to be committed to houses of correction mostly for prostitution or any sign that they were "loose" or "lewed" particularly when they were out of work'. Most of them, it is suggested, were unmarried women 'probably domestic servants out of work'.[25] We have seen Defoe suggesting that for maidservants who had lost their place it was often a question of prostitution or starvation. Defoe blamed their frequent changing of places and their failure to make any financial reserve. In 1749 it was held that the reason London was 'overstock'd with Harlots' was the excess of servants migrating from the countryside.[26] Hogarth's *A Harlot's Progress* could be seen as endorsing such a view. In 1758 the magistrate Sir John Fielding argued that it was the few trades open to women that led so many to enter service. 'For this reason ... there is always in London an amazing number of women servants out of place.' It was this that was 'one of the grand sources which furnish this town with prostitutes'.[27] In the same year Jonas Hanway endorsed Fielding's thesis. 'Domestic servitude' was 'the fruitful supply of prostitutes and female servants in the metropolis, generally much more numerous than can be accomodated.'[28] Colquhoun in 1796 estimated that there were over 50,000 women living by prostitution in London and of these over half had been 'employed as Menial Servants, or seduced in very early life'.[29] Among Paris prostitutes in the 1830s the most

[23] As quoted in M. Dorothy George, 'The Early History of Registry Offices', *Economic History*, 1 (1926–9), 570–90 at p. 584.
[24] 'Domestic Service in London 1660–1750: Training for Life', 10.
[25] Robert B. Shoemaker, *Prosecution and Punishment* (1991), 184–6.
[26] Anon., *Satan's Harvest Home* (1749), 6.
[27] 'The two great causes of the numberless prostitutes that infest our streets', *London Chronicle*, 3 (1758), 327.
[28] *On Prostitution: A Plan for Establishing a Charity-House or Charity Houses for the reception of repenting prostitutes* (1758), 39.
[29] *A Treatise on the Police in the Metropolis*, 39.

common motive for entering the occupation was 'a prior seduction by their employer'. Forced to leave their places, 'ex-domestic servants comprised the largest group of prostitutes'.[30] In the 1850s Acton wrote of domestic servants who became pregnant and who were 'generally driven headlong to the streets for support of themselves and their babies'.[31] Domestic service seems to have been one of the main sources of women who moved into prostitution during the mid-Victorian period. The comment of a doctor in the 1870s might have been made at any time during the eighteenth century. 'They get out of a place', he wrote, 'and they have nowhere to go and they adopt this as a last resort, as a means of livelihood; some go back to service and again return to the streets.'[32] 'Occupational dislocation' writes Judith Walkowitz, 'seems to have been a more decisive factor in women's move into prostitution than pre-marital sexuality and pregnancy.' On the high proportion of servants in London rescue homes and so-called Lock Hospitals (for the treatment of venereal disease) in mid-century she comments: 'at some time or other, most of these women had been servants.' She has estimates that, by 1890, more than 50 per cent of women in prostitution were servants.[33] There is no reason for thinking this was not true of the eighteenth century. If evidence of servants who were out of a place moving into prostitution is difficult to find it is hardly surprising. We know all too little about prostitution in the eighteenth century. We do know that, if contemporary accounts are to be believed, prostitution was noticeably increasing. The most obvious source was those occupations and trades that were poorly paid and where workers were most liable to periods of unemployment such as, among others, domestic service. For many, it appears, it was a temporary expedient resorted to in order to tide them over until a suitable place became available.

[30] R. Bridenthal and C. Koonz, *Becoming Visible: Women in European History* (1979), 289.
[31] William Acton, *Prostitution Considered in the Moral, Social and Sanitary Aspects* (1857), 54.
[32] As quoted in Judith Walkowitz, 'The Making of an Outcast Group: Prostitutes and Working Women', in Martha Vicinus (ed.), *A Widening Sphere* (1st pub. 1977; 2nd edn. 1980), 72–93 at p. 75.
[33] *Prostitution and Victorian Society: Women, Class and the State* (1980), 15–16, 63, 194.

If dismissal of servants was often arbitrary, so was the punishment some employers inflicted on them. William Fleetwood's advice to masters was not always heeded. 'Masters', he wrote, must not be 'over-rigorous in their Punishments, when Servants are faulty, but should inflict them with Deliberation, good Intention, and Compassion.'[34] Sir Richard Newdigate frequently hit his servants, and was then consumed with shame and gave them presents or money to assuage his feeling of guilt. When he gave his 14-year-old boy 'a quick-tempered cuff', he recorded: 'To Ned White because I struck him on a mistake 1s.' Later Tom Cooper was also rewarded 'because he 'worked hard after I broke his head 2s. 6d'.[35] 'Both rewards and punishments', it is said, 'remained personal and arbitrary.'[36] When one of John Gabriel Stedman's maids, Betty Boden, ran away, she was caught next day and 'damnably beat by her father and me'.[37]

One cause of ill-feeling between masters and servants was the practice of giving the latter 'a Month's Warning, or a Month's Wages'. Sir John Fielding thought it 'a manifest Disadvantage to both Parties' and 'attended with very evil consequences, and often the Occasion of Servants having unjust Characters'.[38] Defoe blamed the practice on servant-maids who had become 'their own law givers ... they hire themselves to you by their own rule—a month's wages, or a month's warning'. It was a custom that had 'become a great inconvenience to masters and mistresses'.[39] But clearly it was an advantage to servants who were given some protection against the consequences of instant dismissal. Defoe wanted the practice abolished. Trusler in 1786 advised masters to get rid of servants who were leaving for whatever reason at once 'be it ever so inconvenient'. For once a warning was given to servants, they became 'very impertinent and untractable'.[40] Robert Dodsley, the footman poet, expressed the point of view of

[34] *The Relative Duties of Parents and Children, Husbands and Wives, Masters and Servants*, 2nd edn. (1716), 323.
[35] Eileen Gooder, *The Squire of Arbury: Sir Richard Newdigate (1644–1710)* (1990), 38.
[36] Leonore Davidoff and Catherine Hall, *Family Fortunes* (1987), 390.
[37] *Journal of John Gabriel Stedman*, 314.
[38] *Extracts from the Penal Laws as particularly relate to the Peace and Good Order of the Metropolis* (1768), 140–1.
[39] *Everybody's Business is Nobody's Business*, 11.
[40] *The London Adviser and Guide* (1786), 48.

servants of the practice when he said, he could not see 'that anything in the world could be more just and equitable'.[41]

'The year-long contract', we are told, 'provided security.'[42] But how representative was 'the year-long contract'? Timothy Burrell's diary reveals that he frequently dismissed servants before the year was up and re-engaged them later in order to avoid a continuous year's service.[43] Others did likewise. In 1787 the *London Chronicle* related the story of a female servant who 'having hired herself for a year gave notice to quit at the end of her term. Her mistress in the meantime in consequence of impertinent behaviour, discharged her 8 days before expiration of the year'. The intention was clear—to avoid her getting a settlement and, despite the 'impertinent behaviour' claimed, her discharge seems rather to have been motivated by malice.[44] Her mistress had paid her wages in full but, remarkably, the case came to court to decide whether or not this servant's term of service should gain a settlement. The court decided it should. But, where it existed, how binding on both parties was a yearly contract? What was the legal position of those breaking the contract? Masters were only 'liable in a civil action for damages or wages owing, the servant who broke his contract was punished as a criminal with imprisonment and hard labour up to three months'.[45] If the servant chose to leave before serving his term he lost all his wages, but if his master dismissed him, in theory he was to be paid for the time served.[46] If the master refused to pay the wages due, and they were £10 or less, a servant could take his case before a magistrate. If they were more, only a County Court could deal with it. But few servants can have been aware of their legal means of redress. Since the contract was only verbal it was in any case extremely difficult to prove breach of contract against a master. What tended to happen was that the master denied breach of

[41] *Servitude: A Poem* (1729), 31.

[42] D. A. Kent, 'Ubiquitous but Invisible: Female Domestic Servants in Mid-Eighteenth-Century London', *History Workshop Journal*, 28 (autumn 1989), 111–28 at p. 114.

[43] Violet A. Simpson, 'Servants and Service in Eighteenth-Century Town and Country', *Cornhill Magazine*, 14 (1903), 398–409 at p. 408.

[44] *London Chronicle*, 57 (1787), 558.

[45] Daphne Simon, 'Master and Servant', in John Saville (ed.), *Democracy and the Labour Movement* (1954), 160–200 at p. 160.

[46] Trusler, *The London Adviser and Guide*, 50.

contract and the case of the servant was dismissed. But even if breach of contract could be proved the penalty suffered by masters was only 40s. as compared to imprisonment of a servant who broke a contract.

It has been argued that on the whole servants in larger households had more security of tenure than those in smaller households. Lawrence Stone, for example, makes a distinction between ducal households where 'unlike that of more modest ranks, there was considerable security of tenure for servants'. This 'and the possibility of upward mobility contrasts markedly with most households of the squirearchy and bourgeoisie where the servants were all too often poorly paid casual transients, hired and fired for a few months at a time or at most a few years and with no fixed loyalties to anyone'.[47] But ducal households were representative of only a very small minority of servants.

But just what opportunities were opened up by entry into service? Was it more than just security that service provided? Domestic service has been seen as providing 'unique economic advantages which made it particularly attractive'.[48] It has been described as a real career which women freely chose and saw as providing inviting prospects. 'Domestic service', writes Kent, 'was sufficiently attractive for some women to choose it as a way of life rather than simply as a stage in their life-cycle'.[49] 'Until the early twentieth century', writes Theresa McBride, 'urban household service offered young single women a kind of employment which fulfilled all the traditional expectations women had for work'.[50] But it cannot be too much stressed that for many of those daughters who moved into domestic service there was no real choice. 'There were many parts of England where opportunities outside domestic service were apparently lacking'.[51] 'For many girls and not a few boys', writes Eric Pawson, 'domestic service was the only hope of a station in life other than that of a pauper.'[52] Rosina Harrison's father was a stonemason and her mother a laundry maid. 'The choice of a career for girls born into our

---

[47] *Broken Lives* (1993), 137–8. [48] McBride, *The Domestic Revolution*, 116.
[49] 'Ubiquitous but Invisible: Female Domestic Servants', 112.
[50] *The Domestic Revolution*, 115.
[51] Patrick O'Brien and Roland Quinault (eds.), *The Industrial Revolution and British Society* (1993), 37.
[52] *The Early Industrial Revolution* (1979), 46.

circumstances', she writes of service between the wars, 'presented no difficulty. Almost inevitably we were bound to go into service.'[53] Of course for many daughters of the rural poor, the difficulties of family life in the crowded conditions at home must have made domestic service seem like a welcome escape. Not much thought was given to their future.

The situation in eighteenth-century France was not dissimilar. 'Few rural areas', Sara Maza writes, 'had much to offer by way of employment to a large workforce of single females.' To leave their village was the only option and 'some sort of service was the most likely choice'. There is nothing to suggest, she adds, that 'for most women domestic service' was 'anything but an unpleasant necessity'.[54]

Nevertheless for some servants, and more particularly for men, service does seem to have offered an interesting life—even if at a cost. John Macdonald moved from being a homeless orphan to a place as a postilion and later a groom. He went on to become a valet, body servant, and finally footman. If he is to be believed he had numerous, and enjoyable, sexual encounters with both mistresses and fellow servants. He travelled widely with his masters. Towards the end of his time in service, when he had returned from his travels, he wrote that he 'wanted for nothing. I had my own lodging, with my own furniture.' In the end he had savings enough to invest in a hotel. He clearly enjoyed a great part of his service, but it was at a cost. Between places—and he went through twenty-seven—he frequently had to wait some time before finding an employer. On one occasion he was 'out of a place some months, and lived on the fruits of my labour'.[55] While a servant he never married—although at least at one stage he would have liked to. If he had, his life would inevitably have been far more restricted. There were others, both men and women, who, exceptionally, seem to have lived out their life in service peacefully in one or two households. With kindly employers the life of unambitious servants could be made tolerable, even pleasant. But the households of which evidence is available of the treatment of servants were anything but representative. Of the one- or two-

[53] *Rose: My Life in Service* (1975), 15.
[54] *Servants and Masters in Eighteenth-Century France: The Uses of Loyalty* (1983), 46.
[55] *Memoirs of an Eighteenth-Century Footman, John Macdonald*, ed. John Beresford (1927), 174, 235.

servant households of small merchants, artisans, and tradesmen where the vast majority of servants were employed we know very little. Many of these households had only recently come into the servant-employing population. They would have been much more aware of the slender divide between their servants and themselves, more anxious to assert their superior status and to establish the role of subordination of their employees. Increasingly by the end of the eighteenth century and early nineteenth century 'employers tried to emphasise the gap or social distance between themselves and their servants when in fact that gap had narrowed'.[56] By their treatment of servants they tried to assert their own superiority. The author of a French handbook published in 1785 on lower-class masters insisted they 'usually treat their servants with extreme harshness . . . the lesser the distance between master and servant the more mistreatments the latter had to suffer'.[57]

What were the chances of social betterment for servants? Hecht saw it as 'a path for social ascent'. 'Many who enlisted in its ranks were thereby enabled to improve their social status', he continues, 'some rising a few degrees in the social scale, others radically altering their condition'.[58] It is a view echoed by John Burnett when he writes that 'for the ambitious it provided a clearly defined route to respectable and responsible positions'.[59] There is the extreme case of Elizabeth Cullen, waiting maid to the Duchess of Hamilton who married her fellow servant. From proprietorship of the Thatched House Tavern in St James Street they moved to the Assembly Rooms in King Street where was housed 'the most modish exclusive club in London'. But Elizabeth Cullen was the exception.[60] Nevertheless there seems to be some agreement that service 'in a great house within a graduated hierarchy of servants . . . could lead to a measure of autonomy, a high standard of living and a good deal of authority over others'.[61] On the whole men servants fared much better than women. We have seen the case of John Macdonald. There were other footmen and

[56] Maza, *Servants and Masters in Eighteenth-Century France*, 328.
[57] Ibid. 258.
[58] Hecht, *The Domestic Servant in Eighteenth-Century England*, 177.
[59] *Useful Toil*, 137.
[60] Dorothy Margaret Stuart, *The English Abigail* (1946), 125.
[61] Leonore Davidoff, 'Mastered for Life', in Pat Thane and Anthony Sutcliffe (eds.), *Essays in Social History*, ii. (1986), 126–50 at p. 130.

butlers who 'used service as an entrée into a superior world'.[62] But it is worth while recalling Rickman's conclusion that one-third of servants were upwardly mobile, one-third remained static, and one-third were downwardly mobile. It suggests two-thirds of servants achieved no social betterment.[63] Real social advancement, although not impossible, was rare. 'A great deal', writes Olwen Hufton, 'depended upon good fortune and the kind of qualifications one had at the outset.'[64] In fact there was often, as Rickman suggested, some social retreat—into prostitution, pauperism, and crime.

Service, it is argued, compared favourably with other occupations of the labouring poor. 'The choice of domestic service over some other kind of work', McBride writes, 'demonstrates that service must have been sufficiently attractive to an important segment of the rural emigrants to counteract the disadvantages of virtual loss of freedom, long hours, and frequent mistreatment.'[65] To accept such an argument we would need to be quite certain that there was a choice available to such migrants from the countryside and to weigh up what the choice amounted to. So Mary Ashford certainly chose to go into service rather than become a dressmaker or a milliner, but that was the extent of her choice. Why did she choose domestic service? It was not that she could not sew but that 'she did not much like it'.[66] The comparison between the wages and working conditions of domestic servants and others of the labouring poor is hardly possible. It is to try and compare very different things. It rarely considers the very long, indeed often continuous, hours of day and night that servants were expected to be on call. Nor does it consider the many unpaid or minimally paid servants. From the point of view of the mistress 'a person who is entirely at one's disposal, except for certain "afternoons off", is much to be preferred to a person who is entirely at her own disposal, save for "certain hours on duty"'.[67] And was work in domestic service always preferred to work in a factory? The evidence is conflicting. 'Urban women with access to factory employment', Edward Higgs has written, 'avoided

---

[62] Roy Porter, *English Society in the Eighteenth Century* (1982), 105.
[63] As quoted in McBride, *The Domestic Revolution*, 92–3.
[64] 'Women, Work and Family', 20. [65] *The Domestic Revolution*, 56–7.
[66] *Life of a Licensed Victualler's Daughter, Written by Herself* (1844), 20.
[67] Violet M. Firth, *The Psychology of the Servant Problem* (1925), 62.

domestic service if they could.'[68] McBride uses the example of migrants from alpine regions of France who migrated to Paris and Lyons 'to become domestics when a concentration of industry in and around Lyons offered equal opportunities for employment'.[69] But of the two towns Paris was by far the greatest draw for female migrants whether their journey was accomplished in one or more stages. An early twentieth-century analysis of the psychology of servant–mistress relations has a working-class girl telling her mistress: 'You do not offer us such good hours to work for you in your homes as your husbands and fathers offer us to work for them in their business, therefore we prefer their service to yours because they have moved with the times and you have not.'[70] Who is right?

'Most importantly', Kent writes of eighteenth-century London, 'the female servant was independent; she was valued because of her unmarried status. Her wages may have been low, as they were for all women workers, but they were the wages of an independent woman and not those of a supplementary wage-earner. Domestic service was an occupation which allowed women a measure of choice and relative economic independence.'[71] It is a claim that would have come as something of a surprise to many female domestic servants in eighteenth-century London. Did Mary Ashford feel herself 'an independent woman'? In the second half of the nineteenth century, in that strangest of relationships between Arthur Munby and Hannah Cullwick, the maid-of-all-work, Munby expressed his belief that service gave women 'a sturdy independence, self-reliance and shrewdness'. His obsession with women who did the most menial and dirty work was in large measure sexual. In the early years of their relationship he was at pains to preach to her 'a doctrine of servitude, humility and drudgery'.[72] Hannah herself seems willingly to have embraced servility both out of Christian duty and a desire to

[68] 'Domestic Service and Household Production', in Angela V. John (ed.), *Unequal Opportunities: Women's Employment in England 1800–1918* (1986), 125–50 at p. 145.
[69] *The Domestic Revolution*, 49.
[70] Firth, *The Psychology of the Servant Problem*, 66–7.
[71] 'Ubiquitous but Invisible: Female Domestic Servants', 15.
[72] As quoted in Davidoff, 'Class and Gender in Victorian England: The Diaries of Arthur J. Munby and Hannah Cullwick', *Feminist Studies*, 5/1 (spring 1979), 86–141 at p. 130.

please Munby. The ways in which she expressed that servitude—washing his feet, licking his boots, wearing a collar and chain with a padlock to which only Munby had the key, calling him 'Massa', imply complex sexual and, indeed, sado-masochist motives. But even Hannah Cullwick found aspects of service unacceptable and restrictive of freedom. She saw a prospective employer's demand that she go to church every Sunday and not linger on her way home as 'the imposition of a mistress's will and the denial of her own'. It was not that she minded going to church but that, as she put it, 'I don't like being compelled to go to church'. She was prepared to accept the drudgery of her work—and that is certainly how she saw it—in part from pride in her own physical strength, in part from her religious belief which did indeed make

> drudgery divine;
> Who sweeps a room as for Thy laws
> Makes that and th' action fine.

But sometimes even religion did not sustain her. In 1871, when in service with the Hendersons, she 'found the relentless sameness of her domestic routines stultifying'. Sometimes her remarkable physical endurance snapped. In February 1862 Munby recorded how Hannah 'totally exhausted lay on the floor sobbing about both her hard dirty work and the fact that her employers and fellow servants despised her because of it'.[73] Financially independent she may have been, but one cannot see her as having any freedom of choice. Hannah Cullwick was remarkable not merely in her physical toughness but in her ability sometimes to enjoy drudgery. It is difficult to see her as anything but exceptional.

The suggestion that service was chosen by women in preference to marriage suggests an independence in female servants of which there is little evidence. Judging by the very few women of marriageable age who continued to work as domestic servants rather than marry, even if this was a deliberate choice by the women involved, relatively few seem to have made it. But most young domestic servants saw marriage as their goal and, almost certainly, as the only escape route for them from service. Their decision to marry nearly always meant leaving service. As we

[73] *The Diaries of Hannah Cullwick: Victorian Maidservant*, ed. Liz Stanley (1984), 13, 15, 148, 311 n. 4.

have seen employers were hostile to their servants marrying. It meant disorganization of their households. If servants wanted to marry they had to face leaving service. So servants' tendency to marry late was in part due to their awareness that marriage meant the end of their career as servants. If they were trying to save enough from their earnings to make a dowry that would attract a husband this often meant delaying marriage. Tim Meldrum suggests that while 'service may have been a positive choice in place of marriage for some... most women were opting for choices that took them out of service in their late 20s/early 30s, especially marriage'.[74]

If their time in service was usually limited and ended in marriage, some have suggested, women's experience of service provided invaluable training for their future life. So Tim Meldrum has argued that in service women developed 'skills to last them a life time, even if their achievements were usually made at a later stage in their life cycle, after the ties of service were broken'.[75] In sharp contrast is the view held by Leonore Davidoff that ex-domestic servants were at a 'severe disadvantage when it came to employment after marriage'.[76] What prospects had they but work as washerwomen, charwomen, or fruit-pickers or do sweated outwork? Peter Earle has seen the experience of service as providing 'good experience for a future housekeeper'.[77] Sometimes it seems it was. When David Doyle, Mary Leadbeater's father's servant, married her brother's cook, Winifred Byrne, in 1791, she 'managed his earnings with prudence, prepared his simple meals with neatness, indulged in no luxury but the cleanliness and regularity of her house, and received him with ever cheerful looks and a cheerful fire'.[78] But the experience of running a middle- or upper-class household was not the same as that of making ends meet in a working-class home. There is a late eighteenth-century 'penny-history' in which Ned advises his friend, Harry, against marrying a chambermaid 'for they bring nothing with them but a few old cloaths of their mistresses, and for housekeeping, few of

---

[74] 'Ubiquity and Visibility: Domestic Service in London 1660–1750', paper given at the Economic History Society Conference (Apr. 1993), 8.
[75] 'Domestic Service in London 1660–1750: Training for Life', 1.
[76] 'Domestic Service in the Working-Class Life Cycle', *Society for the Study of Labour History*, 26 (spring 1973), 10–13.
[77] *The Making of the English Middle Class* (1989), 162.
[78] *The Leadbeater Papers*, 2 vols. (1862), i. 194.

them know anything of it; for they can hardly make a pudding or a pye, neither can they spin, nor knit, nor wash, except it be a few laces to make themselves fine withal'.[79] 'Many of the skills servants learned were not much use to working class households', write Leonore Davidoff and Ruth Hawthorn, 'and few servants were responsible for keeping accounts'—an essential for anyone running a home on a limited income.[80] The best that can be said is that experience of service may have helped them to organize their time better.

Service always involved a loss of freedom: of movement, of choice of friends, of free time and where it was spent. A nineteenth-century footman complained that 'the life of a gentleman's servant is something like that of a bird shut up in a cage. The bird is well housed and well fed but is deprived of liberty, and liberty is the dearest and sweetest object of all Englishmen'.[81] 'A disadvantage of being a lady's maid', writes a twentieth-century one, 'was that I could never rely on having time off so I could rarely make any plans. This meant an outside social life was out of the question.'[82] And it was not only lady's maids who were affected in this way. Often servants were discouraged from visiting their families. Even as late as mid-Victorian times, when Hannah Cullwick's father and mother died she was not allowed to go to her home which was only three miles away from her place.[83]

What kind of relationship was it between master (or mistress) and servant? Jonas Hanway in *Eight Letters* compared the attitude of foreign employers of servants with those in England. 'We do not hold it proper to converse so *familiarly* with our domestics', he wrote, 'it is very far from our intention to introduce a *levelling Scheme*, or to destroy all *respect*, except what is *paid for*.'[84] But it was sometimes not just a case of no familiar conversation but of no conversation. 'There is no one so meek or submissive', wrote the author of *The Reveries of Solitude*, 'as not to revolt against continual ill-usage and oppression.' Of a friend with a young servant-boy

[79] *A York Dialogue between Ned and Harry* (1783), 15–16.
[80] *A Day in the Life of a Victorian Domestic Servant* (1976), 88.
[81] As quoted from William Tayler in *Useful Toil*, 185.
[82] Harrison, *Rosa: My Life in Service*, 22.
[83] Davidoff, 'Class and Gender in Victorian England', 107.
[84] *Eight Letters to his Grace Duke of —— on the Custom of Vails-giving in England* (1760), 44.

Tom he wrote that he 'never spoke to Tom, but to abuse him, and as servants have the same feelings, and, where they understand the premises, reason generally as justly as their masters ... servants feel the insult of a contemptuous silence, Lord Anson's brother had made a tour of the East when he came to Aleppo his servant left him and gave for a reason, that his master had not spoken three words to him in a tour of 3,000 miles.'[85] Some mistresses did their best to avoid any direct contact with servants. The mother of Thomas De Quincey, for instance, 'by original choice, and by early training under a very aristocratic father, recoiled as austerely from a direct communication with her servants as the Pythia at Delphi from the attendants that swept out the temple'.[86] Servants in Victorian England, Leonore Davidoff tells us, 'used their bodies to show deference'. They 'stood when spoken to and kept their eyes cast down, they moved out of a room backwards, curtsied to their betters, and were generally expected to efface themselves; doing their work and moving about the house so as not to be visible or audible to their employers'. In some houses there was even the instruction 'to turn their faces to the wall when the employers passed by'. By Victorian times if not before if servants accompanied their employers when they went out they were expected to walk 'a few paces behind masters or mistresses'.[87]

Tim Meldrum has argued that 'the measure of higher servant status ... was the proximity any servant had to the "person" of his or her employer'.[88] But closeness did not necessarily involve affection. As Richard Mayo in his advice to servants of 1693 stressed, 'God has not set you as Companions with your Masters'.[89] Towards the end of his life William Shenstone sadly recorded he 'had been formerly so silly as to hope that every servant I had might be made a friend; I am now convinced that the nature of servitude bears a contrary tendency. It is the nature of servitude, to discard all generous motives of obedience, and to point out no other than those scoundrel ones, interest and fear.'[90] Describing her relations with her employers' children early this

[85] R. Graves, *The Reveries of Solitude* (1793), 34, 36 and n.
[86] Thomas De Quincey, *Autobiographical Sketches* (1853), 159.
[87] 'Class and Gender in Victorian England', 97–8.
[88] 'Domestic Service in London, 1660–1750: Training for Life', 9.
[89] *A Present for Servants* (1693), 29.
[90] *Essays In Men and Manners* (1787), 144.

century Rosina Harrison writes 'we weren't friends...we weren't even acquaintances'.[91]

Writing of eighteenth-century France, Sara Maza has suggested that many employers deliberately stripped their servants of all evidence of their former identity.[92] It was a way of asserting their power and control over them. In some cases even servants' names were changed if they were found 'unsuitable' for their condition. Writing of Victorian employers' attitude to servants, Arthur J. Munby describes how the servants' 'own histories have for them nothing private or sacred'. Servants became accustomed 'to be close questioned about themselves by mistresses and to be called "Anne", or "May" by anyone who chooses to address them. To be asked bluntly "What is your name?" or "How old are you?" by a stranger, does not seem to them at all offensive or impertinent.'[93] For many employers servants had no identity. Frequently employers forgot the names of their servants, called them by their surnames or by names of their own invention. Servants' claim to an identity depended on retaining links with their family, their village, and their friends. The personal belongings of a servant were often subject to the close scrutiny of their mistresses. Some forbade them 'to display pictures or personal belongings in their room'. Some 'supervised the way servants dressed, how they spent their money, and who were their friends'.[94]

The class allegiance of service was always ambiguous. 'Their ambiguity', it is suggested, 'seemed a threat to others.'[95] This perhaps accounts in part for the hostility to domestic servants sometimes shown them by other members of the labouring poor. In the towns and cities in which they were concentrated they were strangers—not really belonging to the urban labouring class. How was domestic service regarded by the labouring poor? 'On the whole', writes Hecht, 'service was considered a somewhat demeaning occupation. A certain stigma attached to much of the servant class.' But he goes on to argue that the stigma must have been 'mild' because of 'the readiness with which both men and

[91] Rose: *My Life in Service*, 220.
[92] *Servants and Masters in Eighteenth-Century France*, 174.
[93] As quoted in Davidoff, 'Class and Gender in Victorian England', 105, from Arthur J. Munby, *Diary* (1860).
[94] Leonore Davidoff and Ruth Hawthorn, *A Day in the Life of a Victorian Domestic Servant* (1976), 82.
[95] Maza, *Servants and Masters in Eighteenth-Century France*, 109.

women' entered service. Nevertheless, he argues, the servant 'was viewed as a person who had temporarily relinquished his freedom; his position was conceived to be but a step or two removed from serfdom'. According to Hecht, only the servants of 'the nobility and gentry were free of all taint'.[96] (For a further discussion of the 'stigma' of service see pp. 196–7.) This then was the stigma carried by the vast majority of servants. If there were few alternative occupations the readiness with which men and women became servants is understandable. They quite simply had no option. Tim Meldrum has used church court depositions to examine domestic servants who appeared as witnesses. Often they were asked 'how they maintained themselves'. Many seem to have emphasized that they had no trade or calling and that going into service was the only option open to them if they were to make a livelihood. 'For some women', he concludes, 'service was one strategy for keeping body and soul together.'[97] We should also remember that for many service was not a career option chosen by them but an occupation into which they were forced by the Poor Law authorities. Under the Statute of Artificers any unemployed person could be 'compellable to service'. Even so many did their best to avoid such a fate. Michael Roberts quotes a case in 1698 when Mary Science, a spinster of Buckinghamshire, was presented for refusing to go to the service into which the local overseers of the poor had directed her. It was said she 'offered nothing material in her excuse' apart from expressing 'an unwillingness to labour, which may be of ill example to lazy and thriftless people'.[98]

As a child, Defoe's Moll Flanders 'had a thorough aversion to going to service'. Her nurse tries to comfort her by promising Moll she will not go to service until she is older. But, Moll confesses, 'going to service was such a frightful thing to me that if she had assured me I should not have gone till I was twenty years old, it would have been the same to me'. Her nurse, exasperated, asks, 'what would you be—a gentlewoman?' Yes, Moll answers. She later explains that all she meant by being a gentlewoman was 'to

[96] *The Domestic Servant in Eighteenth-Century England*, 177, 179.
[97] 'Domestic Service in London 1660–1750: Training for Life', 6.
[98] See Michael Roberts, '"Words they are Women and Deeds they are Men": Images of Work and Gender in Early Modern England', in Lindsey Charles and Lorna Duffin (eds.), *Women and Work in Pre-Industrial England* (1985), 122–80 at p. 158.

be able to work for myself, and get enough to keep me without that terrible bugbear *going to service'*. Her objections to service were, first, that she was ill prepared for the work service involved; what she was good at was needlework, but if she went into service all she could hope for was 'to run of errands and be a drudge to some cook-maid'. Moll was also afraid of the ill-treatment she saw as typical of master–servant relations and the bullying she might experience from her fellow servants. A gentlewoman was 'one who did not go to service, to do housework', one who was independent and self-reliant, not one prepared for the subordination service involved.[99] With Michael Roberts, we need to ask just how representative Moll was in her attitude to service. Nearly a century and a half later Charles Bennett was to ask 'how is it possible for any human being habitually to wear a face of impossible vacuity, to assume an air of formal subserviency ... to bear the gaudy badge of servitude without taking secret revenge upon society which dooms him to such a fate?'[100]

[99] *The Fortunes and Misfortunes of the Famous Moll Flanders* (1722), ed. G. A. Starr (1971), 10–11, 13; and see Roberts ' "Words they are Women and Deeds they are Men" '.

[100] *London People* (1863), 140, as quoted in Phyllis Cunnington, *Costume of Household Servants* (1974), 14.

6

Kin as Servants

'many so-called servants were almost certainly kin. Their status in the household was probably often little different from that of the non-relative who would otherwise have been given the place. The net cost, therefore, was minimal.'

> Michael Anderson of mid-nineteenth-century Preston, in Laslett and Wall (eds.), *Households and Family in Past Time*, 228

IN 1987, in an article on the early censuses, Edward Higgs wrote that 'many of the women described as general servants, housekeepers, nurses, etc., in the manuscript census [1851] were not servants in relationship to the head of the household in which they lived'. He went on to point out that in Rochdale the majority of those described as 'in servant occupations were relatives of the household head or lodgers, as were 25 per cent of those in Rutlandshire in the same year'.[1] It is one example, among many, of how occupational statistics included in censuses can sometimes confuse and tell only half the story. But long before the nineteenth-century censuses the same phenomenon of kin and servants coinciding is in evidence. We know that in medieval times noblemen took on as servants, and dressed in their livery, younger brothers.[2] In this chapter I want to probe this area of domestic service in order to ascertain what groups of women became such kin-servants, what was the nature of their tasks, their status within the household, and how they were treated by the household head and other members of the family.

Housekeepers apparently represented 6 per cent of the servant population in 1861, and 11 per cent in 1871—a rise from 66,000 to

---

[1] 'Women, Occupations and Work in the Nineteenth-Century Censuses', *History Workshop Journal*, 23 (spring 1987), 59–80 at p. 69.
[2] Phyllis Cunnington, *Costume of Household Servants* (1974), 15.

140,000.[3] One problem pointed out by Ann Kussmaul of estimating numbers of housekeepers in the seventeenth and eighteenth centuries is the frequency with which wives were referred to as 'Housekeeper'. She quotes the example of a 1787 listing of the population of Murton in Westmorland where the family of a weaver, Joseph Idle, including his wife, was described as 'housekeeper and four others'.[4] When in 1717 the Revd John Thomlinson and his uncle were keeping house together—both unmarried—John recorded in his diary that his uncle had explained to a neighbour 'that either he or I must marry, for he wanted a housekeeper'.[5] But the problem did not end with the eighteenth century. In the 1851 census 'for some enumerators housekeeper and housewife were synonymous'.[6]

Evidence for the eighteenth century suggests how common it was to find kin serving as housekeepers. Richard Gough in his analysis of the inhabitants of Myddle included 'the daughter of Richard Watkins', a London goldsmith, who 'was a modest comely gentlewoman, and was housekeeper to her uncle, Thomas' (a bachelor).[7] In September 1759 James Fretwell recorded in his diary that 'my niece Mary Woodhouse came to be my housekeeper'. He went on to add that 'it was at her own desire, as I understood; and my mother desired I would take her, and see what I could do with her. So I agreed, very well knowing that they was weary of her at home, for she is of a very disagreeable temper.'[8] Whether it was what her mother had had in mind from the beginning, in just over a year she had left him to marry. In any case the treatment by her family of Mary Woodhouse might be seen as a convenient way of dealing with difficult adolescent daughters. It got them out of the family home for a time and, with luck, if they were married, for ever.

Of the daughters of the Spry family, near-neighbours of the Revd George Woodward of East Hendred, 'one was apprentice to

[3] Higgs, 'Women, Occupations and Work in Nineteenth-Century Censuses', 71.

[4] *Servants in Husbandry in Early Modern England* (1981), 14.

[5] *The Diary of the Rev. John Thomlinson*, in *Six North Country Diaries*, Surtees Society, cxviii (1910), 64–167 at p. 74.

[6] Edward Higgs, 'Domestic Service and Household Production', in Angela V. John (ed.), *Unequal Opportunities: Women's Employment in England 1800–1918* (1986), 125–50 at p. 131.

[7] *The History of Myddle (1701–1706)* (1979), 51.

[8] *A Family History*, Begun by James Fretwell, Surtees Society lxv (1877), 164–244 at pp. 204, 212.

her own sister, a milliner in London and another kept house for her uncle in Bath'. Yet another of the daughters 'is intended very soon to be her brother's housekeeper'.[9] This was a role often filled by unmarried sisters when their brothers remained bachelors or were widowed. Mary, James Fretwell's sister, in May 1726 was 'brought . . . to begin housekeeping' for him. Seven years later she married. Fretwell was anything but happy to lose her. Two years later he wrote of having a sale at his house as he was 'designing to leave that place, being weary of living with servants only since my sister had left me'.[10] While he needed someone to do the housekeeping he was not happy about supervising servants. Robert Bakewell of Dishley was a bachelor but 'an energetic sister looked after his house, and saw to the comfort of his guests; which must have been a heavy task for any woman'.[11] Sometimes it was on the unmarried daughter that the responsibility fell. When Molly Leapor, the kitchen maid–poet, was dismissed from Edgcote House in 1745 she returned to her father's home at Brackley where she kept house for him until the end of her life.[12]

In France, 'during most of the Old Regime', writes Cissie Fairchilds, it was 'customary for prosperous families who needed extra labour to take in poor relations—unmarried brothers, widowed sisters-in-law, orphaned cousins—as servants, who in return for food and board did the housework and laboured in the family enterprise'.[13] Eighteenth-century novels are full of similar examples. In Fielding's *Amelia* for example, there is a Mrs Bennett, the youngest daughter of a clergyman who, when her mother dies, followed very soon after by her sister, takes over the management of the house. Her father 'committed the whole charge of his house to my care, and gave me the name of the little housekeeper, an appellation of which I was then as proud as any minister of state can be of his titles'.[14] In *The History of Lavinia Rawlins*, an anonymous novel of 1770, on the death of her mother, Lavinia wants to go into service but her father, a clergyman, 'made her his housekeeper'. Her father, unlike many such fathers outside

[9] *A Parson in the Vale of White Horse: George Woodward's Letters from East Hendred 1753–61*, ed. Donald Gibson (1982), 31, 50.   [10] *A Family History*, 242–3.
[11] R. Bayne-Powell, *English Country Life in the Eighteenth Century* (1935), 158.
[12] Richard Greene, *Mary Leapor* (1993), 16, 18.
[13] *Domestic Enemies: Servants and their Masters in Old Regime France* (1984), 5.
[14] Henry Fielding, *Amelia* (1906), 291.

fiction, makes quite clear what is involved in the relationship. ' "If I would lay my hand to his affairs, and act therein as his housekeeper"', she records, '"I should never leave him, provided I could submit to his manner of living."' Her father also stresses that '"he desired me not to act the part of a laborious servant, but that of a housewifely mistress"'.[15] She stays with him as housekeeper until his death.

Where unmarried men or widowers had no female kin, it has been suggested, they may have been wary of hiring young female servants. 'Where men had no female kin to act as mistress', they 'were vulnerable to sexual innuendo in respect of female servants'.[16] Some solved the problem by marrying their servants. Julius Hardy, a Birmingham button-maker and a bachelor, had chosen to have a married couple, a workman and his wife, living with him as well as a servant girl. The workman's wife was responsible for the cooking. But when Hardy sacked the workman he also lost his cook and was forced to face up to a new situation. How could he guarantee 'a continuance of even, orderly management or good government in the little concerns of my house?' Should he marry or look for a housekeeper? He was much alarmed on finding his servant-maid was pregnant and, concerned that he would be blamed (but with what justification we are not told), he dismissed her. While looking for a wife he hired an older woman as housekeeper, 'to superintend the new servant girl'.[17]

A kinsman of John Baker the lawyer fell on hard times. He had five children to support. In many ways John Baker was most generous to them. He paid off the mortgage on their house, was constantly giving them money, became godfather to one son, and educated him at his own expense. But when it came to 'Becky, the eldest daughter', aged 17, she was taken into his house and clothes were bought for her. But as Baker reminds us Becky was taken in as a servant. She received no regular wages but only gifts and pocket-money. When she was visited by her father he did not

[15] *The History of Lavinia Rawlins*, 2 vols., 2nd edn. (1770), 41–2.
[16] Leonore Davidoff and Catherine Hall, *Family Fortunes: Men and Women of the English Middle Classes, 1780–1850* (1987), 391.
[17] *The Diary of Julius Hardy (1788–1793) button-maker of Birmingham*, Birmingham Reference Library 669002 (BRL MS 218), transcribed and annotated by A. M. Banks (Apr. 1973), 36.

take his meals with John Baker but 'in the housekeeper's room, and only comes to sit with his second cousin later'. The education of Becky became John Baker's responsibility. With another maid, Nanny Peters, she received 'daily instruction from John Baker in reading, writing and arithmetic'.[18]

Often the need for a housekeeper arose when a man was widowed. The alternatives were remarriage, finding a housekeeper—preferably from among kin, or giving up a household and moving into lodgings. When John Baker's wife died in March 1774, he continued to live in his Horsham house with servants. But without his wife's 'controlling hand the household soon became disorganised. The servants', Baker recorded, 'begin to be troublesome. The grooms throw dung at the maids in the kitchen.' He decided to give up his house at Horsham and move into London lodgings.[19] On the death of Hannah Munby's aunt, 'a cousin of hers who had been a lady's maid in London had to give up her place and go back to Shropshire to "do" for her uncle, as he could not look after himself'.[20] Thomas Turner's housekeeper in 1762 left his service 'to go to Catsfield to keep her uncle Mr. May's house, who came for her'. She did not want to leave. As she explained to Turner it was 'contrary to her inclinations and the most earnest persuasions of her friends, but this uncle, being a widower and having two children, over-persuaded her to live with him in order that she might see the children well done for.' A month later 'as she had not received so good usage from her uncle' she begged Turner to take her back in the spring if he should be without a servant at that time.[21]

Women who became housekeepers to kin were mainly of two groups—either, as we have seen, unmarried daughters of any age, or widows. Both were highly exploitable. 'Single women were often effectively servants for their families, if not in the households of strangers.'[22] Of mid-nineteenth-century Rochdale, Edward Higgs has shown that many heads of households 'regarded their own children as domestic help'. He cites the example of Nelson Brierly of Haugh Heyside, a carder of wool employing

---

[18] *The Diary of John Baker*, ed. Philip C. Yorke (1931), 52–3.   [19] Ibid. 56.
[20] As quoted in Leonore Davidoff, 'The Separation of Home and Work: Landladies and Lodgers in 19th and 20th Century England', in Sandra Burman (ed.), *Fit Work for Women* (1979), 64–97 at p. 76.
[21] *The Diary of Thomas Turner 1754–1765*, ed. David Vaisey (1985), 255, 256.
[22] Louise Tilly and Joan Scott, *Women, Work and Family* (1978), 31.

thirty hands, whose eldest daughter was described as a 'Domestic at home'.[23] The daughter of Lady Osborne (née Penelope Verney) had died early in her childhood. Much later Lady Osborne remarked that 'had God blest me with a Dau^r I had not kept a maid'. She never hesitated to exploit her kin, so when her niece, Penelope Stewkeley, came to stay with her she was given the task of washing 'her old crape and such-like work'.[24] The lives of the womenfolk in the household of William Stout of Lancaster, namely his widowed mother and his unmarried sister, Elin, make the point. In 1691, William tells us, his sister 'freelly offered to come and be my housekeeper'. 'She did it', he adds, 'without a servant, but got one to wash and dress the house once a week and to brew upon ocation.' His mother meanwhile was keeping house for his unmarried brother Josias 'with much industry and care'. Josias 'did not seem willing to marry' although his mother 'desired he would'. She continued to be his housekeeper until at the age of 68 she felt unable to continue, but Josias was still 'not inclinable to marry, or to keep house with servants'. For a time he let the house and moved in with his brother Leonard, but at the age of 76 his mother was again keeping house for Josias, although she had become 'very infirme and uneasy with the care of the house, and was urgent of him to marry'. Finally Leonard did marry: ironically it was the young wife who resented his mother's role in housekeeping and Josias was forced to ask his brother William to take her in. When sister Elin died William continued to rely on kin for his housekeeping. First there was Jennet, his brother Leonard's second daughter, but after three years she married. He then relied on Leonard's third daughter, Elin, and a servant but was 'not very easy with them'. When Elin married he 'sent into Westmorland for Hannah Eglin, who I knew, to be my housekeeper'. Whether she too was a relation we do not know, but she came and stayed fourteen months. Then Stout gave up housekeeping—but not for long. By 1734 he had moved in over his shop and taken 'brother Leonard's two youngest daughters, Margret and Mary, to be my housekeepers'. He hoped they would prove 'capable, diligent, and subject to' his directions. He was to be disappointed. Margret almost immediately, and 'against his advice', married and her sister 'was often out of

[23] 'Domestic Service and Household Production', 133.
[24] Dorothy Margaret Stuart, *The English Abigail* (1946), 46.

health or pretended so'. Once again he gave up housekeeping to lodge with his nephew. Five years later he 'begun to keep house my selfe with a servant, and tooke Mary Hall, daughter of my neece . . . into my house free, in order to improve herself in learning'. Three years later, when his servant left to get married and he was in need of a replacement, the full meaning of Mary improving herself became clear. 'Mary Hall, being now nigh twenty years of age, and having knowledge of my way of living, and having no parents living, I resolved to be served by her.' This turned out 'more to my satisfaction than I could have expected'.[25] For a large part of his adult life William Stout had recruited housekeepers and other servants from his own family and near kin.

Not always was it possible to persuade a daughter to take on the duties of housekeeper. The Revd John Skinner's daughter is a case in point. When Skinner was having difficulty supervising the servants he 'asked her whether she meant to give directions about the rooms being put in order for the reception of our company'; she replied that 'she had given orders to the servants, and that they must do what she ordered; she should not go to look after them, that was not her business'. It is unusual to find daughters resisting so decisively the demands of widowed fathers. John Skinner's daughter wanted to make very clear to her father the distinction between a daughter as mistress of a household issuing general orders to servants, and a housekeeper, an employed servant, responsible for supervising the work of all the servants and seeing that her mistress's orders were carried out. Such independence in a daughter was rare. Skinner concluded that 'as she did not seem inclined to do as my housekeeper I must resume the office myself'.[26]

Edward Higgs has suggested that 'many distant female relatives may have been treated by householders in much the same way as paid domestics'.[27] But was it only distant relatives who were so treated? Or was there in the eighteenth century a very scornful view taken of all dependents? In the early eighteenth

[25] *The Autobiography of William Stout of Lancaster 1665–1752*, ed. J. D. Marshall (1967), 91, 105, 102–3, 131–2, 159, 201, 203, 215, 226, 232–3.
[26] *The Journal of a Somerset Rector 1803–34*, ed. Howard and Peter Coombs (1930), 433.
[27] 'Women, Occupations and Work', 69.

century Sarah Churchill discovered some 'unknown kinsfolk' (in fact, her aunt and family) who were in dire circumstances. The eldest daughter, Abigail Hill, she took home with her to St Albans to act as a sort of companion. 'Exactly what this poor relation's status was in the Churchill *ménage* it is difficult to tell.' Many years later, Sarah Churchill, now Duchess, said she had treated Abigail 'like a sister'. But as Dorothy Stuart comments, 'the girl's calling—whatever her status may have been—was that of a humble and useful confidante.'[28] According to the Revd Joseph Price of Brabourne, Josias Pattenson, Steward of the Manor of Ashford, 'before he married' was 'called "Sir" by his sisters, because dependent upon him and they had not often the honour of dining or sitting in the same room with him'.[29] Consider the way in which Pepys and his wife treated Pepys's sister, Pall, when in 1661 she came to be their servant. In discussing the proposal beforehand with his father, Pepys made clear that if Pall were to come she would 'be as a servant'. Later when he talked to Pall of the proposal he again stressed it was 'to have her come not as a sister in any respect, but as a servant'. If Pepys is to be believed, on hearing of the proposal, Pall 'did weep for joy'. She was to be their chambermaid, as Pepys did not think her 'worthy of being Elizabeth's [his wife's] waiting woman'. From the day she arrived in January 1661, Pepys treated her as a servant: 'I do not let her sit down at table with me, which I do at first that she may not expect it hereafter from me.' Granted, Pepys did not like his sister: 'I find her so very ill-natured that I cannot love her', he recorded. Not surprisingly the arrangement failed to work out. Pepys accused Pall of growing 'proud and idle' and decided not to keep her. In September of the same year she went back to her parents 'crying exceedingly', although Pepys insisted she was 'so cruel a hypocrite that she can cry when she pleases'. By January 1663 Pepys's wife proposed taking Pall on again as her personal maid since 'one we must have'. They hoped that in such a role she would prove a better servant. Pepys complained bitterly of how it was 'a very great trouble to me that I should have a sister of so ill-nature that I must be forced to spend money upon a stranger, when it might be better upon her, if she was good for anything'. But

---

[28] *The English Abigail*, 83–4.
[29] *A Kentish Parson: Selections from the Private Papers of the Revd. Joseph Price Vicar of Brabourne, 1767–1786*, ed. G. M. Ditchfield and Bryan Keith Lucas (1991), 161.

within a week or so his wife had changed her mind and, as Pepys adds, 'nor have I any great mind to it, but only for her good and to save money flung away upon a stranger'.[30] It was not just that Pall was treated as a servant in the Pepys household but that she was paid, if at all, as a very inferior one. Her lot does not appear exceptional. Nearly always, servants who were near kin were poorly paid if paid at all. They were 'at the beck and call of their employers whose equal they socially were; but who often treated them as upper servants, and made them take their meals in the housekeeper's room'.[31]

But the advantages of having kin as servants did not end with the financial saving involved. The very ambiguity of the relationship was easy to exploit to the employer's advantage. Relying on motherly or sisterly affection, much could be demanded of kin-servants by their sons or brothers. As Thomas Turner suggested, it was easy for a widower with children to 'over-persuade' his niece that he had urgent need of her. The employment of servants carried with it a certain status whether they were kin or not. If achieving that status usually cost money, how agreeable it was to achieve the same end so cheaply. For unmarried sons or widowed fathers as anxious to avoid the expense of marriage or remarriage as they were to get their servants cheaply, the employment of kin as servants was the answer.

An interesting case came before the Consistory Court of Norwich in 1723. It concerned a young girl, Judith Carpenter, who five or six years previously, at the age of 12, had been orphaned. She was brought up by her brother, William, a rich yeoman with 300 acres of land, with whom she lived until she married. The case was brought because William claimed reimbursement from the estate for the cost of Judith's board and lodging in the period she lived with him. Crucial was whether she had been treated as William's sister or as a servant. One witness, John Miles, a near-neighbour of William's described how he had seen Judith Carpenter 'riding into the fields with William Carpenter's tyth cart with a Rake in her hand, two or three harvests, and hath seen her go to school with the said William Carpenter's children, attending on them as a servant and carrying their vict-

---

[30] *The Diary of Samuel Pepys*, ed. Henry B. Wheatley 3 vols. (1946), i (vol. iii of diary), 3.

[31] Bayne-Powell, *English Country Life*, 47.

uals, and hath often seen her spinning, and hath seen her measure out malt and help to dress the children and do the other common business of the house'. He was of the opinion that Judith 'deserved to have been allowed something for her attendance care and service' in William's family. Another witness, a childhood friend of Judith's, said that while Judith 'was capable of doing any kind of service' he did not know whether or not 'she wrought amongst the servants of the ministrant . . . not expecting any reward or hire for the same'. But William Finch, who was hired by William Carpenter as a servant on an annual contract at a time when Judith was living with her brother, described how 'she used to go every day with the Tith Cart into the fields and to rake after the cart, and at other times used to do all the common business of the house as looking after ye dairy, dressing of fowls for market, and if ye business of the house was over she used to spin'. He went on to insist that Judith was never 'treated any better or ever fared better or otherwise than as the rest of the Servants did'. He too thought Judith earned her bed and board.[32]

On the other hand William Carpenter's sister-in-law claimed Judith had been 'used and treated as his sister with all the kindness and respect that could be from a Brother to a Sister'. According to her account Judith was 'never look'd upon as a Servant' and she did not do 'any business about the house as such but as a Boarder was maintained and educated'. Other witnesses argued likewise. Judith Carpenter, who was now married, seems to have borne no malice towards her brother. Whether or not she was treated by him as a servant, as seems likely, the case suggests such usage of near kin as servants was not uncommon.[33]

Distant kin, it would seem, were treated no differently from other servants and only exceptionally were near kin treated better. In Sarah Fielding's *The Adventures of David Simple*, David is tricked out of his inheritance by his brother Daniel. But when the evidence against Daniel becomes overwhelming 'his Pride now thought fit to condescend to the most abject Submissions', and he offers to live with his brother as a servant.[34] Daniel clearly thought

---

[32] From the Deposition Books of the Consistory Court of Norwich in 1723, Norfolk Record Office, DEP/60, 1723. A Consistory Court was a Church Court dealing with alleged offences against ecclesiastical law. My thanks are due to Susan Amussen who first alerted me to this case.
[33] Ibid.   [34] *The Adventures of David Simple* (1744) (1987), 24.

that living as a servant with his brother was the greatest humiliation he could experience. One of the best examples from literature comes from Jane Eyre. Mrs Fairfax, the housekeeper at Thornfield, reveals to Jane she is 'distantly related to the Rochesters'. But, she goes on, 'I never presume on the connection—in fact, it is nothing to me; I consider myself quite in the light of an ordinary housekeeper'.[35]

There are numerous references to women employed as kin-servants other than as housekeepers. In 1777 at the Settlement Examination of Martha Winkworth, the daughter of a Micheldever cordwainer, she was anxious that the distinction between living with kin and being a servant to kin should be recorded. She told them she had left her father's house aged 6 to live with her grandfather. She 'lived with him about 20 years', but, she was quick to insist, 'not as servant'.[36] It may have been true, but equally it may have reflected the view, shared by many, of service as demeaning. (See Ch. 10 for a discussion of this view.) The first servant employed by Thomas Wright after the death of his wife was 'B—— B——, a daughter of one of my late wife's uncles.' Wright was clearly preoccupied and distracted by his recent loss but he admits 'this was a very honest girl for aught I ever saw by her'.[37] A more sinister resort to kin as servants was that of his first wife's parents who had never liked him, and, when without a servant, persuaded his daughter Betty to go and live with them 'from no liberal motive'. She was engaged 'to do the servant's work, and had only a little meat to find her, for I myself found her clothes'. Later they found themselves again without a servant and wanted 'to engage Betty to supply the place of one, at a cheap rate, as she had done before'. Betty was finally persuaded and went to live with them again and stayed until her marriage although 'she found her situation very disagreeable; she was obliged to do all their drudgery work'.[38] In November 1752

---

[35] Charlotte Brontë, *Jane Eyre (1847)* (1959), 117.

[36] *Winchester Settlement Papers 1667–1842*, compiled by Arthur J. Willis (1967), 87. A Settlement Examination was an examination by local poor law officials into the parish of settlement of individuals applying for parish relief or those likely to become chargeable to the parish. A legal settlement could be acquired in one of several ways, but where unmarried servants were concerned it was a question of being able to prove a year's service in the parish.

[37] *The Autobiography of Thomas Wright of Birkenshaw in the County of York 1736–97*, ed. Thomas Wright (1864), 139.

[38] Ibid. 166, 192.

William Hutton's 'friend and next door neighbour, Mr. Grace, being a widower took his niece, Miss Sarah Cock... to keep his house'. Hutton fell in love with her—much to the annoyance of Mr Grace—for, as he angrily exclaimed, he 'had given up the thoughts of marriage, because suited with a housekeeper whom [now] he was likely to lose in so short a space as fifteen months'.[39]

There was another class of women servants related—sometimes closely—to their employers; the genteelly educated, unmarried and often unmarriageable, impecunious daughters of middle-class families fallen on hard times. Judging by the numerous examples in eighteenth- and nineteenth-century novels as well as real life, their lot was almost universally hard. For example, the problem of such dependents is discussed in Sarah Scott's *Millenium Hall* (1762): 'the wretched state of those women, who from scantiness of fortune, and pride of family, are reduced to become dependant, and to bear all the insolence of wealth, from such as will receive them into their families; these, though in some measure voluntary, yet suffer all the evils of the severest servitude, and are, I believe, the most unhappy part of the creation'. Their genteel education in no way fitted them for earning their living and their birth made them 'less acceptable servants to many who have not generosity enough to treat them as they ought'.[40] For those 'reduced into service by one of those sudden blows of fate', it is suggested of France, 'entering the service of a relative... mitigated the dishonour attached to their occupation.'[41] But in many cases they are not allowed to forget that it is as servants they are taken in. It has also been suggested that 'in the houses of relatives their lot may have been a happy one but among strangers it must often have been a sad one'.[42] The distinction is not always borne out by the evidence. Mary Wollstonecraft had some experience of both: 'to be an humble companion to some rich old cousin, or... to live with strangers who are so intolerably tyrannical that none of their own relations can bear to live with them... it is impossible to enumerate the many hours of anguish such a person must spend.'[43]

---

[39] *The Life of William Hutton, Written by himself* (facs. of 1841 edn.), 27, 28.

[40] Sarah Scott, *Millenium Hall* (1762), 80–1.

[41] Sara C. Maza, *Servants and Masters in Eighteenth-Century France: The Uses of Loyalty* (1983), 33.

[42] Bayne-Powell, *English Country Life*, 47.

[43] *Thoughts on the Education of Daughters, with Reflections on Female Conduct in the most important Duties of Life* (1787), 69.

The very frequency with which kin-servants are found in literature suggests it was, in fact, common practice. So common perhaps that there was no reason for drawing attention to it unless, as in Pepys's employment of Pall, it brought its problems. There were also reasons why, if you employed kin as servants and treated them no differently from other servants, you might not want to advertise the fact. But it is difficult to gauge just how widespread the practice was before the nineteenth century. A recent work on apprenticeship and service in early modern England suggests there was some caution about choosing relatives as masters. They 'were not a first and preferable choice' and as a member of the family commented when a cousin of John Woodhouse broke his apprenticeship 'it were better for so near relations to be at a greater distance'.[44] The relative paucity of evidence of such kin-servants outside literature makes this a short chapter but it should not be concluded that they were therefore a rare occurrence. The treatment often meted out to kin who had fallen on hard times during the eighteenth and early nineteenth centuries is one of the least endearing aspects of contemporary society. This might be one reason why evidence is hard to come by. It certainly calls for some explanation. It suggests that so great was the need to succeed in a society with increasingly commercial values that those who failed were rejected and despised. It is a measure of how domestic service was regarded by the middle and upper classes that it was considered the most suitable occupation for such family rejects.

---

[44] Ilana Krausman Ben-Amos, *Adolescence and Youth in Early Modern England* (1994), 166.

7
Pauper Servants

'Of what use were parish institutions if they could not be made to yield a supply of domestics?'
                        E. S. Turner, *What the Butler Saw*, 241

'I speak now of a very hopeful class, the young and destitute; those who are receiving a preliminary course of training for domestic service, in those numerous institutions which (thanks to the philanthropic and practical spirit of the times) are to be found in every town, or at least in every county.'
      M. A. Baines, *Domestic Servants as they are and as they ought to be* (1859), 10

IN 1981 an article by F. K. Prochaska was published, entitled 'Female Philanthropy and Domestic Service in Victorian England'.[1] It focused on the numerous societies and institutions in the nineteenth century that had as their main aim the training of girls as domestic servants: the Children's Aid Society, Waifs and Strays Society, the Ragged School Union, and the Metropolitan Association for Befriending Young Servants, as well as workhouses, prisons and charity schools. The training of servants, it was held, was an important aspect of the voluntary work women undertook. It had definite attractions for the women of the middle and upper classes. 'To provide employment fit for the poor while extending their own freedom and influence.'[2] The numbers of such pauper female servants that were placed in employment each year were very considerable. Apparently by the mid-1880s the Metropolitan Association for Befriending Young Servants alone was placing over 5,000. This can only have represented a small fraction of the vast number emerging from all the institutions and societies intent on guaranteeing that a steady flow of servants was available. Very little has been written about such

[1] *Bulletin of the Institute of Historical Research*, 54 (1981), 78–85.　　[2] Ibid. 78.

servants and, as Prochaska concluded, 'when taken into account' they 'must modify findings of some recent scholarship' on domestic service.[3] In 1983 Edward Higgs took up the theme, suggesting that recognition of the existence of a vast body of pauper servants in Victorian England necessitated a fundamental reassessment by historians of hitherto firmly held notions of who were the employers of domestic servants.[4] In this chapter I want to argue that such a supply of servants was not new to Victorian times and that it was just as important a source of supply much earlier—and certainly throughout the eighteenth century. Whether they were illegitimate children of women in the parish, foundlings, orphans, children of those confined to the workhouse, Bridewell, or prison, or the offspring of those in the parish receiving parish relief whose poverty made it impossible for their parents to maintain them, many—and more particularly girls—were apprenticed out as domestic servants. The move into service came via workhouse schools, the London Foundling Hospital, Sunday schools, or, and increasingly from the late seventeenth century, charity schools. How does the existence of such a supply of domestic servants amend our ideas of service in the eighteenth century?

The apprenticeship of parish children had a long history. In the sixteenth century there began the passage of a series of Acts providing for the compulsory apprenticeship of children of the poor. By the Act of 1601 parish children could be bound by parish officers with the agreement of two justices. Boys were bound until they were 24, girls until 21 or marriage. 'Under this Act the occupation', Dorothy George tells us, 'was either farm labour or domestic service.'[5] Parish children could be compulsorily bound to ratepayers in the parish. This was changed when, by an Act of 1691, to the methods of obtaining a settlement there was added that of an apprenticeship in the parish of forty days. It was now to the advantage of parish officers to bind such parish children outside their own parish even though compulsion could no longer be used. From 1601 it became usual to pay the master a small sum of £2–£5. The situation does not appear to have altered much in the next century. In 1725 it was claimed that 'the most

---

[3] Ibid. 81.
[4] 'Domestic Servants and Households in Victorian England', *Social History*, 8/2 (May 1983), 201–10.
[5] *London Life in the Eighteenth Century* (1st pub. 1925; repr. 1965), 221.

that is generally given with these poor Children doth not exceed Five Pounds with a Boy, and is much less with a *Girl*'.[6] Jonas Hanway explained the small sums payable as based on 'an opinion that a parish child's life is worth no more than eight or ten months' purchase.'[7] In some cases the sum was necessary in order to persuade masters to take the children into their households. The Berkshire inspectors for the London Foundling Hospital responsible for finding suitable places for apprenticing its children were appalled when in 1765 the hospital threatened to withdraw its offer of a premium of £10 'to any one . . . who would take the child as apprentice'. Even 'with the premium, let alone without it' it was often difficult to find suitable places. The inspectors expressed their reluctance to bind children out to 'those suspected of wanting cheap labour', but, as another inspector explained, she 'could find none that chuse to take children little more than seven years old at the sum offered'. She proposed that two years' premium should be given at once as some inducement.[8]

The problem for parish authorities with children who had survived being put out to nurse was more one of boarding out than of apprenticeship. The most important qualification of those receiving them was that they had means to support the children rather than what trade they plied. If originally it had been intended that such female parish apprentices should receive some domestic training from their masters, it soon seems to have become a secondary consideration when binding the children. 'Vocational training', it is suggested, 'was a less prominent element of pauper apprenticeship, while support of the child became paramount.'[9] This is not to deny that sometimes they did receive some training but, almost certainly, more often they did not. The London workhouse schools, as Dorothy George has written, aimed at providing at least some 'preliminary training in industry and virtue with a modicum of book learning'. So their children for ten hours of the day under the supervision of a mistress were set 'to spin wool and flax, knit stockings, to make new their linnen,

---

[6] W. Hendley, *A Defence of the Charity Schools* (1725), 32.

[7] *An Earnest Appeal for Mercy to the Children of the Poor* (1766), 29.

[8] *Correspondence of the Foundling Hospital Inspectors in Berkshire*, ed. Gillian Clark, Berkshire Record Society, i (1994), pp. lvii–lviii, 229.

[9] Deborah Lantz, 'The Role of Apprenticeship in the Education of Women 1750–1800', unpublished paper, Aug. 1985.

cloathes, shooes, mark, etc.'[10] Usually such children were apprenticed between the ages of 12 and 14 but, as with the London Foundling Hospital children, they were 'often bound out much younger, even half that age'.[11] In 1769 Jane Yarmouth, who was 'about six years', was bound out to Elizabeth Peck of Adbury in Berkshire, who 'would take her apprentice till she is 21 years of age and would teach her to sew and instruct her to make a good Servant'.[12] Once apprentices were placed what happened to them in the years before their apprenticeship ended was rarely of concern to the institution from which they had come. It is unlikely anyone checked up on whether Elizabeth Peck carried out her promises of training Jane Yarmouth. At such a young age children were often just not 'physically or mentally strong enough to perform the duties expected of them'. Judging by the reports of the inspectors employed by the Foundling Hospital to supervise both the nursing and apprenticeship of such children, many were in poor health. Given that few had received any training for service, these very young girls were often plunged 'at once into a sphere of duty entirely strange to them'.[13] There was always the temptation to bind them as young as possible to free the parish or institution of the burden of maintaining them. As we have seen, they could be as young as 6. Usually they were about 14. But in parishes where the only opening for such girls was domestic service 'they were often several years older before a situation could be found for them'.[14] There is every reason for thinking that the number of such children greatly increased in the course of the eighteenth century. One reason for them becoming more numerous was that, despite mortality among pauper children remaining high, more were surviving than earlier.

The prospects for such parish apprentices were almost always grim. Some of their masters and mistresses ill-treated them. Only the worst cases came to light. Even those 'of respectable character in their station', could, under certain circumstances, become cruel employers. Catharine Cappe, a social reformer who in about 1785 began to take an interest in charity schools for girls, writes of a

[10] George, *London Life in the Eighteenth Century*, 216, 217.
[11] Geoffrey W. Oxley, *Poor Relief in England and Wales 1601–1834* (1974), 58–9.
[12] *Correspondence of the Foundling Hospital Inspectors*, 179.
[13] W. Chance, *Children under the Poor Law* (1897), 71, 81.
[14] Oxley, *Poor Relief in England and Wales*, 59.

couple, the man, a servant himself, and his wife, with seven children, who took a girl from the York Greycoats School for a term of four years 'without any design of using her unkindly'. But when she fell ill they were unable to support her. She was 'continually reproached with the trouble she had brought them till she died of dropsy'.[15] There was the case of Captain Bolton, near Castle Howard, who was 'generally respected'. In 1774 he took 'a girl of 16, an orphan, bound apprentice by the parish'. It was rumoured she was 'unkindly treated'. Then she went missing. Her master claimed she had run away but her body was found 'in a state of pregnancy strangled by her master'. He had not been 'formerly vicious', it was said, but 'the power he had acquired over this unfortunate girl, had supplied the temptation'.[16] While the Foundling Hospital was quick to prosecute employers in such cases, its resources made it impossible to guard against brutal masters. For example, Sarah Drew, a Foundling child, reported on the sexual assaults her master, Job Wyatt, had made on her. He had 'attempted to debauch her at Eleven Years of Age and completed it afterwards and continued the same ill Usage till Christmas last & beat her if she refus'd to submit to his will'. Nor was she the only apprentice so treated. Three other of his female apprentices had suffered similar treatment.[17] The children were frequently driven by the treatment they received to run away. According to William Bailey, the condition of parish apprentices became worse in the course of the eighteenth century. He talked of masters who were 'so inhuman as to regard only the pecuniary Consideration; and having once received that', they regularly ill-treated their apprentices. Many masters were guilty of treating them so badly that, as Bailey claimed, 'few . . . now serve out their time and many of them are driven by neglect or cruelty into such immoralities as too frequently render them the objects of public justice'.[18]

If the possibility of ordinary female apprentices learning a trade was anything but strong (many of them were taught nothing but housework), female pauper apprentices rarely learnt a trade. By far the overwhelming majority of pauper girls apprenticed by

---

[15] Catharine Cappe, *Observations on Charity Schools* (1805), 43 n.
[16] Ibid. 47–9 n.   [17] Ruth K. McClure, *Coram's Children* (1981), 134.
[18] *Treatise on the Better Employment and more Comfortable Support of the Poor in Workhouses* (1758), 5–6.

parish authorities went into domestic service. In the countryside there was often no other option for them. It was a welcome relief for a parish when such pauper children were placed and they were no longer a burden on the rates. Responsibility for maintaining them shifted to their masters. As we shall see, while those taking them in were far from restricted to the poor, the small fee paid by the parish must have been some attraction. In May 1756 Thomas Turner recorded putting out two parish children: 'Lucy Brazer to Edm. Elphick at 18d. per week' and 'Ann Brazer out to Dame Trill' at the same fee.[19] It may well have been a means of keeping their employers from dependence on the parish. For most workhouse girls bound out, although their 'indentures might specify the teaching of some trade or "the art of housewifery" there was often no pretence of teaching anything'. They could end up as household drudges of 'poor families' sometimes even families 'living in one room'.[20]

There are many examples from literature of what being a pauper female apprentice could mean. Defoe's Moll Flanders when only 3 years old is put out to nurse by the parish. She is fortunate in finding her nurse a woman 'who was indeed poor, but had been in better circumstances'. Unlike many she survives—but it is assumed that at a certain age 'they might go to service or get their own bread'. The nurse runs a small school 'which she kept to teach children to read and to work'. When aged 8 Moll hears that the magistrates have ordered that 'she go to service'.[21]

The outlook for such parish girls was almost inevitably domestic service at its most menial. The heroine of Clara Reeve's novel, *The School for Widows*, relates how her landlady, Mrs Martin, 'took a poor girl from the parish to do the under work in my family'.[22] In *The History of Betty Barnes*, a novel ascribed to Sarah Fielding, the heroine, when her mother dies and her father goes to sea, is farmed out to a parish nurse. As a result of an accident a benevolent woman takes her in and puts her 'to the care of her housekeeper, resolving to keep her in the family, and to give her an education that would enable her to get a living without being a vagabond, or at best a meer drudge, which must have been the

---

[19] *The Diary of Thomas Turner 1754–1765*, ed. David Vaisey (1985), 39.
[20] George, *London Life in the Eighteenth Century*, 227–8.
[21] Daniel Defoe, *Moll Flanders* (1722), ed. G. A. Starr (1971), 9–10.
[22] *The School for Widows*, 2 vols. (1791), i. 21–2.

case, if she had been suffered to return with her nurse and continued at the expense of the parish'.[23]

In Tooting Graveney in the eighteenth century most of the parish children were 'bound out . . . with masters living in London'. Some of the girls were apprenticed to 'mantua-makers, ginger bread makers and framework knitters'. But by far the majority 'were bound out to learn the art of the housewife, which in practice meant they became household drudges'. As Dorothy Marshall asked: what else 'could a girl bound out to a "Linen Weaver", who probably occupied one or two rooms, learn that would be of use to her in getting a better place later?'[24]

From Catharine Cappe we learn something of those who applied for these girls as servants. They were 'lodging-house keepers, alehouse keepers, or the lowest manufacturers'.[25] Dorothy Marshall argued that 'it was very seldom that such poor girls were placed in respectable families, since no one, who could afford any other kind of domestic help, would take a child who had been brought up either in a workhouse or in the house of a habitual pauper, because of its lack of training in habits of industry and obedience'.[26] While it is very difficult to quantify, it seems clear that if many of these parish children ended up in the homes of quite humble families, it was not just the poor who took in female pauper apprentices. Although outwardly hostile to the employment of such servants in their homes, many middle-class families nevertheless took them in. In August 1663 Samuel Pepys got home to find 'a little girl . . . a parish child of St. Bride's of honest parentage, and recommended by the churchwardens'. The same evening she ran away, was captured by the parish beadle, returned to Pepys's household, stripped of the clothes provided for her by Pepys and sent away. But the experience does not seem to have discouraged him from immediately taking on another parish girl, Susan.[27] Some time in the 1760s or 1770s a Mr and Mrs Hackman of Lymington, a very respectable couple with a considerable household, found they needed a part-time weeder for the garden. What did they do? 'John the footman was despatched to

[23] *The History of Betty Barnes*, 2 vols. (1753), i. 17.
[24] As quoted in Dorothy Marshall, *The English Poor in the Eighteenth Century* (1926), 194.
[25] *Observations on Charity Schools*, 42.
[26] *The English Poor in the Eighteenth Century*, 194.
[27] *The Diary of Samuel Pepys*, ed. Henry B. Wheatley, 3 vols. (1946), iii. 240–1.

the poor-house, to select a little pauper girl, qualified for the performance of the necessary labour.' The footman returned with 'a diminutive female of eight or nine years of age; pointed out the humble task in which she was to employ herself and left her to her work'. Mrs Hackman was immediately drawn to the girl and decided to remove her from the workhouse 'and attach her to her own kitchen establishment'. She worked first as the 'scullion's deputy'—about the lowest rank of service possible. Later, and exceptionally, she graduated to become Mrs Hackman's lady's maid. What we are not told is what, if anything, she was paid and at what stage in her employment.[28] In 1778 the Revd James Woodforde is enquiring anxiously of Mr Priests, one of the Commissioners, 'respecting my servant Boy whom I take out of Charity, whether I am to pay for him according to the late Act relating to Servants' (presumably the tax on men servants imposed by Lord North).[29]

In the middle of the nineteenth century Atcham Workhouse School was providing servants for 'clergymen, farmers of high reputation, manufacturers, professional gentlemen, and tradesmen'. Nor was the number taken always limited to one. 'Those who have taken one child', we are told, 'generally apply for more, as vacancies occur in their establishments.'[30] Alcock claimed 'a prejudice, unfortunately, exists against receiving workhouse servants', but it did not always prevent them being employed—if perhaps surreptitiously.[31] It was only when something went wrong that their origin was revealed. So when the Revd Skinner complained about two servants, 'daughters of the parish' who left his employ in 1803/4, 'leaving us without a person to answer the bell', he was quick to point out their origin. 'The gross ingratitude of the older girl, Betty', he wrote in his diary, 'is beyond all parallel. I took her absolutely a pauper . . . I clothed her, and gave

[28] Richard Warner, *Literary Recollections*, 2 vols. (1830), i. 48–9.
[29] *The Diary of a Country Parson: The Reverend James Woodforde 1758–1813*, ed. John Beresford, 5 vols. (1924–31), i. 234. In 1777 Lord North, on the basis that taxes should fall on luxuries and non-necessaries, placed a tax on male servants claiming that, like carriages, cards, and newspapers, they were luxuries. Bachelors were required to pay a double tax while families with children were in part exempted. See Ch. 2 above, where the possible effect of such a tax on employers choosing male or female servants is discussed.
[30] Chance, *Children under the Poor Law*, 18.
[31] Thomas Alcock, *Observations on the Defects of the Poor Laws* (1752), 10.

her wages, beginning at £5 and ending at £10 per annum.'[32] If she was a parish apprentice, she was unusual in getting paid a regular annual wage.

The training of children of the poor as servants was the main objective of much of eighteenth-century philanthropy. It was a form of philanthropic activity in which middle- and upper-class women were conspicuous. Ensuring a sufficient supply of servants for the future was an object that appealed to many of them. 'Do we wish our daughters to have modest, discreet, trusty maid-servants?' it was asked. The answer was clear. Then 'let us unanimously resolve to give a helping hand towards infusing good principles into the minds of poor girls'. Such philanthropy was 'a species of charity which forms a part of the prerogative of our sex', women were told, 'and gives to those who have leisure for it an opportunity of doing much good with very little trouble and expense'.[33] As Donna Andrew has emphasized, such charity was 'entirely practical'.[34] Such charitable work was regarded as particularly suitable for unmarried ladies, and if there was a danger from too close contact between those 'from whom genteel behaviour and elegance of expression is expected' and 'a set of vulgar low-bred children', they were reassured by the advice of Sarah Trimmer 'to conduct themselves in the schools so as to preserve the respect due to their station, by keeping the children at such a proper distance as to maintain their own consequence'. The contact, it was stressed, was particularly important for the children of the poor. It might 'improve the manners of the lower sort of children so as to prevent their being disgusting', but it would not 'refine them to such a degree as to place them on a level with young ladies who have a regard to real refinement'. They were not to be 'instructed in languages, geography, history, and other articles that constitute a polite education; but merely in such a knowledge of the English language as shall enable them to read the scriptures; in the plain duties of Christianity; and in those modes of conduct which their station requires'.[35] When in 1724 the Bishop of London addressed the teachers of London charity

[32] *The Journal of a Somerset Rector 1803–34*, ed. Howard and Peter Coombs (1930), 345.

[33] Sarah Trimmer, *The Oeconomy of charity: or, an Address to the Ladies concerning Sunday Schools etc.* (1787), 28, 48.

[34] *Philanthropy and Police: London Charity in the Eighteenth Century* (1989), 23.

[35] Trimmer, *The Oeconomy of Charity*, 37, 41, 43.

schools, he emphasized that 'fine singing, like fine writing and fine needlework had no place . . . in the schools'.[36] Much the same points were made by Patrick Colquhoun in his plan for a free school 'for the Labouring People' in Westminster. It was not proposed, he emphasized, 'that the children of the poor should be educated in a manner to elevate their minds above the rank they are destined to fill in society, or that an expense should be incurred beyond the lowest rate ever paid for instruction'. To give them more education than this 'would be to confound the ranks of society upon which the general happines of the lower orders, no less than those that are more elevated, depends'.[37] When Hannah More was attempting to set up a Sunday school in one of the Mendip villages, the wife of 'the big man of the village' went further. As the poor 'were intended to be servants and slaves', it was 'preordained that they should be ignorant'. If the promised school was set up 'it would be all over with property, and if property is not to rule what is to become of us?'[38] In 1754 the governors of the London Foundling Hospital raised the question of teaching all their children to write, but nothing came of it, and when they appointed a mistress it was to teach their children 'spinning, knitting, and needlework in such a manner as may enable them to make useful servants'.[39]

In considering what education charity school children should receive there was 'simply no conception of any liberal education'. This was equally true of all so-called educational provision for poor children. Those responsible for setting up and administering the schools saw them as fitting neatly into 'a stratified society based upon a rigid class system'.[40] In 1792 Mrs Trimmer was at some pains to stress that not all the children of the poor could be trained in charity schools—nor was it desirable that they should be. For such an education, she argued, 'will probably raise their ideas above the very lowest occupations of life, and disqualify them for those servile offices which must be filled by some of the members of the community'. They 'should not be educated in

[36] C. Birchenough, *The History of Elementary Education in England and Wales* (1920), 81.
[37] *A New and Appropriate System of Education for the Labouring People* (1806), 12–13.
[38] M. G. Jones, *The Charity School Movement* (1964), 169.
[39] McClure, *Coram's Children*, 220–1.
[40] Jones, *The Charity School Movement*, 73.

such a manner as to set them above the occupations of humble life, or so as to make them uncomfortable among their equals'. She would have liked to establish a hierarchy among schools catering for children of the poor, with charity schools 'for the first degree among the lower orders'. This would include those 'who have been born to good prospects' but whose parents had fallen on hard times, as well as others 'whose bright genius breaks through the thick cloud of ignorance and poverty'. They would go as servants to 'respectable families'. Day schools of industry, on the other hand, would train those called *'common servants'*. The nature of the education children would receive at such schools would also be graded according to the status of the inmates. Instruction in 'the genuine principles of the Church of England' was to be given only to a *'limited number* of children' who would then 'deserve to be preferred to the highest places in great families for their exemplary conduct'. They would have 'learnt to write a tolerable hand, and to do common sums in the four first rules of arithmetic'. In schools of industry, however, 'the business of literary instruction may be contracted into a narrower compass'.[41]

The teaching received in workhouse schools with one or two exceptions such as the well-endowed London Workhouse, was 'perfunctory to the last degree'.[42] Similarly the education received in many charity schools was minimal. At a school in Attleborough, for example, the woman who ran it 'had been illiterate up until its foundation'. What teaching there was in the school 'was rudimentary and consisted of the daily ministrations of one man for two or three hours to the school's three score students'.[43] It was a continuation of the policy behind workhouse schools. 'Why should poor children that must be put out to poor trades, where they must work hard, and fare hardly', Thomas Firmin had asked in 1681, 'be . . . taught farther than is necessary for such Trades?' Poor children, he argued had no need of schooling from the age of 7 to 15. Two hours a day was quite adequate and children should only be kept at school until, in the case of boys, 'they are fit to go

[41] Sarah Trimmer, *Reflections upon the Education of Children in Charity Schools* (1792), 7–8, 11, 18–19, 23.

[42] George, *London Life in the Eighteenth Century*, 217.

[43] As quoted in Tim Hitchcock, 'Paupers and Preachers: The SPCK and the Parochial Workhouse Movement', in Lee Davison, Tim Hitchcock, Tim Keirn, and Robert B, Shoemaker (eds.), *Stilling the Grumbling Hive*, (1992), 145–66 at p. 155.

to Prentice, or to do other business' and in the case of girls 'till they are fit to go to Service and no longer'.[44]

The setting up of charity schools was one of the most popular forms of philanthropic endowment in the eighteenth century. It was, we are told, the 'favourite form of benevolence'. A reason for its popularity, it is suggested, was that charity schools 'encouraged the feeling for class prerogative which animated the charity of the wealthier classes'.[45] It was also charity in which self-interest was a major motive. If these poor children were not taught to work they would become a charge on the parish. There was a considerable expansion in the number of charity schools founded in the course of the century. 'Thousands' were 'set up and hundreds of thousands of children for whom no other means of education existed were instructed by its means.' In London and Westminster alone in the first thirty-three years of the century, charity schools 'bound out 3,873 girls and 3,366 boys as domestics'. Such charity schools were not confined to England. In Scotland in the period 1709–39 an additional 500 such schools were founded. In the early years of the century in Ireland, 170 schools were established 'on the English pattern', and in the next half-century fifty more. In Wales there was a marked expansion of such schools between 1737 and 1761 which accounted for the education of 158,000 children. Nor were the schools only the product of the Anglican church. Many were founded by dissenters—Quakers and Methodists being particularly prominent. If it is impossible to estimate with any accuracy their number, there is 'evidence of a widespread and continuous Charity School movement in the eighteenth century'.[46] From their start charity schools had close links with parish workhouses, and children from workhouses would often be sent to local charity schools.

Closely connected with the charity schools in organization and finance, and pursuing much the same policy towards their pupils, were Sunday schools. They were particularly designed for the children in poor families, whose parents demanded their labour during the week so that their schooling had to be confined to one day only. Robert Raikes, whose pioneer work in setting up Sunday schools started in Gloucester in the late 1750s, explained their

[44] Thomas Firmin, *Some Proposals for the Imployment of the Poor* (1681), 5, 9.
[45] Marion Ardern Burgess, *A History of the Burlington School* (1949), 5.
[46] Jones, *The Charity School Movement*, 3, 51, 23–5.

main aim as that of 'establishing notions of duty and discipline at an early stage'. Other Sunday schools were set up all over the country but more particularly in Wales and the industrial towns of Yorkshire. Hannah More, in the schools she set up in the Mendips, believed the children should be 'taught to read, and be instructed in the plain duties of the Christian Religion with a particular view to their future character as labourers and servants'. Her idea of what instruction was appropriate she described as 'very limited and strict'. It was to learn 'such coarse works as may fit them for servants'.

The education provided by Sunday schools suffered from the same difficulty experienced by all schools for the children of the poor—the absence of suitable teachers. At Congresbury, when no other teacher was to be found the More sisters resorted to a schoolmaster and his wife who 'ran a pay-school in the locality' and whose learning, as they readily acknowledge, was 'very moderate'. After three years' continuous work the children had learnt nothing. They were 'still in the fifth chapter of Genesis'. At Shipham, after a prolonged search, they heard of 'a young dairymaid, better educated than her fellows' who 'had raised a little Sunday School' for children of her neighbours.[47] In the last two decades of the century many more Sunday schools were created, accounting, it is said, for a quarter of a million children. In 1791, according to Hannah More, those of the ten parishes in the Mendips for which she was responsible alone accounted for nearly a thousand children.[48] In 1787 a Sunday Schools Society was created to which 201 schools were affiliated representing 10,232 children. By 1797 these numbers had grown to 1,086 schools with 69,000 pupils.[49]

In the second half of the century concern for foundlings, orphans, and vagrant children increased. 'The Foundling Hospital, the Magdalen Hospital, the Asylum for Orphan Girls, the Orphans' Working School, and the Philanthropic Society', according to Hecht, 'prepared most of their girls for service, apprenticing them at an early age.'[50] The London Foundling Hospital, opened

---

[47] Jones, *The Charity School Movement*, 146–7, 152, 164, 167–8.
[48] Ibid. 26; *The Mendip Annals: or, A Narrative of the Charitable Labours of Hannah and Martha More*, ed. Arthur Roberts, 2nd edn. (1859), 48.
[49] Jones, *The Charity School Movement*, 152.
[50] *The Domestic Servant in Eighteenth-Century England* (1956), 21.

in 1741 to cope with the increasing number of abandoned children, sent many of its children into the country to be nursed, In 1740 the governors were given the authority to apprentice the children under their care. Some remained in the countryside where they had been nursed and were bound out locally—the girls mostly as servants. Of the first fifty-nine children apprenticed twenty-three were girls who went into domestic service. Other children returned to London to be apprenticed out as servants in the city. Although for a period there was mass apprenticing to manufacturers, most of the girl apprentices seem to have ended up as household servants. In the period 1760–70, 4,407 children were apprenticed out by the hospital.

Lack of funds at first severely restricted admissions to about 500 a year. In 1756 the hospital petitioned parliament for financial help. A sum of up to £10,000 was granted on condition that the hospital would henceforth admit all children under 2 months old who were brought to it. In consequence, in the last six months of 1756 alone the number of entrants exceeded 13,600. Nearly ten years later, perhaps dismayed by the prospect of mounting costs in a period of economic depression and widespread social unrest, the government became increasingly critical of the running of the hospital and reluctant to continue its support. A Committee of the House of Commons was appointed in 1765 to investigate and make recommendations. Its report condemned the hospital's educational and apprenticeship policies, claiming that the education its children received made them unfit for labour, and that apprenticeship should start much earlier than was hospital policy. It recommended that the hospital should apprentice its children 'with all Convenient Speed' at the age of 7 or earlier, and that a fee of not less than £5 nor more than £10 should be paid.[51] This, it was argued, would put such pauper apprentices on the same basis as ordinary apprentices. In the period between 1757 and 1762 branch hospitals had been set up in Ackworth, Aylesbury, Barnet, Chester, Shrewsbury, and Westerham to meet the need for some provision for foundlings outside London. The Committee report recommended their closure. It announced the withdrawal of parliamentary support, although provisionally it was prepared to make *ad hoc* annual grants from year to year for those children

---

[51] McClure, *Coram's Children*, 116.

already admitted. In consequence the Foundling Hospital finances were put under severe strain. Its branch hospitals were closed and the number of places for entrants drastically cut. In 1771 all financial support from the government ceased. The real object of the Committee's recommendations was to enable the Foundling Hospital to cope with far more foundlings by placing them out to useful toil at an earlier age and saving a great deal of money. The recommendations of the Committee are very close to those expressed by one of the governors of the hospital, Jonas Hanway, in 1764. He had argued that such a policy of fee-giving would 'exonerate the Public by £30 or 40 Expence on the Child, by a well-timed Application of £10 or 12'. The attitude of the government was that held by many. 'When so many of the labouring poor were contributing towards their own support at 7 or younger, why ... should foundlings be given more education and be maintained in greater comfort than these children enjoyed for an additional three or four years at public expense?'[52]

Some kind of formal apprenticing of foundlings was essential to their future; it was their means of achieving eventual independence in adult life and the only way in which they could gain a settlement, as well as, in theory, the means to acquiring a knowledge of a trade, but if these benefits were gained by some it was at a heavy cost for the many. 'At its worst', writes Ruth McClure, 'it was a system conducive to exploitation and semi-slavery, in which masters profited from cheap labour, gave little instruction in return, and ... abused their apprentices brutally.'[53] Given the small number of governors and supervisors, it was difficult to investigate the suitability of all employers in advance and virtually impossible to check up on all apprentices after they had been placed.

The majority of the governors of the hospital wanted to raise the age at which their children were apprenticed. They argued in favour of more education and training before apprenticeship, claiming that 'the best masters and mistresses took them readily at a proper age without any fee' while 'small girls were ... unequal to the laborious household service that families with no other servant would expect, and these were the households that most often took the girls'.[54] Faced by financial crisis

[52] McClure, *Coram's Children*, 117, 121.   [53] Ibid. 136.   [54] Ibid. 117.

they had to at least temporarily abandon such a policy in favour of one of disposing of the children as quickly as possible by earlier apprenticeships. Only by the early nineteenth century did the governors succeed in making the minimum age of apprenticeship 14. If this meant the hospital could admit fewer children it had longer to provide them with an education and training. Foundling homes, it was argued, 'would become "nurseries" where upper class women would pick out Servants for the meanest offices of their houses'.[55] Local clergy also seem to have benefited. In October 1766 the Revd Mr. Ellis St John of Frenchhampstead in Berkshire, 'a gentleman of a good fortune', approached one of the Foundling Hospital's inspectors about a child put out to nurse in his locality. 'He was desirous of taking apprentice the child Augustine Hide.' He promised 'to give the child a suitable education and afterwards to take him into his family as a footboy'. 'A more fortunate circumstance', the inspector wrote, 'could not well have happened to the child.'[56]

About the same time as the Foundling Hospital was launched, the Magdalen Hospital was founded. Its declared aim was the reclamation of prostitutes, although in fact many of those it took in were not prostitutes at all but women who had 'been seduced under Promise of Marriage, and afterwards deserted by their seducers'. Admissions for any year between 1762 and 1848 varied between 52 and 113. Most of the women were between 15 and 21 and in the early years of the hospital they stayed about three years. Apart from being given 'a proper acquaintance with the principles of the religion of Christ' the hospital aimed to give inmates the means to earn a living 'by honest labour'. Under supervision they worked 'at spinning, knitting, household work, and various manufactures'. Later laundry work was introduced. At the end of their stay if they were not reconciled with their friends and family they were placed 'primarily in domestic service'—preferably outside London.[57] Rewards were given to those who did well and who remained in their places a year.

Quite apart from the various institutions set up to educate poor children there was a great deal of small-scale philanthropy with

[55] Hecht, *The Domestic Servant in Eighteenth-Century England*, 24.
[56] *Correspondence of the Foundling Hospital*, 209.
[57] Stanley Nash, 'Prostitution and Charity: The Magdalen Hospital: A Case Study', *Journal of Social History*, 17 (1984), 617–28 at p. 620.

the same purpose. The Revd William Jones records in his diary in 1802 the existence of four maiden sisters, his neighbours, who 'show great benevolence' to the local poor. 'They have always some of their children under their roof, whom they themselves instruct in reading, etc., [and] train them up useful servants.'[58] The same object was shared by Hannah More, who in the Sunday schools she conducted in the Cheddar area at the end of the eighteenth century aimed 'to train up the lower classes in habits of industry and piety'.[59]

In Sarah Scott's novel, Millenium Hall is a female retreat for widows and unmarried women, where the education is undertaken of daughters 'left destitute of provision by their parents' deaths'. The aim is to 'render them acceptable, where accomplished women of an humble rank and behaviour are wanted, either for the care of a house or children'. Those destined for service—the majority, we are told—work under the supervision of the regular servants of the house. It is claimed that such admirable servants are produced that 'it seldom happens that any one takes an apprentice or servant, till they have first sent' to the house 'to know if they have any to recommend'.[60]

By far the greatest amount of time in all schools for the education of the children of the poor was spent on religious instruction. If the object was to turn out good and loyal servants then it was necessary to instruct the children in the Christian religion which, it was held, 'would instil industrial and social discipline'.[61] It was no accident that the Society for Promoting Christian Knowledge was responsible for co-ordinating the charity schools set up by Anglicans. It was part of the church's fight against popery. The overwhelming majority of the female pupils of these charity schools were destined to be domestic servants and the instruction they received, at least in theory, was meant to be appropriate to this end. At a charity school for girls founded in 1699, for instance, most of the time 'was spent on housework'.[62]

By the turn of the century many were increasingly critical of the whole nature of parish provision for children of the poor, and

[58] *The Diary of the Rev. William Jones 1777–1821*, ed. O. F. Christie (1929), 135.
[59] Hannah More, as quoted in E. S. Turner, *What the Butler Saw: 250 Years of the Servant Problem* (1962), 75.
[60] *Millenium Hall* (1762), 140, 151, 190.
[61] Hitchcock, 'Paupers and Preachers', 152.
[62] Burgess, *A History of the Burlington School*, 31.

their apprenticeship. Catharine Cappe in 1805 talked of 'the incalculable evils that arise from suffering children to remain in our poor-houses as they are now constituted'. She wanted children removed from contact with the 'inmates of those wretched abodes'—which only ensured that sooner or later they too would descend into the underworld of vice, petty crime, and prostitution. The answer, she thought, lay in more charity schools, and better ones, designed 'to procure for their inmates greater advantages than a mere parish education could be expected to supply'.[63] That meant better instruction and more education. Many charity schools, she recognized, were urgently in need of far greater regulation and reform. Some of the matrons and masters of such schools sought by cutting down on the food given to their pupils to maximize their earnings. What determined where the children were sent, and when, rested entirely with the matron, who not unusually put her own convenience before the well-being of her charges. The very suitability of most charity school children as servants was called into question. 'Instead of being each instructed in all the different branches, which should fit them for Servants, or enable them to maintain themselves when out of place, many of them will never have been instructed at all, or at least but very imperfectly, in the very things, which it would have been the most important for them to have been taught.'[64] Cappe had a special interest in the charity schools for girls at York. In the Grey Coat School the rules laid down that all girls on leaving the establishment were to be bound out for four years as domestic servants. She thought it 'a most ruinous practice' and was against binding out children for long apprenticeships. But if the way in which such schools were conducted came under scrutiny their object was never in any doubt. It was to turn out a steady stream of children looking for places as servants. Charity schools for girls must be better regulated because they were 'highly important' in 'fitting them for servants'. Some of the pupils of charity schools, she argued, should be educated 'for mere House Servants', others to be servants 'of a higher order'.[65] Her comments reveal not only the crucial importance to their employers of the work done by domestic servants, but the conviction that the female poor primarily existed to provide cheap labour for their social betters. They

[63] *Observations on Charity Schools*, pp. viii, 3, 10.
[64] Ibid. 13.   [65] Ibid. 22.

also reveal the deep class distinctions which divided servants from those they served. If the object of the Grey Coat School at York was to provide 'the means of a better education ... than they could have obtained in a Parish Poor-House', by the end of the century—thanks to Cappe's efforts—it seems to have achieved this end for, we are told, those girls leaving the school 'went out to service on the same footing as other young women, generally at about the age of 16 or 17'. They had no difficulty in placing them. 'On the contrary', she explained, 'they were so much sought after ... that they were engaged 3 or 4 months previous to leaving school.'[66] Of the 114 girls leaving the school after its reorganization in 1787, forty-seven had gone into service. The only other occupation mentioned—mantua-making—accounted for two. One girl had become an assistant mistress at the school. The rest of the girls were married, were sick, had died, or had disappeared from York.[67] Olwen Hufton has concluded that 'the charity school girl enjoyed some solid advantages over other seekers of posts in affluent households ... [she had] been taught deference and a respect for honesty and sobriety'.[68] There is no doubt that both Cappe and Trimmer shared the notion of a hierarchy of sorts existing in the various institutions turning out pauper servants. At the bottom were the workhouse schools from which came the most menial of servants, at the top, and almost certainly still a minority, were some charity schools, the source of better-qualified servants. It was a hierarchy that extended to the inmates. Some, as Mrs Cappe had written, were destined to be 'mere house servants' while others were 'of a higher order'.

At the end of the eighteenth century Priscilla Wakefield outlined the education that was needed by the female labouring poor. 'In addition to reading', she included instruction in 'Plain work, knitting, marking, cutting-out, and mending linen', as well as 'washing, ironing, and cleaning house'. This 'with every other qualification that will prepare them to become useful as servants'.[69] If such aims were very seldom realized, by the end of the

[66] Catharine Cappe, *An Account of Two Charity Schools* (1800), 17; Cappe, *Observations on Charity Schools*, 55.

[67] Cappe, *Observations on Charity Schools*, 41.

[68] 'Women, Work and Family', in Natalie Zemon Davis amd Arlette Farge (eds.), *A History of Women* (1993), iii. 21.

[69] *Reflections on the Present Condition of the Female Sex with Suggestions for its Improvement*, 2nd edn. (1817), 138.

century the standards of some schools had improved. In the Grey Coat School at York, in many ways an exceptional school, girls, by the end of the century, were taught 'to read, write, sew, knit and spin worsted' and 'to wash, and do other household work'.[70]

If such schools were often the creation of those who felt a real sympathy for the poor and a responsibility towards them, there was also, as has been emphasized, a 'determination to reform them by application of what Defoe called "the great law of subordination"'.[71] In charity schools 'children are made more tractable and submissive', an account of 1708 explained, 'by being early accustomed to Awe and Punishment and Dutiful Subjection. From such timely Discipline the Publick may expect Honest and Industrious Servants.'[72] That such philanthropic effort came mainly from the middle classes was not surprising. It was they who felt the need to redefine the essential class differences between themselves and their servants. And, after all, it was mainly from them that, in the course of the eighteenth century, came the expanded demand for domestic servants. The provision of domestic servants was not regarded as something that could safely be left to the laws of supply and demand; it needed to be actively promoted. It suggests middle-class concern at the increasing expense of keeping servants and a desire to find cheaper sources of supply. It is possible that pauper servants were far more widely employed by the middle classes than we have previously thought, but in any case the existence of a large body of pauper servants might well have the effect of keeping all servants' wages down.

Charity schools—even at their best—provided a restricted training for poor girls destined to become domestic servants. Betty, the wife of Benjamin Shaw, had had from the age of 8 'a long period in the workhouse as a child'. Later she was sent to the Bluecoat Charity School in Lancaster where her education included 'instruction in household management'. Her marriage was not a happy one. In her husband's eyes one major fault in his wife was her inability to run the house efficiently and economically. He blamed her education which, he said, was 'more practi-

---

[70] Cappe, *An Account of Two Charity Schools*, 17.
[71] As quoted in Jones, *The Charity School Movement*, 4.
[72] *An Account of the Charity Schools lately erected* (1708) as quoted in Jones, *The Charity School Movement*, 72.

cal than financial, being to prepare girls for going into ordinary domestic service'.[73] It is a story which throws some doubt on just how useful a period as a domestic servant was to the future life of women.

Quite apart from female parish apprentices there were also girls apprenticed by their parents to learn a trade, for which they paid a premium. But many of them are now recognized to have ended up doing housework. Not all such cases have come to light, but the case of Sarah Gibson who in 1715 was 'discharged from her apprenticeship to Joanna Worthington of St. Andrew's Holborn, widow, mantua-maker, upon proof that the said Sarah, instead of learning the trade of mantua-maker had been employed in common household work, cleansing and washing lodgers' rooms and had been immoderately beaten and not allowed sufficient food' was by no means exceptional.[74] But such apprentices were very few in comparison with the number of female pauper apprentices. Nevertheless it means that, alongside female pauper apprentices, there was a considerable body of girls entering domestic service for whom no wages or very small wages were payable. Many of them when first bound out would have been of limited use as servants. They were frequently too young and physically weak as well as too untrained. But if they survived in a household they might in time become effective servants. There was, for example, the parish apprentice Elizabeth Beech bound to William Wakeley of Myddle, who 'proved a good servant and lived in the family above twenty years, and was married from thence'.[75] What effect has the existence of such a rich source of cheap servants on historians' perception of the nature of service in the eighteenth century?

Any discussion of servants' wages must take into account this pool of labour in service which was paid little, if anything. It seems more than likely that its existence helped to depress the wages of female servants in relation to male. If some male pauper apprentices were bound out as servants they were always fewer than female, and in the course of the eighteenth century their

---

[73] *The Family Records of Benjamin Shaw, Mechanic of Dent. Dolphinholme and Preston 1772–1841*, ed. Alan G. Crosby, Record Society of Lancashire and Cheshire, cxxx (1991), p. lviii.

[74] George, *London Life in the Eighteenth Century*, appendix IV, p. 416.

[75] Richard Gough, *The History of Myddle (1701–1706)* (1979), 158.

numbers declined still further. So one would expect the effect of the availability of pauper servants on wages to be greater for non-pauper female than non-pauper male servants. Yet this has not been taken into consideration by historians when discussing wage differentials of male and female servants in the eighteenth century.

And what was the relationship between such pauper apprentices and ordinary servants? It was a question that Catharine Cappe posed. 'What sort of treatment is a young woman so circumstanced likely to receive from the other servants . . . in the family? Will they in general be disposed to treat with tenderness the poor Apprentice Girl? neither imposing upon her in respect to labour or wounding her feelings by upbraiding her with her degraded situation? Which may she fairly reckon upon, their kindness and pity, or their contumely and reproach?'[76] Although she gives no example, there is no doubt of the answer Catharine Cappe would have given. One might speculate that often pauper servants were as badly treated by their fellow servants as by their employers. Parish children must have been the butt for much servant frustration. Many of them would have occupied the lowest rung of the service hierarchy as kitchen skivvies or general household drudges. They were almost certainly made to feel their inferior and lowly position in relation to other servants. Certainly their fellow servants had some cause for grievance against them for cheapening their labour and undermining their wages.

Recognition of the existence of these pauper servants and just how many of them there were means that any suggestion of a certain level of income below which the employment of servants was impossible is no longer a valid thesis. Pauper servants could be employed by the humblest of households—and often were. Their existence and widespread employment also fundamentally undermines the notion of servants as an aspect of the middle-class 'paraphernalia of gentility'.[77]

[76] *Observations on Charity Schools*, 47.
[77] J. A. Banks, *Prosperity and Parenthood* (1954), the title ch. 6: 'The Paraphernalia of Gentility'.

8
Nicholas Blundell's Servants

> Margaret Blundell, a descendant of the diarist, comments on his servants: 'An interesting point about this household is the extreme independence of its members, who usually came from the farmhouses and cottages of the district. The men remained for years in the service of the Squire, leaving the continual arrivals of maids to tell their own tale of an unreasonable mistress.'
>
> *Blundell's Diary and Letter Book*, 98

AN analysis of the servants employed by one household, of whatever size, cannot provide conclusive evidence for servants as a whole. But where, as in the case of Nicholas Blundell's journal, we have a mass of carefully indexed information about his servants, both men and women, over a period of twenty-six years of the eighteenth century, an analysis can pinpoint questions about domestic servants in general. The three volumes of the diary, produced by the Record Society of Lancashire and Cheshire, have been edited and annotated with great care. Each volume is extensively indexed and the references to individual servants make it possible to build up a continuous account of their working lives while in Blundell's household, and, often, after leaving it. Such standards of editing and indexing make this diary readily accessible and of great value. The original, while legible, is made very difficult to read by the diarist's extensive use of abbreviation of both people and places as well as his idiosyncratic spelling. It is true he too had constructed 'Tables of Index' but they are 'most complicated' and 'of little value.'[1] If it is asked what motive he had for keeping a diary with such care the answer appears to be that it was mainly as an *aide-mémoire*. He had a bad memory. His diary was a very necessary and full record of the day-to-day

---

[1] *Blundell's Diary and Letter Book 1702–28*, ed. Margaret Blundell (1952), p. xii.

happenings at Little Crosby to which he could constantly refer back.

Recently it has increasingly been stressed that most studies of English servants have tended to concentrate on those in large, rich households which are unrepresentative and misleading of the great majority of servants, who were mainly employed in small households with often no more than one servant. Among those in large households, it has been suggested, the hierarchy among servants was rigid, important, and reflected in the wages earned. So Hecht writes 'it was...in the large households, where specialisation of function was carried furthest, that such distinctions were most marked.' Although the social standing of the master of the house exerted some influence on the occupational status of its servants it was not the most important factor. Above all 'nominal rank defined a servant's occupational status'. 'The scale of wages suggests the main differences in status.'[2] The degrees of skill represented by 'lady's companion', 'housekeeper', 'chambermaid', and 'milkmaid', it is held, determined that hierarchy and, although over time any individual servant might ascend the hierarchy, it took time, training, and experience. In his analysis of the Pepys household—a relatively modest one—Peter Earle has talked of its 'strict hierarchy' particularly among the female members. It was, he writes, 'a hierarchy headed by his wife Elizabeth and then, in descending order, her waiting-woman or companion, the chambermaid, cookmaid and under-cookmaid'.[3] How far does a study of one large, moderately rich household—the Blundell's—bear out such a thesis?

Nicholas Blundell was a north country gentleman whose seat, Crosby Hall, was about seven miles north of Liverpool and twenty-three miles from Preston. It lay in the parish of Sephton, described in 1773 by Thomas Pennant as 'placed in a vast range of fine meadows, that reach almost to the sea and in a great measure supply Liverpool with hay. It is watered by the Alt, a small trout stream; but after the first winter flood is covered with water the whole season, by reason of want of fall to carry it away.'[4] Nicholas Blundell's 'diurnal' starts in 1702 and ends in 1728. In all those

---

[2] J. Jean Hecht, *The Domestic Servant in Eighteenth-Century England* (1956), 35, 38.
[3] *The Making of the English Middle Class* (1989), 226.
[4] As quoted in the *Victoria County History: A History of the County of Lancaster*, iii (1907), ed. William Farrer and J. Brownbill, 58.

years only once did he omit to record the day's happenings. When his father died in 1702 Nicholas, at the age of 33, inherited the estates. Under his father he had already learnt something of their management. The estates extended well beyond Little Crosby where Nicholas was born and grew up, and included land and property in Great Crosby, Ince Blundell, Thornton, Hindley, Marchhouses, Orrell, Warrington, and Liverpool. It was an extensive estate and when, as a 'papist' he registered it, it was valued at £482. 12s. 2½d. When he inherited the estate it was encumbered with debt. Nicholas was one of fourteen children, as his father and grandfather had been. In consequence there were heavy demands on the estate in the form of dowries, annuities, and maintenance costs. In the period of the civil wars the estate had been sequestered, and was only regained by the payment of a crippling sum. In these circumstances Nicholas was very aware of the importance of making 'a provident marriage' and producing an heir, but his father appears to have been unable to meet the demands of the parents of eligible young women for marriage settlements and Nicholas only married after his father's death, at the age of 34. The evidence suggests his marriage to Frances Langdale was not for love 'but for the sake of the dowry and the necessity to have a son and heir'.[5] Nicholas gained £2,000 by it.

Luckily for the estates Nicholas was not just a landowner but an efficient and hard-working farmer prepared to try out new methods and to experiment. He grew wheat, oats and barley, rape and flax, and tobacco. He kept sheep, cattle, and horses, and a well-stocked poultry yard. The household was largely self-sufficient. It was this that enabled the Blundells to embark on what has been called a 'life of intense sociability which they were to pursue together for the next thirty three years'.[6] The farm supplied the family with all its vegetables and fruit, and with meat and poultry. What was excess to their needs in eggs, cheese, butter, potatoes, and fruit was sold in Liverpool. From their home-produced wool and flax came much of the family's clothes. Nicholas kept a tight hold on the purse-strings and kept detailed accounts. Under him, despite a period of exile, the estate prospered. During

---

[5] *The Great Diurnal of Nicholas Blundell of Little Crosby, Lancashire*, ed. J. J. Bagley, Record Society of Lancashire and Cheshire, 3 vols. (1968, 1970, 1972), i. 3.

[6] *Blundell's Diary and Letter Book*, 17.

his lifetime Crosby Hall, already a large house, was significantly extended.

In assessing just how representative his household was of the larger and wealthier, it is important to stress factors that were unusual. One of these was the fact that Frances, the daughter of Lord Langdale, whom Nicholas married in June 1703, was, as his editor puts it, 'an extremely difficult person'.[7] Both Nicholas's mother and his great aunt at times found it impossible to live in the same house with her, and moved out. It is not entirely surprising, therefore, to discover that female servants were constantly leaving the Blundells' employment after only a few weeks or even days. The presumption must be that made by the editor of the journal, that their often precipitous departure was 'because of treatment received from the mistress'.[8] Particularly difficult were her relations with female servants in the early years of her married life when her two children were infants.

In sharp contrast, but perhaps to be seen as equally exceptional, was the fact that Nicholas was a very tolerant and liberal employer who frequently showed 'solicitous care' for his servants, both male and female.[9] He would visit them when ill, lend them a horse to take them home on a visit, and when any of their family died, would lend his coach for the use of the bereaved. This difference in attitude between the two Blundells could, at least in part, account for the differences in length of service of male as compared with female servants in their household.

One other unusual factor about the Blundells needs mentioning. They were a strong and active Catholic family. At the time of the Jacobite Rising of 1715 Nicholas was forced to flee to London, and from there to Flanders, where he remained in exile for two years, his family joining him early in 1716. The family's Catholicism may well have affected their recruitment of servants. When, for example, Nicholas wrote a recommendation for Mary Barton, a chambermaid, in 1705, he specifically mentioned that she was a Catholic as well as 'a brisk mettled work woman'.[10] In May 1709 three of Blundell's servants 'were confirmed at Morehall' where a Catholic priest was serving.[11] Betty Gorsuch of Gorsuch Hall, a relation of the Blundells' and, it would seem, at one time a servant

---

[7] *The Great Diurnal of Nicholas Blundell*, i. 3.
[8] Ibid.   [9] Ibid. 5.   [10] Ibid. 69 n. 90.   [11] Ibid. 216.

of Mrs Blundell, wanted to become a Poor Clare nun at Dunkirk. In July 1716 she went into a monastery 'to try if she were able to do service there'.[12] It is likely that it was to a network of Catholic friends and acquaintances that the Blundells turned when anxious to recruit servants. This said, Nicholas appears to have had the best of relations with his non-Catholic neighbours, and among his friends there were several local Anglican clergy.

In the first edited volume of the journal, which covers nine-and-a-half years, an astonishing fifty-seven names of female servants appear in the index. They include dairy maids, chambermaids, Blundell's wife's maids, nursery maids, cooks, housekeepers, and at least one example of a 'companion' to Mrs Blundell. Admittedly the list also includes the names of servants who came in search of a place and were turned away (see p. 61). In the second volume, covering seven years, there are twenty-three female servants listed, and in the third, which covers eight years, twenty-one. The figures for the early years of the Blundell's marriage (volume i of the diary), when they went through fifty-seven female servants, contrast sharply with the twenty-seven male servants that are listed for the same period. This, it seems, was a difficult period in relations between Mrs Blundell and the female servants. The second volume indexes twenty-one and the third twenty-three men servants—figures very close to those for female servants.

One thing revealed by the nature of the servants employed by the Blundells, whether male or female, is just how irrelevant a narrow definition of domestic service as work in the house was in this period of the early eighteenth century, when much of such work blurred into farm work. Dairy maids, cowmen, ploughmen, and shepherds existed alongside chambermaids, cooks, and butlers. And when the need arose all were expected to switch roles, whether inside or outside the house, and help with the harvest or give additional assistance in the kitchen or at table when visitors were staying.

The numbers of servants' names occurring in the diary are of only limited value unless the number of female servants as compared to male employed at any one time is known. This is not a figure easy to estimate. The full complement of female servants

---

[12] *The Great Diurnal of Nicholas Blundell*, ii. 172 n.

kept at Crosby Hall appears to have varied between three and five, but this can only be a rough guess. Normally Blundell's wife employed either a cook or a housekeeper, but in at least one period of seven months she employed both. Then often, as we shall see, and particularly in the early years of the diary, servants were appointed for the dual role of nursemaid and 'wife's maid', or as dairy maid and chambermaid. It is also far from clear when Blundell refers to his 'wife's maid' whether she was the chambermaid or an additional servant. At one period early on in their marriage when their children were young Blundell sought—not altogether successfully—to employ a 'companion' to his wife.[13] On the basis of this rough estimate of female servants employed at any one time between 1702 and 1711, the full complement of female servants in the household could have been changed as much as twice a year.

What of his male servants? In the same period the total number of male servants employed at any one time was greater than that of female and probably as many as seven or eight. In the nine-and-a-half years the full complement appears to have changed three to four times—that is once every two or three years. Such a contrast is confirmed by the longer period most male servants stayed at the Blundells in comparison with females. Very few male servants stayed less than a year and most considerably longer. There are of course exceptions. Thomas Gower, hired as a butler in February 1707, stayed only a few weeks.[14] On the other hand there are several references to 'old and faithful' servants like William Arnold, who died in August 1702.[15] He had been 'brought up from a Child at this hous', wrote Blundell in 1702, and had acted in his time as 'Groome, Coachman & Butcher'.[16] John Bannister, hired as cowman in February 1704, was still with the Blundells in 1725, but no longer as cowman. He had become butler.[17] John Kerfoot was miller at Crosby Hill for thirteen years.[18]

---

[13] Ibid. 27; see also i. 205 and n. 11. In Mar./Apr. 1709 both Nicholas's young cousins, Frances and Catherine Gorsuch, came to act as companions to Mrs Blundell, but seem to have been treated as guests. Later, however, Blundell's other cousin, Ann Gorsuch, came 'to be as a Companion & an Assistant to my wife' (ii. 27). She stayed for four months.
[14] Ibid. i. 129.   [15] Ibid. 15.   [16] Ibid.   [17] Ibid. i. 51, iii. 169.
[18] Ibid. i. 287 n. 25.

This is in sharp contrast to the length of service of the majority of female servants, who often stayed less than a month. Dairy maids, particularly in the early years of the diary, appear to have presented special problems. They changed places frequently. Ann Hill, for example, was employed as dairy maid on 2 January 1707, and left on the 29th.[19] Ailes Finch, hired as dairy maid on 14 February 1711, left on the 22nd.[20] Many, like Betty Atherton and Jane Smith, both dairy maids in the early years of the diary, left after three months or less.[21] Very few dairy maids stayed longer. The same pattern—if not so extreme—is found among other female servants. Jane Lydiate, hired as cook on 12 August 1708, departed on the 27th of the following September.[22]

Despite all this coming and going of servants, which is recorded in such detail by Nicholas, the diary still manages to convey the impression of order. If sometimes the dismissal of servants produced tensions between Nicholas and his wife, there never seemed to be a major interruption to the day-to-day working of the household. Perhaps this was in part because of the ease with which local labour could be hired when needed. It was also not unrelated to the flexibility in function of all his servants.

One interesting aspect of Blundell's servants, both male and female, is the way in which they switched jobs. Indeed Blundell, in July 1704, recorded 'Jane Smith Cook and Mary Formby Dary Maid changed offices'.[23] A strict hierarchy, which, it has been argued, was common among servants in large households, does not seem to have been the case at Crosby Hall. Take the example of Ellen Eaves, who was first employed by the Blundells as housekeeper in July 1709. Less than three months later there was, as Blundell so graphically expressed it, 'A Grand falling out with Eves', and she left her service. Yet two years later she reappeared as Mrs Blundell's maid.[24] Mary Howard in 1708 acted as both dairy maid and chambermaid.[25] In the following year Mary Bell was hired as chambermaid and nursery maid.[26] Mary Scott who had earlier been approached by Frances Blundell with a view to becoming housekeeper, was appointed as 'Nursery Maid & Chamber Maid' and later designated 'Head maid, nursery maid,

[19] *The Great Diurnal of Nicholas Blundell*, 127, 134.
[20] Ibid. 279.   [21] Ibid. 137, 145, 56, 62.   [22] Ibid. 182, 186.
[23] Ibid. 61.   [24] Ibid. 225, 233.   [25] Ibid. 302.   [26] Ibid. 230–1.

and chamber maid', but apparently with no corresponding increase in wages.[27] Between July 1708 and October 1709, Betty Harrison at different times occupied the positions of cook, nursemaid, and chambermaid. After only a month her job as cook was given to Jane Lydiate and Harrison 'who had been Cook for some weeks was made Nursery Maid'. Not surprisingly she seems to have resented the change, and a fortnight later she left Crosby Hall. Nevertheless, after less than four months she reappeared and was re-employed as chambermaid and dairy maid.[28] When Jane Smith left her employment in July 1704, after only three months, Blundell recorded that 'she was first Cook & now Dairy-Maid'.[29]

There is the same diversity in the work done by Blundell's male servants. John Bannister, who as we have seen was one of Blundell's longest-serving servants, was described at different times over the whole journal as cowman, gardener, and butler. In one wages list he is described as both 'Gardiner and Butler' but his wage remained unchanged. Charles Howard, in 1709, was hired as 'ploughman, coachman, etc', but by 1712 he is listed in the quarter's wages as 'Head-Hind, Groom and Coachman'.[30] Henry Sumner in 1704 was taken on as 'Ploughman, Groom & Coachman'.[31] In 1718 James Barnes was acting as both butler and gardener.[32] Perhaps the most interesting example is that of Richard Cartwright, butler to the Blundells from December 1703, and a much trusted member of the household. But the skill for which he was most valued was not among those usually associated with the work of a butler, for he was a blood-letter. Over the years he was employed by the Blundells, and after he had left them to become—naturally—a butcher, there were numerous occasions on which he was called on to exercise this skill, particularly where Blundell's wife was concerned. So we read that on 23 April 1710, he 'let my wife Blud in ye foot. She fainted, having parted with 20 oz. of Blud as is supposed'. On 14 June 1714 he again 'let my Wife Blood in her Arme. He took about 13 ounces of Blood from her'.[33] At first it was as part of his duties as butler that

---

[27] Ibid. 246, but see also 231.
[28] Ibid. 178, 182–3, 195.   [29] Ibid. 56, 62.
[30] Ibid. 203 n. 8, 235, and ii. 5 n. 12.
[31] Ibid. i. 203 n. 8.   [32] Ibid. ii. 234.   [33] Ibid. i. 252, ii. 102.

he was asked to let blood, but when Cartwright had left service he was still employed by the Blundells at blood-letting but now at 'an economical fee'.[34]

What Richard Cartwright's career as butler also demonstrates is the wide-ranging nature of his duties—duties that are little associated with the usual tasks for which a butler is employed. Over the period of his service he was called on to take apples to Liverpool to be sold, 'to trace Rabets in the Snow', to climb 'some Chimbneys for young swallows', to bottle wine, to trim trees, and on one occasion to 'read old writings' to Nicholas.[35] As Margaret Blundell, a descendant of the family, has noted, whatever the life of a butler in Blundell's household was like it was not 'monotonous'.[36]

In addition to living-in and permanent servants, Blundell from time to time hired others to do particular jobs. In fact the distinction between casual and permanent servants is blurred by the frequency with which casual labourers lived in during the period they were working at the Hall. Many were from local families. For instance, Elizabeth Blundell is referred to as a 'daughter of a tenant, who sometimes helped as a servant at Crosby Hall'.[37] In May 1705 Ellen Nelson was employed to weed in the garden.[38] Blundell records settling his account in July 1709 with 'Ezabell and Margery for weeding in the gardens & with Ann Blundell for Wheeling Turf'.[39] When Blundell's daughter, Fanny, was married in 1733, the Disbursement Book records taking on the temporary services of Ellen Eaves, a former housekeeper in his employ, and Betty Crofts to help 'in the kitchen for a few days'.[40] Dorothy Blundell, we are told in August 1719, 'came hither and began to prepare against tomorrow'. For her help in cooking on this occasion she earned 5s. 0d.[41] For the same occasion the Blundells also employed extra charwomen to come in and help in the house. Ann Bradley, in July 1718, came form Preston 'to be Cook here awhile, being we expected my Lord Langdale and Sister

---

[34] *Blundell's Diary and Letter Book*, 104.
[35] *The Great Diurnal of Nicholas Blundell*, i. 63, 75, 87.
[36] *Blundell's Diary and Letter Book*, 104.
[37] *The Great Diurnal of Nicholas Blundell*, i. 29 n. 14.
[38] Ibid. 84 and n. 48.   [39] Ibid. 221.   [40] Ibid. iii. 261, appendix.
[41] Ibid. ii. 266 and n. 51

Midleton to come'. But by the next day Mrs Blundell had decided she 'would not do well in the kitchen and sent her to Leverpoole'.[42]

The rural position of Crosby Hall made it almost imperative that those coming from any distance should live in or at least lodge for a night or two, but local women would come in on a daily basis. Sometimes the Blundells took on servants who were 'temporary' in the sense that they were fill-ins during a crisis or until something better turned up. So in November 1714 Frances Harrison 'came to supply in the Chambers until we were better provided'.[43] In February 1715 'Margaret Lurting came to supply here till we get a Cook'.[44] When Jane Withington and Nelly Howerd, Blundell's wife's maid and chambermaid, went to Derby to stay two or three nights during Wakes Week in 1721, a Betty Carefoot 'came to supply in their place'.[45] In January 1725 a Mrs Ann Wilding came to lodge at Crosby Hall. 'She came to assist us', Nicholas wrote, 'being at present in want of Maides'. Later in 1727 she was again with them 'attending my Wife in her Sickness'. She was no ordinary servant. She seems to have been a friend of the family, for the Blundells on one occasion dined with her, and on another Blundell's wife lodged with her when she visited Liverpool. It was not only the Blundells who employed her from time to time. In April 1724 she went to 'Mr Crisps to stay some time to sew for him.'[46]

Men also came to work casually for the Blundells. In fact Nicholas in his journal differentiates between 'my servants', that is those in his regular employ, and 'my workfolk' who consisted of casual labourers who 'weeded, reaped, sheared sheep, "push-ploughed" '.[47] According to Margaret Blundell, the majority 'had their own holdings and eked out a livelihood by such seasonal employment'.[48] In February 1710 Nathan Howard left Blundell's employment after staying for a period 'to help his Brother', Charles, who was 'Ploughman, Coachman, etc.'[49] James Barnes was employed temporarily during the summer of 1718 to provide

---

[42] Ibid. 235. For further discussion of the role of local hired labour see pp. 176–8.
[43] Ibid. 116.   [44] Ibid. 125.   [45] Ibid. iii. 52.
[46] Ibid. 149, 224, 91, 132.   [47] *Blundell's Diary and Letter Book*, 115.
[48] Ibid.   [49] *The Great Diurnal of Nicholas Blundell*, i. 245.

extra assistance during Lord Langdale's visit.[50] In September 1721 'Humphrey Blundell came to supply the Miller's place a while being he went ill home on Sunday'.[51] Then there were the two Piningtons—father and son—who were taken on to do some ditching for Blundell.[52] In 1726, when Jackson Blundell, a gardener, died, 'young John Lunt came to trim my Trees & supply his Place where I have occation'.[53]

Blundell's hiring of a Mrs Mills as a companion for his wife in the early years of their marriage when his wife was recovering from childbirth deserves some attention. The Blundells seem to have met her casually at the home of Lord and Lady Gerard at Dutton Lodge. She was invited to act as companion to Mrs Blundell for three months, and when, in September 1706, their daughter Fanny was born, John Bannister was sent 'to bring Mrs Mills from Warrington to live here some time'. If she was asked to stay for three months, in fact she remained at Crosby Hall a further five months as a 'tabler' or paying guest. She is one example of Blundell's appointing a servant as a result of his Catholic connections. Mrs Mills seems to have been a devoted Catholic. But when she finally left Crosby Hall at the end of April 1707 to go to London, she still owed the Blundells money. The outstanding debt amounted to £1. 4s. 3d. She was not allowed to forget it. Mrs Blundell wrote to her enclosing an account, and, when that produced nothing, Nicholas suggested she pay the debt in the form of coffee sent from London. Again she failed to respond and a bitter correspondence ensued until, in July 1710, Nicholas refused to send on to her a trunk she had left at Crosby Hall. Only in November 1711 was the dispute resolved and the trunk dispatched.[54]

How were their servants recruited? A quite surprising number of would-be servants came to Crosby Hall to offer their services to the Blundells. In fact few seem to have been accepted. Whether servants approached the Blundells because they had the name of good employers is at least questionable given what we know of Mrs Blundell's difficult relations with them. So was it simply that in the country there were relatively few positions available in relation to those seeking places?

[50] *The Great Diurnal of Nicholas Blundell*, ii. 238 n. 61.
[51] Ibid. iii. 55. [52] Ibid. 198. [53] Ibid. 185.
[54] Ibid. i. 120, 130, 137, 146, 196.

Elizabeth Johnson, in January 1704, 'came hither to offer her Service to be my Cook, I think she will not be accepted of'.[55] She was not and left next day. In April 1704 Ann Hilton 'came to proffer her Service to be my Wives Maid' and, in this instance, was taken on.[56] There were many others; the services of Ellen Boucher in May 1704 were not accepted.[57] Molly Ashton, in June 1708 'came to see what work my wife had for her to doe'. She was, added Blundell, 'to stay here some time' but her name does not reappear so presumably her services were not wanted and she moved on.[58] In August 1709 Frances Howard 'came to proffer herself to be housekeeper', but 'she was not accepted of'.[59] Howard, when she approached the Blundells had apparently been, and may have remained, 'servant to Lady Gormonstown'. Despite her rejection at this time she was to become the Blundell's housekeeper the following December—but only for eight days. A month later Ma Billington approached Nicholas Blundell and 'desired to know whether I was against her coming to serve here'.[60] Blundell does not say what answer he gave her, but she was not employed. In the following month an old servant, Dorothy Chaddock, came to see Blundell 'and to look about her'.[61] Mary Heatley came 'to offer her service to be Dary Maid, etc.' in November 1714, but, Nicholas Blundell went on to add, 'I did not accept of her for Nanny Blundell came againe to-night to be Dary Maid & Chamber Maid'.[62] In September 1724 Jane Launsdale came 'to proffer herself to be Servant here' but with what result is not recorded.[63]

The offer of their services was sometimes accompanied by a recommendation from a friend or neighbour. So in July 1709 Ellen Eaves, who had come to offer her services as housekeeper, 'was recommended by Mrs Poole of Burchley'.[64] Often Nicholas or his wife would seek out local girls, first getting information about them from their local contacts. In 1705, for instance, Nicholas went to 'Ailes Meling to discours Pat Wofold concerning Mary Carys being my Nursery Maid'.[65] Subsequently she was appointed. In 1709 Mrs Blundell went to 'Carr Side & discoursed Betty Blundell about Catherine Carys'.[66] A week later Carys was

[55] Ibid. 50. [56] Ibid. 55. [57] Ibid. 58.
[58] Ibid. 174. [59] Ibid. 225. [60] Ibid. 230. [61] Ibid. 233.
[62] Ibid. ii. 117. [63] Ibid. 140. [64] Ibid. i. 273. [65] Ibid. 89.
[66] Ibid. 235.

taken on as housekeeper. The same year, Blundell recorded, 'my wife went to Cappoli and discoursed Ann Hodgson about coming for some time to supply the place of Ho'.[67] One wonders whether 'Ho', whoever she might have been, was informed. In May of the same year Mrs Blundell went to Derby 'to see if Mary Winstanley would come to be my houskeeper'. Mary Winstanley seems to have been in a rather special position. She may have been related to the Blundells or to have been a woman of gentility known to them for some years who had fallen on hard times. Blundell emphasizes that she was 'to stay some time to assist in the Hous but not just as a servant, yet to work and overlook'. When two months later she left 'to serve Lord Mountgarret', Blundell once more stresses that she had been at Crosby Hall 'not as a Servant, but yet partly in the Nature of one to assist my Wife'. That she was different from other of Blundell's servants there is no doubt. Later she was to buy a cow from Blundell which was 'hiered out to my Lord Mountgarret'. Another time Blundell paid her '30s. for interest on £30'.[68] Nevertheless the wages she received as housekeeper in no way distinguished her from others. Her quarterly earnings amounted to 10s. Still without a housekeeper in October 1709, Blundell's wife 'went to Sutton to discourse Mary Scott about coming to be Houskeeper here'.[69] The search for servants would sometimes take Blundell's wife to Liverpool where in April 1711 she went 'to discourse Mary Heyes about coming to be servant here', but she never arrived.[70] On 29 May 1715, accompanied by Ellen Eaves, she 'went to Leverpoole . . . and discoursed Mary Woodcock about coming to serve her'.[71] Later she 'went to the Hall of Lidiat & spoke to Jane Heys about her coming to be Chamber-Maide here, but they did not bargain'.[72]

On occasion other servants already in their employ were sent to make the initial enquiries. For example, when in November 1712 Betty Harrison was thinking of leaving Crosby Hall, John Bannister approached a Catherine Molyneux about coming to replace her. The following month it was Bannister who 'Hired Catty Molineux to be Dayry Maid & Chamber Maid here'.[73] Meanwhile, however, Betty Harrison had changed her mind and decided to stay on, so Catherine Molyneux never arrived. The Blundells

[67] *The Great Diurnal of Nicholas Blundell*, 206.
[68] Ibid. 217, 218, 244, 296–7, 287.   [69] Ibid. 231.
[70] Ibid. 285–6.   [71] Ibid. ii. 136.   [72] Ibid. iii. 173.   [73] Ibid. ii. 42, 44.

seem to have had no qualms about approaching servants of their friends and neighbours with a view to inviting them to enter their employment. On 29 August 1725 Blundell's wife 'went to Mr. Crisps and discours'd Ellen Eastom about her coming to be servant here'.[74] In January 1727 she 'went to Francis Farers intending to speak to Mary Wogden about coming to be Cook here, but she saw her not'.[75] Yet a week later Mary Wogdon arrived at Crosby Hall as cook. In March of the following year his wife 'went to Timothy Muches about a Maid but to no purpose'.[76] On one occasion in 1728 Mally, one of the Blundell's daughters, 'went to Matthew Withington & hier'd his Daughter Ann to be my Wive's Maide & Chamber Maid but she came not'.[77]

Nicholas Blundell recruited his men servants. Sometimes, as in the case of William Ainsworth in January 1709, Blundell would hire a servant on the recommendation of a neighbour or acquaintance. Ainsworth came 'with a Letter of Recommendation from Mr. Walmesley Senior of Showley'.[78] In April 1718 he 'discoursed Richard Ashcroft about coming to be' his servant, but, as he was to add, 'we did not Bargain'.[79] In June of the same year James Barnes 'came to discourse me about being my Servant'.[80] He was taken on but stayed only two months. Joseph Rigby, one of Blundell's servants, in December 1721 'brought Baraby [sic: Barnaby?] Hargrave to be my Butler', apparently with a recommendation. But Blundell did not employ him. He was 'too little'.[81]

What wages were paid by Blundell to his servants? Were there great differences between the wages of cooks, housekeepers, dairy maids and chambermaids, or between those of ploughmen and grooms? The Blundell experience suggests not. £2 per annum seems to have been a fairly standard wage for their female servants. It was the amount paid in 1711 to Ann Armetrading, maid to Mrs Blundell, and to Betty Harrison in 1712 as chambermaid and dairy maid. But it was also the wage paid to Catherine Howard and Margaret Jackson, both cooks in the Blundells' employ. Holcroft Bradley, who combined the work of Mrs Blundell's maid with that of nursemaid, was paid £3 per annum in 1708.

---

[74] Ibid. iii. 165. [75] Ibid. 204–5.
[76] Ibid. 236. [77] Ibid. 231. [78] Ibid. i. 201. [79] Ibid. ii. 227–8.
[80] Ibid. 234. [81] Ibid. iii. 200.

Whether her 'constantly threatening to leave' had anything to do with the enhanced wage is not related.[82] Catharine Fisher, who was cook when the diary opens, and may well have been some time in the Blundell's employ, was paid £3. 10s. 0d. per annum. Among the highest paid was Ann Hilton, who in 1704 was paid an annual wage of £4 as housekeeper. Exceptional was the wage paid to Mary St Legar, a much valued servant, although for what reasons is anything but clear. In 1704 she was paid £6 per annum, yet even such a wage was not apparently sufficient to persuade her to stay at Crosby Hall.

On average the male servants earned more—but not significantly so except in the case of Blundell's millers. Henry Kerfoot, coachman in 1713, like many of Blundell's female servants was paid only £2 per annum. Henry Bilsbury was hired as groom in 1704 at an annual wage of £2. 10s. 0d. Charles Howard in 1707 combined the work of groom, ploughman, and head hind, and was rewarded with an annual wage of £3. The same year Robert Tompson, coachman and plough driver, was hired at the same wage. The much trusted John Bannister, who was both butler and gardener, earned £3. 15s. 0d. annually. A cowman in 1713, William Weedow earned £4 per annum. Even Blundell's steward, William Ainsworth, earned the same £4 per annum, as did Edward Pinnington, appointed butler in 1728. But John Kerfoot, 'Miller at his own Board', was paid £9 per annum and his successor John Rigby £10.[83] When the latter threatened to leave unless Blundell 'would come upon a New Bargan with him', his annual wage was increased to £11. 10s. 0d. with an extra 2s. 6d. for 'lite and licker'.[84] Eleven years later he was succeeded by R.P. who was paid £2. 15s. 0d. a quarter (£11 per annum) plus 1s. 3d. for 'lite and licker'.[85]

What do we learn from the journal of the reasons for servants leaving Crosby Hall? Unfortunately, all too often, the reference to their departure is non-committal. It is simply recorded that a servant 'left his/her service'. But sometimes something of the background to their departure is hinted at. In October 1703 Nicholas records that Mary St Legar, Mrs Blundell's maid, 'gave my Wife warning'. There is no further explanation, but the fol-

---

[82] *The Great Diurnal of Nicholas Blundell*, i. 171 n. 31.
[83] Ibid. ii. 5 n. 12.   [84] Ibid. iii. 172 and n. 1.   [85] Ibid. 175.

lowing April she left for Liverpool saying she would not return to Crosby Hall. She must have been greatly valued by Blundell's wife for, remarkably, Mrs Blundell leaves for Liverpool in an attempt to persuade Mary St Legar to return with her to Crosby Hall—'but without success'.[86] In 1707 Nicholas Blundell returned home to find that Catherine Melling, a dairy maid, 'had given warning'.[87] The same year Betty Atherton, another dairy maid, 'went away in a Passion' after 'serving three months'.[88] Holcroft Bradley, who in 1707–8 combined the jobs of Blundell's wife's maid and nursemaid was constantly threatening to leave his employ. In fact she stayed at Crosby Hall from September 1707 to March 1709, when Blundell recorded 'a Grand falling out with Bradley upon which she went out of the Hous with an intention to goe quite away but she came back againe'. The cause of this falling out had been some disagreement between Mrs Blundell and Bradley, although on what matter we remain ignorant. Bradley departed a week later.[89]

In the summer of 1707 Mary Molyneux 'went away in a Passion & stayed away all night'.[90] The same summer, Mary Brown, the Blundells' cook, 'would needs have gon away in a fret at Night though the Doors were Locked'.[91] This summer seems to have been a particularly tense one for relations between Mrs Blundell and her female staff. Catty Weedon, a nursemaid in 1712, left 'upon account of a Fawling out as had ben'.[92] Ellen Sergeant, who was cook at Crosby Hall in 1715, 'declared to some of the servants that she intended to leave her service to-morrow but she has since changed her mind'.[93]

Frequently, particularly in the case of their female servants, departure was the result of dismissal. Not always, it would seem, would servants go without offering some resistance, which led to departure being postponed. So Ellen Nelson, cook in 1706, was paid her wages 'with orders to be gon, upon account of some words that past, but she went not'.[94] Only a year later did she finally leave the Blundell's service. Similarly Margaret Jackson, cook in 1711, 'had her wages paid but with orders to be gon forthwith, but she went not'.[95] She only left eight months later.

[86] Ibid. i. 43–4, 55–6.   [87] Ibid. 136.
[88] Ibid. 145, 47.   [89] Ibid. 151, 204–5.   [90] Ibid. 147.
[91] Ibid. 148.   [92] Ibid. ii. 35.   [93] Ibid. 136.   [94] Ibid. i. 107.
[95] Ibid. 278.

It is rare for Nicholas Blundell to give the reasons for a servant's dismissal. In 1705 he gave Henry Bilsbury, groom, 'warning to leav my Service'.[96] He had worked for Blundell nearly three years. No reason was given for his dismissal. But there are exceptions. In October 1714 he wrote of how 'I intercepted a Peece of Beef as Margaret Ridgate was sending to her Mother for which I turned her out of my house for this Night, but upon her great Submission I took her the next day'. Twelve days later Blundell went to Liverpool to get a warrant 'to Apprehend' Ridgate and to search 'her mother's and her brother John's House'. When a constable came to take Ridgate before a Liverpool JP, somewhat surprisingly Blundell recorded his wife 'begd me to pardon her'. Whether or not he did so, Margaret Ridgate 'left her Service'.[97]

It was not always that misdemeanours in servants resulted in their immediate dismissal by the Blundells. In November 1708 Blundell set off to visit a neighbour, 'but hearing he was not at home I turn'd back and found Grace Pilkington endeavouring to open the Dining Roome dore with some keys she had got to get Apples to give to Ince servants that were here'.[98] Was she given a severe reprimand? We are not told but it does not appear that she was dismissed, for a month later Blundell recorded in his journal her return to Crosby Hall. 'She had been abroad for some days'.[99] Catty Howard, cook on and off from January 1712 until February 1715, was constantly in trouble. In January 1713 Blundell recorded—but without comment—'the Half plucked Goos by Catherine Howerd brought to her Sister'. Less than a fortnight later she was paid her wages and left Blundell's service. But only a little over a month later she is back as cook. In May of the same year Blundell recorded that 'Catty Howerd and Nanny Blundell should have set up in the Night with their Sweet-hearts but they were discover'd and prevented'. The only consequence was that next morning Nanny's father, John Blundell, came to the Hall and 'chaptered his Daughter for her last nights Project'.[100] In sharp contrast, in August 1724, 'before three this morning', Blundell 'disturbed two Cupple of Woosters Jane Withington, Nelly Howerd and their Sparks'. Both 'left their Service' three days later.[101] The offence of stealing wood—always a serious one in the

[96] *The Great Diurnal of Nicholas Blundell*, 86.
[97] Ibid. ii. 112–15.   [98] Ibid. i. 193.   [99] Ibid. 197.
[100] Ibid. ii. 46–7, 55, 62.   [101] Ibid. iii. 138.

eighteenth century—caused the dismissal of one servant. Blundell 'turned off Ailes Davy from working for me because she took some wood more than I gave her'.[102]

But misdemeanours were not confined to female servants. When Richard Ainsworth, ploughman, was found to have 'got hold of the key to the cellar of Crosby Hall' and 'to be making use of some of the goods stored there', he was dismissed at once. Nor did Blundell leave the matter there. A warrant was obtained to search Ainsworth's house. In July 1708, just before he was brought to the Assizes, he asked Blundell to pardon him, but 'I told him noe & advised him to make what provision he could against his Tryell'. Brought before a judge he was found guilty of robbery, fined, and burnt in the hand.[103] A less serious confrontation occurred in October 1711, when Blundell 'found Robert Tompson & Henry Kerfoot playing of Reed Pip[e]s when they should have been getting Potatoes'.[104] They may have been reprimanded but they were not dismissed. When, after many years service to the Blundell family, Walter Thelwall, steward, was discovered to have long been slightly fiddling the accounts he agreed to go, but Blundell appears to have remained outwardly friendly with him, for a few days after his dismissal he is back helping Blundell with a particular task.[105] But when, in December 1713, he disturbed 'Mary Hole who had recently been appointed as cook, and Henry Bridge in the Gatehouse Chamber about four in the morning', she was dismissed forthwith.[106] We are not told what happened to Bridge.

It is not always clear which of the Blundells was responsible for dismissing female servants. In September 1708 Blundell recorded that 'my wife gave warning to Mary Howard, the Dary-maid'.[107] She left a month later. But as, whenever servants left, Blundell had to settle the wages account with them, effective dismissal was always in his hands. When Blundell's mother sent word that she expected 'Mary Barton should be turned away ere she would

---

[102] Ibid. i. 121.
[103] Ibid. 96 n. 92, 178, 181–2. Burning in the hand was a customary punishment for theft. Usually the ball of the thumb of the left hand was burnt so that the prisoner would be known in future. In court prisoners were often requested to show their hand in order to ascertain whether it had been burnt for an earlier offence.
[104] Ibid. i. 304.   [105] *Blundell's Diary and Letterbook*, 113–14.
[106] *The Great Diurnal of Nicholas Blundell*, ii. 82.   [107] Ibid. i. 186.

come', it took Nicholas from April until October to decide to tell his wife his 'intention to part with Mary Barton'.[108] His wife was expecting her first child and he wanted to avoid upsetting her. Subsequently Mary Barton was given three months' notice. Yet the disagreement between his wife and his mother and aunt over Mary Barton did not prevent him writing her a warm letter of recommendation which gained her another position. The same year Blundell gave one of his men servants, Thelwall, 'warning to leave my service'.[109] Another time Blundell told Mary Scot, chambermaid and nursemaid in 1710, that his wife 'designed to part with her'.[110] She left three months later. On one occasion Blundell gave the loyal and long-serving John Bannister 'a Quarter's warning but', his journal recorded, 'since we have peeced againe so he dose not leave my service'.[111] Very unusually Blundell, on 30 September 1715, 'gave warning to four' of his men servants that he was going to dismiss them.[112] Equally exceptional was the occasion when three of his servants, Robert Weedow, Thomas Marrow, and Edward Blundell came to beg their master's pardon 'for a Misdemaynor'. They were made to pay over to him some money 'which was this day distributed to the Poore'.[113]

Some of his male servants were provided with livery, although it is not always clear who bore the responsibility for paying for it. That it was a very expensive charge on employers there can be no doubt. One year liveries cost Blundell £13. 6s. 2d.[114] So Blundell records the making of a livery suit for Henry and Robert Weedow and Henry Kerfoot, but only in the latter case is it made clear that Kerfoot had to pay part of the cost in instalments. He seems to have paid £1. 13s. 8d. in all. Robert Thompson probably paid only 15s. towards his.[115]

That the wages of Blundell's servants were in general very low cannot be denied. Much was expected of them. They were asked to turn their hands to a great variety of tasks and, at times, to accept considerable responsibility. Their lives were disciplined and if they fell out with their employers there was a strong prospect of dismissal. Yet within the household they were treated as members—if not equal members—of the family, and they seem to

---

[108] *The Great Diurnal of Nicholas Blundell*, 55, 69.
[109] Ibid. 195.   [110] Ibid. 271.   [111] Ibid. ii. 39.   [112] Ibid. 148.
[113] Ibid. iii. 209.   [114] *Blundell's Diary and Letterbook*, 103.
[115] Ibid. 103–4.

have enjoyed a certain independence not available to all domestic servants. There was always free lodging for a night or a few days for their friends and family when they came to visit. And when Nicholas decided to take a holiday very often his servants also benefited. Nicholas seems to have been a keen skater and when he went skating his servants frequently accompanied him. So on 3 January 1709 he recorded 'Skating again with servants'.[116] When earlier Nicholas and Mr Aldred went sledging to Formos-poole (Nicholas's spelling of Formes Pool, a favourite place for sledging on the Little Crosby estate) 'the Maids went with us'.[117] In 1708 when *The Soldiers Fortune* was staged locally, 'most of my Servants went'.[118] With his children the servants 'went to Formby Fair'.[119] Nicholas's Disbursement Book in 1707 records '25 July Fairing for the Servants... 1s. 2d'.[120] When the miller, a pipe-player, came to play, the whole household joined in the dancing. Nor do the servants seem to have been so confined as in some households. They entertained the servants of neighbouring households and in their turn were entertained by them. In September 1706 'most of the Servants went to be Mery at Great Crosby', in January 1708 'most of my Servants if not all went to Ince to the Merry Night'.[121] When Mrs Blundell went to Liverpool she would often take a servant with her. On one occasion in February 1708 she and three servants walked there.

The Blundells had only two children, both girls, Mally and Fanny. Despite his disappointment at the absence of an heir Nicholas was a devoted father. The girls' upbringing was unusual and enlightened. At a young age they were given a great deal of freedom and encouraged to be independent. When still very young they were taken on visits to neighbours and when there were festivities in the neighbourhood—fairs, feasts, even balls—Nicholas often sent them with his servants. In 1711 for example Blundell recorded 'My Children & the Maids went to Formby Fair'.[122] When, aged 6, Fanny was sent to Ditton to convalesce after an illness, two servants, Betty Harrison and Catty Howard, 'went towards Ditton' to see her.[123] Mally's birthday was celebrated by the miller playing to the servants after supper. When

---

[116] *The Great Diurnal of Nicholas Blundell*, i. 198.
[117] Ibid.   [118] Ibid. 183.   [119] Ibid. 294.   [120] Ibid. 145 n. 63.
[121] Ibid. 119, 159.   [122] *Blundell's Diary and Letter Book*, 52.
[123] Ibid. 107.

Robert Tompson, the coachman, broke his thigh falling from his cart and getting run over, the two girls, apparently on their own, went to Ormskirk to see him. When in 1728 the maid to Mally and Fanny, Ailes Chantrell, went home on account of ill health, 'Fanny went to see how' she 'did of her Ague-Fits'.[124] If in many households the triangular relationship between parents, children, and servants was fraught with dangers, there is no evidence at all in this diary that anything but harmonious relations existed between servants and children.

In so far as Blundell's diary departs radically from the usual picture of servants in a large household, we need to ask how exceptional it was. In the flexibility of his household, and the absence of any rigid hierarchy among his servants or specialized function reflected in their wages, was this household unique or were there others like it? There were certainly other households where no strict hierarchy appeared to prevail and where the same flexibility of function among servants is found. There may be something in the claim that 'in many a nobleman's home . . . there is greater simplicity and economy in the household arrangements than in many a commoner's'.[125] Elizabeth Purefoy in 1741, for instance, was seeking a dairy maid 'who can manage a small dairy and clean an House'. Two years later in looking for a maid she asked that she be 'a thorough servant & capable of seeing the sending in of 5 or 10 dishes of meat upon occasion. Tho' I keep a cookmaid', she went on to add, 'she must understand that part, and she is to wash the small Linnens & clean part of the house and make some beds.' When finding it difficult to recruit a good cook who would also be prepared to 'do the dairy of 4 Cows', she was prepared to settle for 'a young healthy girl to help who can stand at the Buck Tubb [a large wash of clothes particularly of the coarser kind] & milk the Cows & serve a couple of Hogs & pluck ffowlls & help clean the house & scald the milk vessel or any other thing she may be set about'. For this work the wage was to be 40s. a year. Her job description for a footman is instructive: she wanted 'a footman to work in the garden, lay the Cloath, wait at Table' and 'go to cart . . . when hee is ordered, or do any other business, and', she added, 'was not too large sized a man that Hee

---

[124] *The Great Diurnal of Nicholas Blundell*, iii. 231.
[125] Henry Mayhew, *London Characters* (1874), 323.

may not be too great a load for an horse'.[126] There is the advertisement—apparently authentic—which read:

Wanted, for a family who have bad health, a sober steady person, in the capacity of doctor, surgeon and apothecary. He must occasionally act in the capacity of butler, and dress hair and preach a sermon every Sunday. The reason for this advertisement is that the family cannot any longer afford the expense of the physical tribe, and wish to be at a certain expense for their bodies and souls ... A good Salary will be given.[127]

John Macdonald, the footman, writing of one of the households in which he worked, described how rarely were his duties 'closely defined'. He 'was part of everything there. I marketed, kept the books, and had the keys of everything in the house. I was steward, valet, butler, housekeeper, head cook and footman'.[128] Not always was even a servant's sex a restriction on flexibility in occupation. Steele has Isaac Bickerstaff's maidservant acting as footman or body servant, when on staying late at his club, 'my *maid* came with a lantern to light me home'.[129] The more modest the household the less occupational labels seem to have meant anything. If the master took on two male servants, they were required 'to do the work of footmen, valets, gardeners, and handymen'.[130] There is some evidence that even where occupational labels were attached to servants they were in practice pretty meaningless. Henry Mayhew tells the story of Jane Bell taken on as her 'la'ship's' personal maid by Lady Belmontine. In fact she was nothing more than a general servant. 'I did all the work of the house, except what an old charwoman did for an hour or two in the morning ... I was maid, and housemaid, and cook, too, sometimes.'[131] Such evidence suggests we should view with immense caution any attempt to characterize servant-owning households—whether large or small, rich or poor—as necessarily tightly structured hierarchies in which a servant's occupational label defined exactly the role he or she was to fill.

---

[126] *The Purefoy Letters*, ed. G. Eland, 2 vols. (1931), i. 136, 139, 142, 145.
[127] As quoted in Violet A. Simpson, 'Servants and Service in Eighteenth-Century Town and Country', *Cornhill Magazine*, 14 (1903), 398–409 at p. 406.
[128] *Memoirs of an Eighteenth-Century Footman, John Macdonald*, ed. John Beresford (1927), 71.
[129] As quoted in Phyllis Cunnington, *Costume of Household Servants* (1974), 12, from the *Tatler*, no. 132.
[130] E. S. Turner, *What the Butler Saw: 250 Years of the Servant Problem* (1962), 18.
[131] *London Characters*, 308–9.

9

Serving the Clergy

Teach me, my God and King,
In all things Thee to see,
And what I do in any thing
To do it as for Thee.

. . . . . .

A servant with this clause
Makes drudgery divine;
Who sweeps a room as for Thy laws
Makes that and th' action fine.

George Herbert

IN 1775 Trusler estimated that 'a Gentleman, with a wife, four children and five servants, may, residing in the country with a few Acres of Land, live as well as, and make an Appearance in Life equal to, a Man of 1,000l. a year, and yet not expend 400l.'[1] As Woodforde's biographer writes, 'it was possible to maintain open house, keep two maidservants, two men-servants and a boy . . . on a little over £400 a year'.[2] My intention when originally framing this chapter was to illustrate the life of servants in households of a moderate but comfortable income. The three households chosen were not selected because they were those of clerics but because they were households of about the same size and represented approximately similar levels of income. They were also chosen because in their diaries and letters these three clerics were particularly informative about their servants.

Is it coincidence that many diaries of country clerics contain so much information about their servants? Servants seem to loom particularly large in their households. On the basis of a census sample it has been estimated that clerical families 'possibly living

---

[1] John Trusler, *The Way to be Rich and Respectable* (1775), subtitle.
[2] *The Diary of a Country Parson: The Reverend James Woodforde, 1758–1813*, ed. John Beresford, 5 vols. 1924–31, vol. ii, p. ix.

up to the expectation that they should help to train young girls, were well served with three times the average percentage of four or more servants; half the upper middle-class clergy ran this full complement'.[3] Edward Higgs confirms this 'high servant-employing ratio amongst the clergy of the established church'.[4] When parents of a country girl decided she should be sent to service they often consulted the local clergy and, not infrequently, owed their daughter's first places to them. Such employment seems to have been a good recommendation: when Elizabeth Purefoy is corresponding over her need for a maidservant she mentions that she would welcome 'one as has lived in a Clergyman's House'. Later, she writes to a Priscilla Higgins that 'the Revd. Mr William Ffletcher was here on Monday last and informs mee that your mother desired him to get you a Place in a Gentleman's family'. Or again, in 1753, she writes anxiously to Mrs Mary Harris about a girl 'who had lived with a Clergyman as head maid' and who, she thinks, would suit her well. When her son, Henry Purefoy, is endeavouring to get a tenant's son a place he writes in recommendation of him that he 'has lived with a clergyman three years'.[5] In 1847 Henry and Augustus Mayhew published the *Greatest Plague of Life* which described 'the adventures of a lady in search of a good servant'. Her idea of what constituted a 'good servant' was made clear. Apart from stipulating that she must be 'a devout Christian' she required 'a ten years excellent character from her last situation, which had been with a clergyman in the country'.[6]

It must sometimes have been convenient when servants left such clerical households for the latter to be able to fill the gap so easily and take on the local girls anxious to present themselves. It was usual for the clergy to function in local charities for the poor, on poor house committees, and at orphanages. They were often JPs. They certainly played a prominent role in the administration of charity and Sunday schools. In Biley, Gloucestershire, 'the Minister here, with great Application, has found Means to erect 8

---

[3] Leonore Davidoff and Catherine Hall, *Family Fortunes: Men and Women of the English Middle Classes, 1780–1850* (1987), 388.
[4] 'Domestic Servants and Households in Victorian England', *Social History* 8/2 (May 1983), 201–10 at p. 207.
[5] *The Purefoy Letters 1735–53* ed. G. Eland, 2 vols. (1931), i. 144–5, 153, 154, 156.
[6] As quoted from J. F. C. Harrison, *The Early Victorians 1832–51* (1971), 111.

Schools in this Parish, wherein are taught about 130 children'. At Wem in Shropshire, '40 children are taught to read and work here at the Charge of a Reverend Divine'.[7] There are numerous other examples of the involvement of clerics or their families in charity school organization. The Blue Coat School at Bishops Auckland was under the care of the son of a clergyman. Another school for girls was under the direction of a clergyman's widow.[8] Clerical families, it has been suggested 'took the training and placing of young servants as part of their philanthropic duty'.[9] Frequently they must have been made aware of the need to find places for pauper and orphan girls and boys as domestic servants. Not infrequently they recommended them to households and, if they themselves were in need, they took them into their own households.[10] 'Care is taken to place these Charity-Children', wrote Hendley in 1725, 'with *Church-Men*, where they may preserve in their *Prenticeships* those sound Principles they learn's at *School*.'[11] In Myddle when baptizing the eleventh child of one Parks, Mr Kinaston, the rector, 'merrily' remarked 'Now one child is due to the parson'. Apparently Parks agreed and 'Mr Kinaston chose a girl, that was about the middle age among the rest, and brought her up at his own house, and she became his servant'. When she married after several years he gave to her husband 'thirty, some say sixty pounds portion'.[12] In the early nineteenth century the daughter of the Revd William Marsh, Catherine, 'befriended a young Irish girl who was placed in a training school for servants for four years and then joined the Marsh rectory as under housemaid'.[13] When the Revd John Skinner was faced with a serious lack of Sunday school helpers he persuaded his boy George 'to assist' with the bribe of an extra 6d. a time over and above his wages.[14] One of our three clerics, James Woodforde, in 1778 refers

[7] *Methods used for Erecting Charity Schools*, 16th edn. (1717), 27, 29.
[8] Thomas Bernard, *The Barrington School* (1812), 20–1.
[9] Davidoff and Hall, *Family Fortunes*, 393.
[10] See e.g. Flora Thompson, *Lark Rise to Candleford* (1977), 162, on how mothers consulted the daughters of the manse about placing their daughters; and Frank Victor Dawes, *Not in Front of the Servants* (1984), 54–61 on relations between the clergy and domestic servants.
[11] W. Hendley, *A Defence of the Charity-Schools* (1725), 34–5.
[12] Richard Gough, *The History of Myddle (1701–1706)* (1979), 16.
[13] Davidoff and Hall, *Family Fortunes*, 393.
[14] *The Journal of a Somerset Rector 1803–34*, ed. Howard and Peter Coombs (1930), 337.

to 'my servant Boy whom I take out of Charity'.[15] It would seem that there was something unique about clerical households in their ease of access to servants, if nothing more.

I want to look mainly at two diaries and a collection of letters of clergymen written in the second half of the eighteenth century, which describe households in which the complement of servants is between three and five. They could be described as occupying a middling position within the clergy, having 'adequate provision to maintain their position in their parishes and to mix on terms of equality with their wealthier neighbours'.[16] In each case the employing cleric was known as a kindly man who treated his servants well. Two of the three were bachelors. The diary of the Revd George Woodward of East Hendred covers the period 1753–61.[17] By his own account he received a stipend of £210, but this almost certainly excluded additional fees from marriages, baptisms, etc., as well as his prebend at Salisbury. As his biographer emphasizes, his stipend alone made him a moderately rich man. Apart from the stipend Woodward also had about fifty acres of glebe land. While he let the larger part to a tenant he retained enough to supply his household, which consisted of his wife, their two children, and three servants—one male and two female.[18]

The diary of the Reverend James Woodforde, Parson of Weston Longville, near Norwich, covers a much longer period of time from 1758 to 1813. Woodforde was probably as wealthy as Woodward. Although reputed to have had an income of only £30 a year—that is one-seventh of Woodward's income—his real income has been estimated at about £300 per annum.[19] Woodforde never married, although for much of the diary his sister, Nancy, lived with him. But he kept more servants than Woodward, his household consisting of himself, his sister, two servant-maids, two male servants, and a boy.

The third diary, covering the years 1765–7, is that of the Revd William Cole of Blecheley.[20] We do not know his income, but he

---

[15] *The Diary of a Country Parson*, i. 234.
[16] *The Diary of Benjamin Rogers, Rector of Carlton 1720–71*, ed. C. D. Linnell, Bedfordshire Historical Record Society, xxx (1950), p. xiii.
[17] *A Parson in the Vale of White Horse: George Woodward's Letters from East Hendred 1753–61*, ed. Donald Gibson (1982).   [18] Ibid. 20–1, 23, 72.
[19] J. Jean Hecht, *The Domestic Servant in Eighteenth-Century England* (1956), 7.
[20] *The Blecheley Diary of the Rev. William Cole 1765–7*, ed. Francis Griffin Stokes (1931).

was said to have inherited 'a handsome estate from his father'.[21] Also unmarried, he kept a cook, a gardener whose wife also helped out in the house, a man servant, and a boy. So the households of Woodforde and Cole were very similar.

In all three households kin relations play a large part. In Cole's household, his main man servant, 'my Tom', was the son of William Wood. When Wood's shop went bankrupt Cole gave him the post of parish clerk and, when the diary opens, he had, it seems, for six years been in the habit of sleeping in the rectory.[22] Tom's younger brother Jem was also in service to Cole—doing all the jobs of a boy servant. When Woodward was in need of a new under-servant, it was the niece of Sarah, his maid of long standing, who came to fill the position. A sister of Joe Shepherd, his gardener, was recommended to Woodward's friend at Ditton, George London, with—at least initially—not entirely satisfactory results.[23] Woodforde, when in need of a maidservant, employed the daughter of the old woman, Elizabeth Crick, or Cricks, who looked after him at Babcary Parsonage.[24]

If five was the full complement of their living-in servants, all of them employed in addition a great deal of part-time labour. Sometimes these were kin of their full-time servants. So in Cole's household there were two brothers, Tom and Jem Wood, employed full time. But when Cole had ploughing to be done on his land he took on their elder brother, Will Wood junior, to do the job. And he employed Tom's sister, Molly, to fill in when his cook was away for a month, on occasion to help out in the kitchen, and to assist with the harvest. His gardener's wife, Sarah Tansley, frequently helped out in the kitchen, filling in when his cook was away, 'picking & sorting feathers', and helping with the washing.[25]

But apart from kin relations of existing servants there appear to have been a number of local people on whom Cole could call for special services as the occasion arose. Will Travel, 'an old servant', and William Chenels came in to help with the mowing. Hannah Holdom arrived to survey his linen, taking what needed mending away, and making him new shirts. When he moved house Mary

---

[21] *Dictionary of National Biography.*
[22] *The Blecheley Diary of the Rev. William Cole,* 6, 30, 60.
[23] *A Parson in the Vale of White Horse,* 77.
[24] *The Diary of a Country Parson,* i. 36.
[25] *The Blecheley Diary of the Rev. William Cole,* 24, 58, 77, 78, 96, 143, 207, 210, 260.

Phillips came to help with the packing. She and Catherine Gifford helped with the washing and ironing.[26] There seems to have been no problem in recruiting such part-time labour whenever it was required. When Woodward's children had smallpox, and his wife and servants were sent away from the house for fear of infection, it was the local blacksmith's wife and Woodward's clerk's wife who came to nurse the children and help in the house.[27] Woodforde employed gardeners—one Spraggs, Edward Gooch, and 'John Piper of Mattishall, Gardner and his Man', from time to time. Mary Norton and Elizabeth Mace were employed by him to weed in the garden, Thomas Cushing and Nathaniel Heavers for hedging and ditching. When both his maids were indisposed, Widow Greaves came in 'to assist' them. 'My two old washerwomen, Mary Heavers and Nan Gooch' came in regularly to wash or help with the washing. At other times Anne Downing and Anne Richmond came in to wash.[28] In William Cole's household local labourers were recruited to help Tom with the harvest—sometimes as many as twelve or thirteen. At the supper he gave in July 1766 'to all my Haymakers & Helpers' at the end of the harvest there were thirty sat down in the kitchen.[29] This extensive use of local labour for odd jobs about the house and garden was far from restricted to these three clerics. John Skinner, the Somerset rector, 'not knowing where to hear of a servant... engaged old widow King who lived at Claverton, to come over for a time till I could suit myself'.[30]

It is worth pausing and considering the extensive use made of part-time local labour in rural households all over the country. Little has been written on this labour. In an illuminating article Jessica Gerard talks of it as 'an essential component of the country-house community, an indispensable support of its way of life'.[31] Her study is on the country house in Victorian times, but

[26] Ibid. 68, 278, 288, 295–300, 303.
[27] *A Parson in the Vale of White Horse*, 103.
[28] *The Diary of a Country Parson*, ii. 24, 78, 154, 195, 336, iii. 299, 311, v. 60, 198.
[29] *The Blecheley Diary of the Rev. William Cole*, 70, 75.
[30] *Journal of a Somerset Rector 1803–34*, 14. Apart from clerical households there are many examples of households such as that of Mary Hardy, the Norfolk diarist and the wife of a farmer and brewer, which employed such casual local labour extensively. See *Mary Hardy's Diary*, with an introduction by B. Cozens-Hardy, Norfolk Record Society, xxxvii (1968).
[31] 'Invisible Servants: The Country House and the Local Community', *Bulletin of the Institute of Historical Research*, 57/136 (Nov. 1984), 178–88 at p. 178.

the evidence suggests the phenomenon considerably predates the nineteenth century. It existed throughout the eighteenth century—but perhaps more particularly in the second half. Where there was little or no local industry and only seasonal employment in agriculture, many villages must have had an abundance of unemployed or semi-employed labour, more particularly female (Gerard has noted the wide use made of widows and 'middle-aged or older' women), on which the country house could draw. But it was not just the grand establishment that employed such labour. In quite modest establishments such labour was extensively used when and as the need arose, whether from the 'events of family life, guests and social activities, seasonal and intermittent household tasks and staff absences'.[32] Sometimes village labour was sought for nothing more than helping out with the washing, coping with the mending, or doing a bit of charring—work involving at most a day or two's labour. But in larger households, Gerard suggests, some such labour was almost continuously employed right through the year.

One thing that distinguished Woodward's servants is that he had employed two of them—Joe Shepherd and Sarah—for a considerable time. When the two decided to marry in 1760 they had worked fourteen years in the Woodward household and Sarah was already 40. Woodward was lucky in having two such good devoted servants, and when they told him they intended to marry but would like to keep their places he readily agreed. 'They are both such good servants', Woodward wrote in his diary, 'and have such a regard for the interest of us and our family, that we cannot help being willing to comply with their requests'. He was confident they were irreplaceable and that there could not be 'two people of more upright principles in all respects'. But Woodward is careful to add that if 'any inconveniences are likely to arise from their having children, they have agreed to part'. In fact despite Sarah's age Woodward was called on to baptize three of her children. When the first was born the Woodwards were agreeably surprised that they suffered no inconvenience. But as Sarah had a woman who acted as nurse and who also 'has done what she otherwise would have done herself' there was no problem. In addition the child, they had to admit, was 'the quietest thing that

[32] 'Invisible Servants: The Country House and the Local Community', *Bulletin of the Institute of Historical Research*, 57/136 (Nov. 1984), 178–88 at p. 180.

ever was, for it is very seldom we hear it cry'.[33] The retaining of two such good servants in his employ over a long period perhaps accounts, at least in part, for the absence of many references to servants in his diary. On the whole he seems to have had fewer problems with them than other employers—but then the diary only covers nine years.

What exactly did their servants do? Both Cole and Woodforde employed boy servants, or as they were sometimes called 'livery boys' or 'husbandry boys'. Some appear to have been paid no wages at all. Sir Richard Newdigate in 1684 had employed two boy servants aged 17 and 14. While they were provided with food and lodging and kept in clothes, they were paid nothing.[34] Trusler estimated the cost of keeping a boy servant in 1775 as £5 per annum, adding 'no wages, but cloathed from his master's old wardrobe'.[35] Although miserably paid—if paid anything—they seem to have had a very varied set of tasks and responsibilities given to them. Trusler described their role as 'to drive the plough occasionally, or ride and drive when the carriage is used as a post-chaise, or to send out messages'.[36] In 1768 Woodforde took on a new boy, George Hutchins, almost certainly the son of his gardener. His father negotiated the conditions of his employment with Woodforde. His wages were to be £2. 2s. 0d. a year. During his stay in Woodforde's employ he was to be provided with 'a coat, a waistcoat and hat etc.', but while Woodforde would buy 'shoes, breeches and shirts' for him, the sum expended would be deducted from his wages.[37] Such a deduction in wages to meet in part or whole the cost of clothes and livery seems to have been a normal practice. (When Sir Richard Newdigate paid his servant William Etherington £4 as his wages, he recorded in his diary 'next Time £2. 15s., because of livery'.[38]) In 1768 Woodforde spent time teaching George Hutchins 'to wait at table'. Wherever Woodforde went his boy tended to go with him—to Oxford to elect a new Warden at New College, and to Bath. A later boy, William Coleman, went with him to stay in New College to help him carry his portmanteau. When Woodforde went to Norfolk his

[33] *A Parson in the Vale of White Horse*, 150.
[34] Eileen Gooder, *The Squire of Arbury, Sir Richard Newdigate (1644–1710)* (1990), 38.
[35] *The Way to be Rich and Respectable*, 19.   [36] Ibid.
[37] *The Diary of a Country Parson*, i. 74.   [38] Gooder, *The Squire of Arbury*, 39.

boy accompanied him; with Woodforde's man servant the boy went to Norwich to collect wine, dishes, and plates. They only returned in the evening—both the worse for liquor.[39] Jem Wood, William Cole's boy, took messages, conveyed invitations to dine, delivered gifts of cucumbers and fruit to friends and neighbours—and on one occasion was sent 'to Newport with a Spare rib to Mr Pomfret'. Such duties provided wonderful excuses for delaying returning to the house. In August 1766 Jem was 'cudgelled' by Cole for 'staying so long on an Errand to Newton Longueville'. Clearly he failed to learn his lesson for in November Woodforde had his Father come who 'heartily threshed' him 'for staying too long on Errands'.[40]

Most boys stayed only a short time until, like Woodforde's Jack Wharton, who had been 'a very good lad', they got 'too old for their place'. In October 1784 Jack told his master 'he is advised to get another Place being too old for a Skip-Jack any longer. He wants to be a Plow Boy to some Farmer to learn the farming Business.' Woodforde encouraged him in his plans. He was 'very right to try and better himself'.[41] Some, like Will Coleman, moved into other roles within the household. Thomas Hankinson, one of Sir Richard Newdigate's boy servants, became 'under gardner and pond keeper' but his master still kept him in 'cloathes, shoes, stockings, leather breaches, boots, coat, suit of cloathes, two aprons' and a hat.[42] Boy servants were recruited at about 13 or so—the age at which Jack Wharton's successor, John Secker, was employed in 1785. He was not previously known to Woodforde, and perhaps for this reason, after negotiating with his father, the boy was only paid £1. 1s. 0d. He too was to be given 'a Coat and Waistcoat and Hat when wanted' and in addition Woodforde agreed 'to allow him something for being Washed out and mended'. 'His friends' were left to provide him with shoes and stockings.[43] In 1787, when Secker moved on, a local woman, Mrs Crossley, came to see Woodforde with her son, Charles, 'desiring me to take him in place of my present Boy'. He too, was paid only £1. 1s. 0d. a year. He stayed nearly eighteen months before being replaced by one John Dalliday, who came for a wage of £2. 2s. 0d.

[39] *The Diary of a Country Parson*, i. 78, 83, 132, 176, 202.
[40] *The Blecheley Diary of the Rev. William Cole*, 14, 70, 95, 115, 154.
[41] *The Diary of a Country Parson*, ii. 155.
[42] Gooder, *The Squire of Arbury*, 39.   [43] *The Diary of a Country Parson*, ii. 172.

a year and moved on after two years' service with Woodforde. Only one boy servant seems to have been a total failure from the beginning. He was John Brand who, taken on in June 1796, must have been given notice almost immediately as 'being the most saucy swearing lad that ever we had' and what was worse 'profligate'.[44] There was also Henry Daines, who in October 1800 was sacked by Woodforde after serving nine months. He was 'not behaving in a manner that I expected from him, as he could not be trusted to do anything if not overlooked, and also a very saucy, foul-mouthed lad'.[45]

Woodward employed only one male servant, the gardener Joe Shepherd. He was 'employed largely out of doors, sometimes as a porter/companion on his master's travels', and on occasion indoors when the need arose.[46] The relationship between Woodward and Joe was close, and in September 1754 Woodward writes of how on a journey home from a visit to the Bishop of Salisbury 'Joe was entertaining me (as he often does when we travel alone together) with matters of intelligence', that he had picked up in the servants' hall—in this instance the prospects of a canonry.[47] In addition Woodward employed Sarah, Joe's wife, as his head maid, and one under-maid. Sarah seems to have been cook and housekeeper rolled into one. What work exactly the under-maid performed we are not told, but we can guess it was mainly cleaning and helping out in the kitchen.

Both Cole and Woodforde employed two male servants. Like Woodward, Cole kept a full-time gardener. Thomas Tansley, 'my gardener', who went 'a Fagotting' 'fetches a load of Fire wood from ... Woburn Abbey', brewed, beat 'down apples' to make cider for Cole, spread dung, laid gravel paths, played a leading role in both harvest and hay-making, dug potatoes, lopped trees. He married another domestic servant, Sarah Tarrey, cook to one of Cole's neighbours.[48] Cole's other male servant was Tom Wood—'my Tom'—who when the diary opens has already been six years with Cole. He acted as coachman, and was responsible for keeping both 'Chaise & Harness' clean and in good repair. As coachman he wore a livery. He also helped in hay-making and

---

[44] Ibid. ii. 303, iii. 55, 78, iv. 285.
[45] Ibid. v. 277.   [46] *A Parson in the Vale of White Horse*, 23.
[47] Ibid. 61.
[48] *The Blecheley Diary of the Rev. William Cole*, 25, 41–2, 61, 114, 142.

harvest. Cole sent him to buy grain for the pigs. At times he went fishing and shooting (on 23 August 1766 he brought home a brace of partridge).[49] His main female servant, Sarah Turvey, was both cook and housekeeper.

Ben Leggatt, one of Woodforde's two male servants, was hired on 30 September 1776. He was a skilled farm servant and had considerable responsibility in the household. He was sent to buy horses, to sell Woodforde's 'brinded [sic] Cow and Calf', he went to Norwich to sell barley, oats, or a 'Wagon Load of Wheat and Straw', to fetch letters, and sometimes just to get the newspapers. He regularly had the responsibility of going round the parish informing the farmers of Woodforde's Tithe Audit—an occasion it would seem for much drinking, for he returned from one such tour 'very full indeed of liquor'. Whether or not Woodforde reprimanded him we do not know, but when the next tithe audit came round Ben returned 'Very well'. 'He never returned so sober before', added Woodforde, 'on any former occasion of the same kind.' The reformation, however, does not last and in 1800 Ben returned from his tour of the parish 'quite drunk'.[50] Sometimes he ploughed. Often he was accompanied on his journeys by the other male servant, his subordinate, as assistant. Being less directly concerned with Woodforde's farm it was this under-servant who accompanied his master on his frequent journeys. Sometimes the two servants worked together shearing wheat and mowing oats.

Unfortunately neither Woodward nor Cole reveal what they paid their servants, but Woodforde includes considerable detail of the wages of all his servants. By far his most expensive servant was Ben Leggatt. When he was appointed in 1776, his father came with him to negotiate a wage. It was fixed at £10. per annum, but by 1782 it had risen to ten guineas. The wage of his male under-servant varied between £3 and £4. 4s. 0d. When Luke Barnard was taken on at £3 per annum, 'a coat and waistcoat and hat besides victuals and drink, washing and lodging' he protested it was too little and that unless Woodforde could increase the wage he would leave. But until his time was up Woodforde agreed to pay

---

[49] *The Blecheley Diary of the Rev. William Cole*, pp. liii, 30, 43, 70, 78, 93, 94, 97, 109, 114.

[50] *The Diary of a Country Parson*, i. 58, 179, 222, ii. 114, 214, 244, 359, iii. 10, 390, iv. 81, v. 285.

him £5 per annum but without any new clothes. The boys rarely receive more than £2. 2s. 0d., which seems to have been the standard wage, and, as we have seen, sometimes only half that sum.[51] Woodforde's main female servant, his 'Head Maid', was a cook/housekeeper. In 1774 he was paying Elizabeth Crick three guineas. There was Molly Salmon, first heard of in November 1776 when she was dismissed by Woodforde, who received an annual wage of £5. 5s. 0d. Sukey Boxly her successor, who left in 1778, was paid £4 a year. When Woodforde took on Elizabeth Claxton in 1778 she was about 40 years of age and she was paid £5. 15s. 6d. But Woodforde made it clear that 'out of that she is to find herself in tea and sugar'. When in Michaelmas 1784 Betty left to be married, her successor, Sally Barber was given £5. 5s. 0d. per annum 'but no Tea at all'. Sally Barber thought the wage too low but finally agreed to it.[52] It seems probable that Woodforde only employed an under-maid from 1778. Nanny Lillistone started in October of that year at £2. 0s. 0d. a year plus 10s. for tea, but by the following January she had left. The annual wage paid to Lizzy Greaves in January 1782 was £2. 0s. 6d. And this included something for tea. By 1784 she was receiving £2. 12s. 6d.[53]

How were their servants recruited? We have seen that when Woodward's friend, George London, was in need of a maidservant, Woodward consulted his own servants. He recommended Molly, Joe Shepherd's sister, despite the fact he described her as having 'a bad mouth', and she was dispatched to London.[54] As we have observed in Nicholas Blundell's household, when it was in need of a servant no qualms were felt at pinching one's neighbour's. In December 1766, William Cole records, 'Mr Batty, Lace Buyer of Newport Pagnel came to enquire after my Cook'. Cole generously told him that 'she was much at his service', adding 'though I had not provided myself' and suggested he speak to her. In September 1767, William Cole reached home to find 'Mr and Mrs Dicey at' his house. 'They hired my maid to go to Walton at Michaelmas.'[55] Sometimes servants already in a place, hearing a more attractive one was vacant, would take the initiative and approach the master or mistress. So in August 1784, Woodforde

[51] Ibid. i. 61, 68, 189, ii. 55, 172.
[52] Ibid. i. 236–7, ii. 147, 150.   [53] Ibid. ii. 55, 114.
[54] *A Parson in the Vale of White Horse*, 40, 137, 265.
[55] *The Blecheley Diary of the Rev. William Cole*, 137, 265.

tells us, 'one Sally Barber (Servant Maid at present to Mr Hewitt of Mattishall) came here to offer as a Servant in Betty's place who is going to be married at Michaelmas'. Another time a 'Molly Perchman' approached Woodforde 'to offer herself as a Servant', but Woodforde decided not to take her as 'she did not chuse to wash Dishes'. When in November 1784 another 'servant maid came to offer her Service here, who lately lived at Mr Eatons at Elsing and but a very little time indeed only a Quarter of a Year', Woodforde was out. His sister Nancy had forgotten her name but her account of the girl decided Woodforde against taking her 'she being rather high and her late wages 8 Pounds per Annum'. Within two days of Will Coleman deciding to leave Woodforde's employ, '2 young Men offer themselves' in his place. But, Woodforde records, 'neither would do as they never waited at Table in their lives'.[56]

Often servants were recruited locally and their parents came to negotiate terms. So 'Mr Legate and his son Benjamin called on' Woodforde, 'and talked about my taking his son at old Michaelmas as a servant'. Woodforde agreed and they bargained about wages. The local squire's wife, Mrs Custance, in December 1782, came to consult Woodforde about a servant-maid. He recommended his own servant 'Lizey's sister Sukey', and Mrs Custance apparently 'seemed to approve of her by recommendation'.[57]

Why did servants leave the employ of these clerics other than because they had been dismissed? In the case of boy servants it was because they got too old for the job. By the time they were in their early teens they started looking out for a better paid and more responsible adult servant's position. Often the reason for leaving a place was for higher wages. When in 1755 Woodward's cook left she did so 'only for another place where she has more wages' adding 'this being a liberty that my wife had given her, whenever she could meet with one to her liking'.[58] It is an interesting use of the word 'liberty'. When Lizzy Greaves left Woodforde's service in July 1784, she did so with Woodforde's encouragement. Presumably she was attracted either by higher wages or the experience a new job offered. Woodforde had rec-

[56] *The Diary of a Country Parson*, ii. 150, 158, 159, 184.
[57] Ibid. i. 189, ii. 49.   [58] *A Parson in the Vale of White Horse*, 77.

ommended her to the neighbours at Weston House.[59] Sometimes servants were lured to the metropolis. Tom Walls, a young local man known to Cole and who consulted him about becoming a servant, was 'determined to go to London for a Place'.[60] Sometimes, as in the case of Cole's main female servant, Sarah Turvey, they left to get married. Woodforde's 'head maid Elizabeth Claxton' suddenly one day 'after tea [gave notice] that she should go at Michaelmas next'. Woodforde explained that she gave no reason for leaving. He thought the notice was short. But all was revealed the day after she left her service, when Woodforde married her to Charles Cary.[61]

Apart from complaints about low wages we hear little of the reasons for servants deciding they must leave a place. We do, however, learn a great deal about what irritated employers in their servants. According to these three clerics drunkenness was a perennial problem. When drunk, servants tended to talk too much, to answer back and be 'saucy'. References such as that in Cole's diary for 17 April 1766—'Will Wood so drunk unable to carry out his duties'—abound. In the course of the harvesting of July 1766 Tansley was drunk and Cole notes he 'quarrelled with his Companions all Day long'. Again in September of the same year Cole records 'Tansley drunk all the Day', and again later in the same month 'Tansley drunk'. A year later he records: 'my Gardiner Tho: Tansley, as usual, very drunk, & in the Evening went to help Will Wood to unload a Load of Beans, & fell off from the Top.'[62] One of Woodforde's men servants, Luke Barnard, is described as 'indolent and too fond of Cyder'. In May 1778 his servant Will 'came home rather intoxicated and was exceedingly impudent and saucy towards me'. In October 1780 Will once more 'came home drunk . . . and he and my head Maid had words and got to fighting'. Again 'Will behaved very saucy and impudent and very bold in his talk' to Woodforde. Another time in November 1782 Will dined with the servants at the Squire's house. They 'made him too welcome by making him rather merry which made him very saucy after he got home'.[63]

[59] *The Diary of a Country Parson*, ii. 142.
[60] *The Blecheley Diary of the Rev. William Cole*, 52, 291.
[61] *The Diary of a Country Parson*, ii. 147, 156.
[62] *The Blecheley Diary of the Rev. William Cole*, 42, 68, 112, 124, 266.
[63] *The Diary of a Country Parson*, i. 68, 225, ii. 45.

A great source of complaint against servants was their returning late from a night out, or from delivering a message. When in April 1777 Woodforde sent his two servants Will and Ben to Norwich for 'some wine from Mr. Priest and some dishes and plates etc. from Mr. Beloc's' they only returned at seven in the evening. 'They might have come home much sooner I think' records Woodforde, adding significantly that they 'were both rather in liquor, and as for Will, he behaved very surly.' When in May 1784 Will, with most of Woodforde's other servants, went to a Smock Race, all but Will returned 'in good time'. Woodforde sat up waiting till 11 o'clock for Will to return. He then went to bed but later was woken by Will coming and making 'a noise under my window'. Only Nancy's intervention saved Will this time from dismissal. But it was not for long, as in April 1785 he once again stayed 'out all Evening till just 11 o'clock—came home in Liquor behaved very impudently to me indeed'. Woodforde 'was determined never more to bear with such behaviour' and told him he must go next morning. This time he did go, but not without Woodforde giving him a character and, although he got another place, within ten days he was back again, apologizing for his past behaviour, and asking Woodforde to employ him. Woodforde took him on as a gardener with a shilling a day and board for two days a week. But he had to find lodging somewhere other than at Woodforde's. It was not only male servants who annoyed employers by staying out too late. In May 1785 Woodforde became 'very angry with my Maid Molly this Night for staying out after 11 o'clock, just as I was going to bed'.[64] The point being that Woodforde had to go down and let them in when they returned.

Another source of annoyance to employers was the way servants entertained friends and relations in the kitchen, and often overnight. Even the otherwise kindly and charitable William Cole in December 1766 was cross when he found 'no less than 8 people round my kitchin fire. I told Tom to send them away before they got their supper.' Earlier the same year he had not been pleased to find his 'gardener's brother, all the afternoon & Evening in the kitchen with my Cook, whom he courts'.[65] Woodforde was only

[64] *The Diary of a Country Parson*, i. 202, ii. 137, 183, 186–7, 189.
[65] *The Blecheley Diary of the Rev. William Cole*, 3, 163.

told of his maidservant Sukey going out one afternoon at 10 o'clock the same evening after she had returned with her sister, who then 'laid at my house'. As he commented: 'I think it is taking too great liberties with me to bring home a stranger to sleep here. I do not like it at all.' Woodforde 'did not speak one word to her, as she came unasked'. Another time in September 1785 when he recorded his 'Maids Father (Dade) dined here today', he comments: 'he makes rather too free and comes too often to see his daughter.' When in March of the following year he came again Woodforde went 'out into the Kitchen and told him that he had better have his Daughter home, as I did not like for him to make too free here'.[66] Betty Dade was given notice to leave the next Lady Day on her father's account.

These three clerics showed a liberal and kindly attitude towards their servants. It was not one shared by all employers or, it must be said, by all other clerical employers of servants. In William Cole's diary we meet Mrs Goodwin, the wife of a neighbouring cleric, who with Mrs Holt frequently dropped in for coffee and a chat. In January 1766 they complained of 'Mr. G's ill Humours at Home, except with the Maid, who was going away with child'. In October of the following year they told Cole of 'Mr Goodwin's offering the Maid, soon after she came to them, in November last, to lie with her'. The maid, when further harassed by Goodwin, had given him 'a slap in the Face & made it black for some Time'. Or there was Dr Pettingal, Prebendary of Lincoln, admittedly heartily disliked by Cole, who 'on calling his Maid, & her not coming so soon as he expected, went out & beat her very severely'. Not altogether surprisingly Mr Goodwin excused Pettingal on the grounds that the maid 'was a very bad one'.[67] The Revd Joseph Price of Brabourne records that he was told the Wiltshire clergy always asked a prospective servant 'if he can write a good hand' because they used their servants to write out their sermons while they went hunting.[68] It is a story that throws new light on the desirability of servants having some education.

We must remember that, when it came to the production of pious tracts directed at telling servants their duties to their bet-

---

[66] *The Diary of a Country Parson*, i. 216, ii. 206, 229.
[67] *The Blecheley Diary of the Rev. William Cole*, 5, 272–3, 253, 256.
[68] *A Kentish Parson: Selections form the Private Papers of the Revd. Joseph Price Vicar of Brabourne, 1767–1786*, ed. G. M. Ditchfield and Bryan Keith-Lucas (1991), 153.

ters, the clergy were always most prominent. They had 'a vested interest in keeping the domestic servant class properly subservient because they themselves needed at least a small staff to run the rectory or vicarage'.[69]

Not all clerical households were as grand as those of Woodward, Cole, and Woodforde. The Revd Francis D'Aeth, vicar of Godmersham, whose living was reputed to be worth £145 per annum, employed one man servant and a housekeeper. In the 1770s the latter was paid fourteen or fifteen guineas a year 'for waiting upon him, cleaning his house, drssing his victuals and washing all his linen (fouls six shirts a week)'.[70] The Revd David Davies of Barkham in Berkshire, whose income was something over £200 a year, also employed two servants, a housekeeper and a male servant, possibly only a boy, for in the 1780s he was paid only £5 a year, or half that paid to the housekeeper. Only in 1812, when he suffered a long illness, did he employ a second female servant.[71] From the diary of the Revd William Jones, vicar of Broxbourne (1781–1821), one might conclude that he kept no servants at all. He was by his own account poverty-stricken, and in order to augment his income to support his wife and children, he took pupils—most of them foreigners—some of whom were boarders in his house. It is only right at the end of the diary he casually lets slip a remark about his under-maidservant. It would seem he had at least two servants and very probably more.[72]

Nor were all diaries of clerics as informative about their servants as those of Woodward, Cole, and Woodforde. Benjamin Rogers, rector of Carlton (1720–71), who also belonged to the middling income group of clergy, hardly mentions his living-in servants in the whole fifty years he kept a diary. Yet his family included his wife and at least eight children (four out of their twelve children died in infancy). Like Woodforde and Cole, Rogers farmed his own glebe. Yet while he employed a great deal of casual day labour there is almost nothing recorded of his living-in servants. That there were some we only learn when in June 1728 he records in his diary: 'William Bugby went away from

[69] Dawes, *Not in Front of the Servants*, 54.
[70] *A Kentish Parson*, 152–3.
[71] Pamela Horn, *A Georgian Parson and His Village* (1981), 16.
[72] *The Diary of the Rev. William Jones 1777–1821*, ed. O. F. Christie (1929), pp. xix, 160, 174, 216.

me . . . and John Grant came to work here on the Thursday following.' In June 1730 he mentions the confirmation of Eleanor Woolston and Elizabeth Wilworth, two of his female servants. Later the same year he records the death 'of a violent fever', of his servant, John Palmer. It is impossible to gauge how many servants he kept at any one time. Was the reason for such silence about his servants that they caused him so little trouble? Certainly the John Grant he hired in 1728 was still with him nine years later. And when there *were* problems relating to his servants he mentions them in his diary. So when on 16 February 1736 'Elizabeth Neale went away from her Service here, without any known Cause, and did not return til the 27th in the Evening', we hear of it. And when a new servant, George Ives, took Roger's son Jack to Olney Fair 'upon my little Horse', met up with friends, and let Jack start alone for home on the horse, and the boy lost his way, was taken in by a friendly farmer, and only returned home next morning—much to the relief of his parents—the event is recorded. But we hear nothing more of what happened to George Ives in consequence. It seems reasonable to conclude that Rogers's household was an unusually peaceful one.[73]

If far from representative of the experience of most domestic servants, the households of Cole, Woodforde, and Woodward were not untypical of a considerable section of comfortably off clerics who ran relatively modest households with between four and five servants. The more I studied their households the more I began to see 'clerical' as frequently defining a particular kind of household with clearly defined characteristics. It is perhaps this particularity of clerical households that in part accounts for the wealth of material their journals, diaries, and letters provide about their servants. Perhaps more than any other occupational group the clergy were responsible for many eighteenth-century diaries and journals in which servants are given particular prominence. The fact that, like many others, two of our clerics were unmarried meant that the full recruitment, management, and organization of the work of their servants fell on them and not, as in the case of most married men, on their wives.

Our three clerics were all living in the countryside where their parish duties were less than onerous. They had the time to record

[73] *The Diary of Benjamin Rogers*, 4, 19–20, 21, 67, 85.

the day-to-day happenings of their households. Indeed it could be argued that those who remained celibate were particularly dependent on their households not just for their work but for company. It is significant of this dependency that there were often far closer relations between master and servants than in the households of married men with children. The exception among our three is Woodward who married late, and, unusually, had only two children. Before he married he had had time to become accustomed to managing his household. Unlike town households all three were able to recruit their servants locally, often from within the parish from families well known to them. I have suggested that by no means were all clerical households as well ordered and calm as those of our three examples. If anything it serves to authenticate these accounts of relatively good servant–master relations, for other employers, clerics among them, do not seem to have felt any qualms in revealing just how chaotic were their households and how much of their time was spent dealing with servants, dismissing them frequently only to face the problem of recruiting others.

10

A London Domestic Servant: Mary Ashford

> 'It occurred to me that the various events of my own life—not merely "founded on facts", as is sometimes expressed, but the real truth—might afford amusement to matter-of-fact persons.'
>
> *A Licensed Victualler's Daughter*, p. iv

WE know a great deal about servants in large establishments but it is difficult to discover much about those in humbler households. So the autobiography of a female domestic servant at the end of the eighteenth and beginning of the nineteenth centuries is doubly welcome.[1] But what do we know of Mary Ashford? The answer is very little except what we learn from her own account. According to this she was born in 1787. Her father, Joseph Ashford, was the son of a barber and wig-maker in a small Shropshire town. Aged 12, Joseph with his brothers went into service. Even at this age he showed an anxiety to learn to read and write for, as his daughter relates, he would 'spend the evenings in reading, writing and cyphering, under the eye of his master'.[2] Apprenticed to a master skinner and tanner, and later, when his master died, to the trade of leather breeches and glove-making, on the completion of his apprenticeship he went to London. It was here he met his future wife, whose parents were Scots and kept the City Arms at 1 Lombard Street. Her mother had been well educated by her parents at 'one of the best schools' and they had nursed ambitions of putting her to 'some genteel business'.[3] When she met with Mary's father, her parents thought Joseph not good enough a match for their daughter, and a promise was

---

[1] *Life of a Licensed Victualler's Daughter, Written by Herself* (1844).
[2] Ibid. 6.   [3] Ibid. 10.

extracted from her that she would never marry him. But the death of Mary's grandmother intervened and they married. Mary was their second child.

If her account is true Mary Ashford decided to write her experiences as a domestic servant when, in July 1842, she came across a billboard on which an advertisement read 'Susan Hopley, or the Life of a Maid Servant'. She had been surprised that any such account existed for, as she said, 'although female servants form a large class of Her Majesty's subjects', she had 'seen but little of them or their affairs in print'.[4] In fact the title of the novel she was then to read was *The Adventures of Susan Hopley, or Circumstantial Evidence* (1841). The novel was published anonymously, but the author was Catherine Crowe (1800?–1876). It was her first novel and almost certainly the most successful of the many she went on to write. Earlier she had published *Aristodemus, a tragedy in verse* (1838). A writer on the supernatural, she was also to publish a much acclaimed collection of supernatural stories, *Night Side of Nature* (1848). *The Adventures of Susan Hopley* meanders its slow path—it is in three volumes—to a conclusion. It is a curious novel, less concerned with the life of a maidservant than the adventures that arose through her changing places and having new employers. In these adventures it is her employers who are mainly involved. It starts off realistically enough describing the background of the heroine Susan Hopley. She is the daughter of a day labourer at Mapleton in the south-east of the country, whose wages were barely sufficient to 'supply the family with the necessaries of life'. Any education she has is due to her mother, who teaches her daughter 'to spell out words in the Bible'. When her mother dies Susan is 13. With her brother Andrew, aged 10, she is taken in by a Mrs Leeson and placed under the care of an older servant to 'do what little she was able in the house, till she had learned the duties of a servant'.[5] If Susan is more fortunate than most children orphaned at an early age, her background is representative of many female domestic servants who were the daughters of impoverished agricultural labourers.

The households in which she is employed are modest ones and indicative of the kind of humble households in which the majority of domestic servants, more particularly female, were found. The

[4] *Life of a Licensed Victualler's Daughter, Written by Herself*, p. iii.
[5] *The Adventures of Susan Hopley*, 3 vols. (1841), i. 5–7, 9–10, 175.

Leeson family 'had not much money' and they seem to have only the one elderly 'worthy excellent servant' apart from Susan. The second household she works in is that of the Wentworths, to whom she is recommended by Mrs Leeson. Mr Wentworth is a clerk in the post office and Mrs Leeson's uncle. Susan then moves to London and, on the recommendation of the Leesons' servant, she goes to a Mr Wetherall. 'He's a clerk, or something of that sort in the post-office', she is told, 'and she's sister to our baker's wife.' It is an example of how employers recruited servants and servants got to know about places. The Wetheralls have lived until this time in lodgings 'where the people of the house did for them', but Mr Wetherall has just got a rise so they have moved into a small house and 'mean to keep one servant'. As this one servant, Susan is told: 'You'll have everything to do, and the wages are low; but you mustn't mind that for a beginning.' The Aytouns are her next family, where the husband is 'a foreign traveller for a great mercantile house'. They keep two female servants: 'one for cooking and cleaning lower part of the house and the other, who acted as housemaid, had charge of upper rooms and waited at table'. It is to fill the latter role that Susan Hopley is taken on. There is little or nothing about her work as a domestic servant in the novel. In Susan we have a model servant, all of whose energies are directed at doing good to her employers.[6] No wonder Mary Ashford failed to find it convincing.

Ashford had obtained a copy of the novel and admitted she was bitterly disappointed on finding it was fiction. Then and there she decided to write up her own life—'the real truth'. She thought it might be of some interest to 'matter-of-fact persons'.[7] But can we accept Mary Ashford's word that this was 'the real truth'? Is there any reason for thinking her account is more than a realistic fiction? I think there is. Regenia Gagnier has observed how with many working-class autobiographies 'little is known but the one work'.[8] Unlike Catherine Crowe, Mary Ashford made only this one attempt to put pen to paper. The account is more a series of experiences than a story. If she had wanted, it would have been relatively easy to make those experiences the basis of a work of fiction but there is no attempt to do so. At the time she wrote

[6] Ibid. i. 7, 9, 175, ii. 177–8.
[7] *Life of a Licensed Victualler's Daughter*, p. iv.
[8] *Subjectivities: A History of Self-Representation in Britain* (1991), 139.

Ashford was 57. Of her life so far only one-third had been spent in service, but it had occupied seventeen years. Mary Ashford's work not only provides us with a rare account from someone who had experience of domestic service over a considerable period of years but it throws some light on those humbler households about which it is normally so difficult to learn anything.

Mary Ashford's second employer, for example, was the head waiter at Garraway's Coffee House, who lived with his wife at Hoxton.[9] Later she was employed by 'an old lady who lived in the City Terrace, in the City Road', who was the daughter of a Scottish earl but was 'penurious in the extreme'.[10] There was the clergyman's widow who employed her as a servant-of-all work, and the household in Canterbury Place where one of two sisters living with their brother had married, so they decided to cut down the number of servants from two to one.[11] But neither of their existing two servants wished to be left on their own so both left and Mary was taken on. Another household in which Mary became servant was that of the head clerk of a solicitor in Great Winchester Street 'who lived rent free'. It too was almost certainly a one-servant family.[12] So in all these households Mary was probably the only servant employed. None of the households in which she was employed kept many servants. Perhaps the grandest was the one at Staines where besides herself they employed a nurse and housemaid as well as a lad. We hear nothing of how many other servants there were at her Bromley place other than that, in addition to Mary, they kept a footboy. At Epsom the family she lived with had just parted with their cook and housemaid in order 'to keep one thorough servant, and the stable lad to come and assist in the house'.[13] Later they parted with the stable lad for a girl and finally decided to keep only one servant. One of the final places we learn about from her account was a Chelsea household, that of a clergyman attached to some sort of institution—almost certainly part of the Royal Hospital, Chelsea—for the children of soldiers, where besides Mary Ashford as cook there were two other female servants. But after she had been there a year they also cut the number of servants employed, to just two.

This experience in modest households must have been that of the great majority of female domestics in London. Only a min-

[9] *Life of a Licensed Victualler's Daughter*, 23.   [10] Ibid. 27–8.
[11] Ibid. 35, 38–9.   [12] Ibid. 42.   [13] Ibid. 44.

ority were employed in large and grand households. Most, like Mary Ashford, spent their life in domestic service moving from one modest household to another.

What persuaded Mary Ashford to go into service? At the tender age of 4 months she was put out to nurse with a Mrs Long, who was responsible for all the washing from the City Arms. When she was 12 her father became ill and during the time his wife was nursing him the business fell off. After having enjoyed comfortable circumstances they found themselves bankrupt. The shock of finding herself ousted from her family home, poverty-stricken, and with a very sick husband, combined to kill Mary's mother. Her father died soon after.

Mary Ashford had first attended a day school and was sent at the age of 8 to Mrs George's boarding-school as a day-scholar. For a girl destined to become a domestic servant she had had a good education. It was this that later enabled her to write an account of her life. Her relations on both her mother's and father's side discussed among themselves what was to be done with Mary. They agreed to subscribe sufficient money to pay for her apprenticeship, 'for at least five years', as a dressmaker or milliner.[14] This was considered a suitably genteel occupation for a girl of Mary's background. But Mary Ashford was not at all sure she wanted to become a dressmaker or milliner and went to consult Mrs Bond, an old friend of her father's, who advised her that while it was 'all very well for those who have got a home and parents to shelter them, when work is slack ... many clever women find it, at times, a half-starved kind of life'.[15] She recommended that she go into service, but suggested that, before Mary finally decided, she should consult her father's aunt Margaret. When Mary explained the intention of her relations to place her genteelly, Margaret responded that was all very well but, as an old proverb had it, 'gentility without ability, was like a pudding without fat'.[16] She too encouraged Mary to enter service. As Mary admitted, she was good with her needle but did not enjoy the work so was determined to become a domestic servant.

Her relations—more particularly on her mother's side—were clearly aspiring middle-class, anxious that Mary Ashford should enter a trade suitable to a woman of a genteel education. When

[14] Ibid. 20.   [15] Ibid.   [16] Ibid.

she told them her decision to enter service she was sent to talk to a cousin of her mother's whose husband was employed as a bank clerk and who, as Mary Ashford writes, made it quite clear that by going into service she would be ruining all her future prospects. 'I could not be introduced into society by her or any other of my respectable friends if I was a servant'. If she was unlucky enough to fall out of a place 'they would have nothing to do with me'.[17] It is an interesting comment on how domestic service was regarded by at least some of the lower middle class. The desire of her mother's parents to place their daughter in a genteel occupation was the same as that motivating the opposition to Mary Ashford entering domestic service. It was not considered a suitable occupation for a girl of genteel education. But there is more behind their opposition: there was a real stigma attached to service. If servants were 'out of place' they were regarded much as dependents who became kin-servants: their dilemma was their own fault. There is also more than a hint that 'out of place' servants were seen as no better than prostitutes. Mary Ashford's lower-middle-class relations represented those beginning to enter the servant-employing class. They were of all such employers the closest in background and upbringing to the servants they were employing. Almost certainly some of Mary Ashford's relations on her mother's side had earlier been servants themselves. The divide between them was extremely narrow. It was therefore all the more important to distance themselves from servants and establish their middle-classness. It also perhaps accounts for such employers' bad treatment of servants. But perhaps above all else it was the servility of service that lay behind the stigma. To be so totally dependent on employers, to owe them complete obedience, was anathema to the pride of the lower middle classes.

Meeting with such discouragement from her mother's family Mary Ashford fell back on Mrs Bond, who offered her a home at any time she needed one. When her time at her first place ended, her relations renewed their efforts to get her to leave service, but finally they 'gave up the contest'.[18] The treatment Mary later received from them makes clear the genuine shame they felt that a member of their family was a domestic servant. Mary found, she wrote, that she had '"lost caste"; for if I called on any of my

[17] *Life of a Licensed Victualler's Daughter*, 21.   [18] Ibid. 23.

relations, if anyone came in, I was requested to step into another room, and kept in the background'.[19]

She was 13 when she first started in service. She changed places twelve times in the next seventeen years but, as she proudly said, 'never had warning given' to her except in her last place, where she was asked to find other employment in order to make way for an old servant who wished to return to her former employ. As she tearfully explained to prospective employers when asked why she had left this place, 'all I knew of it was, to make way for another'.[20] Her mistress, who was away in Brighton for a month, had written to Mary explaining that 'a servant whom it has long been my intention to engage if ever I heard she was out of place' was disengaged, so would Mary now 'look out for a new situation'.[21] Her first employer had been a head clerk of a banking house who took her on without asking her age, 'supposed she could do the work', and hired her at £6. 10s. 0d. a year. The family consisted of his wife and four children—the youngest a baby. When a rumour started that the banking house at which her employer worked had been opened solely for the purpose of doing a young man of fortune out of his money, she was advised to leave his employ. But, on leaving, her mistress refused to pay her. Very luckily for Mary Ashford, and very exceptionally among domestic servants, she had a knowledgeable adviser who brought her employer before the Court of Requests and in consequence she was ultimately paid.

How long did she stay in any one household? It varied enormously from a week or so to several years. She stayed two months in the banking house in Exchange Alley, at Hoxton Well over two years, at Bromley ten weeks, with the old lady in the City Road seven months, at the West Indian merchant's only 'a little time'.[22] At the 'kind' Mrs Pearce's she stayed six months, at her next place something over six months, although she made every effort to leave.[23] At Miss W's in Canterbury Place she stayed nearly three-and-a-half years. At the Jewish family in Goodman's Fields only 'a short time', at the head clerk in Great Winchester Street ten months, at Epsom nearly two years.[24] At the military institution she stayed a year and a half, at Edgeware 'not . . . many weeks'.[25]

One of her main reasons for leaving a place seems to have been

[19] Ibid. 40.   [20] Ibid. 56.   [21] Ibid. 54–5.   [22] Ibid. 34.
[23] Ibid. 39.   [24] Ibid. 41.   [25] Ibid. 53.

financial—and to get new experience—but if she liked her employers, regardless of the wages, she tended to stay longer with them than if she did not. Other reasons for her leaving a particular household were dislike of the work involved; so, for example, at Hoxton, where the cellar regularly flooded, she 'gave warning, as I would not run the risk of another winter's pumping'.[26] Another very important reason for moving on was the unpleasant character of some of her employers, and a further reason was not wanting to be left on her own in a house for long periods—sometimes weeks—while her employers were away. This was why she preferred not to be the sole servant in a household—she enjoyed company. Often her reason for moving or not accepting an offer of a place was dislike of the mistress. When a place with Mrs R's mother was recommended to her with assurances that it 'was a very good place', Mary Ashford declined the offer. As she commented, Mrs R's mother 'was a lady I did not at all like'.[27]

Her wages seem to have fluctuated wildly. In 1801 her first employer, as we have seen, undertook to pay her £6. 10s. 0d. Her next, later the same year, paid her only £2. 10s. 0d., but rising by a £1 a year. Her next in September 1803 gave her £5 a year, but she was to find her own tea and sugar. It was, she thought, an inadequate wage on which to 'find me in apparel' and she left after ten weeks. 'I left', she wrote afterwards. 'on account of the low wages'.[28] In February 1805 she was employed by a clergyman's widow in Lambeth, who had given £7 a year to her housemaid, but promised that if Mary would come to her as a servant-of-work she would give her nine guineas. After six months she left for a place at which she was paid ten guineas. The only consistency in the wages she was paid is that with one exception she only moved on to higher wages. Did she manage to save anything from her wages? It would seem so, for in February 1814 when she had been in service for thirteen years she had savings of £9 and 'a good stock of useful clothes in my possession'.[29]

One hears a great deal about her employers; of the methods used by mistresses to retain their servants. At one place Mary was made to nurse the child 'and do everything that was laborious', but when it came to anything 'that required any art or knowledge, she not only would not let me do it, but would send me out of the

[26] *Life of a Licensed Victualler's Daughter*, 23.   [27] Ibid. 51.
[28] Ibid. 24, 25.   [29] Ibid. 52.

way, with the little boy, while she did it herself'. It was done, she insists, so that 'I should not leave her, or think myself qualified for a better place'.[30] One learns much about the treatment of servants by some employers. One of Mary's mistresses was constantly away and left her 'very little to subsist on'. When on one occasion she complained, her mistress replied 'My dear Mary, when I was young, there was a famine, and ever since I have had such a veneration for all the necessaries of life that I cannot bear to see anything used profusely'.[31] It provoked Mary to answer that she would 'always think of a famine' whenever she thought of her place.[32] What the lodger left on his plate used to eke out her dinners. One day her mistress after looking at Mary for some time said, 'Mary, child, you would be very handsome were it not that your cheeks are too large; if you would eat less, they would soon be thinner'.[33]

On her mistresses in general she commented that 'many ladies, when they wish to part with a servant who is not guilty of any particular fault, instead of being candid, and warning them to quit, they find fault about trifles, and teaze and aggravate them to give warning themselves'.[34] The mistress who provoked such a remark was reconciled with a past servant who she had wrongly assumed was responsible for stealing a counterpane. It was Mary who, feeling an injustice might have been done, contacted her and brought her to the house to give an account of the affair. It turned out that the counterpane had been lent to the lodger. As a result of the reconciliation between the servant and her mistress Mary was henceforth given little peace and 'I could hardly ever do anything to please her'.[35] Mary thought the old servant better suited to the place, for 'as she was above forty years old, I dare say her appetite was not so sharp as that of a girl not seventeen!'[36] When she finally 'gave warning' there was still the month's notice to serve.[37]

When another of her mistresses heard that the marriage of a former servant, a cook, had broken up and that she wished to return to her former mistress's employ, Mary Ashford observed that so much did she desire her old servant to come back 'she contrived to aggravate me till I gave warning'. Another mistress tyrannized her 'by scolding almost continually', gave her very

[30] Ibid. 29.   [31] Ibid.   [32] Ibid.   [33] Ibid. 300.   [34] Ibid. 31.
[35] Ibid.   [36] Ibid.   [37] Ibid. 33.

little meat to eat, and 'kept' the bread 'till it was mouldy before it was cut'.[38] Another, of whom Mary was genuinely fond, left her alone for weeks in the house while she visited her sister. At one place in Edgware she found out after a few weeks that 'it was the rule of the family . . . to go to a watering place on the continent in the summer—let the house, and discharge the servants'.[39] She always commented on the turnover of servants in the places she went to: at the place at Wickham (sic: High Wycome?), during the ten weeks she remained they had 'no less than five-footboys: it was one of those places that have got a bad name; and that is worse in the country than in London'.[40] On one occasion when she was looking for a place as a cook and had been directed to a doctor's house in Sloane Street, a cheesemonger intercepted her and, after asking her whether she was coming for a place, told her 'you may as well live with old Nick as come here; for they have had four cooks in three months'. She 'walked on'.[41] One of her mistresses, Mrs Taynton, when a new servant was expected in the place of another, 'made it a rule that the one coming in should not see the one going away'.[42] One can see why. Mrs Taynton had one other rule—that servants' boxes should not be brought into the house, 'for fear of her being overrun with importations of London bugs'.[43] As Mary ironically comments, 'to be sure, for anybody that is always changing servants, it may be a very necessary precaution'.[44]

If a mistress chose she could provide such a bad reference for a servant that it would totally prejudice her chances of getting a place. Or, as in Mary Ashford's experience, a mistress could bedevil efforts to get another place by refusing to give her servants a wholly good character. So when Mary wanted to leave one place she found that whenever 'ladies came for my character' her mistress 'always said something that broke it off'.[45] The experience of being 'between places' cannot have been a pleasant one for female domestic servants. For Mary Ashford it was made easier by the fact that, if she did not have a parental home to resort to, she did have the kind Mrs Bond who took her in whenever she was out of place. Nevertheless, there were periods when there seemed no

---

[38] *Life of a Licensed Victualler's Daughter*, 36, 37. [39] Ibid. 53.
[40] Ibid. 24.   [41] Ibid. 49.   [42] Ibid. 25.   [43] Ibid. 26.
[44] Ibid.   [45] Ibid. 38.

permanent place accessible to her and she made do with odd jobs. On one occasion she writes: 'I went to mind some children for a short time, and then to stop with a lady whose servant was ill; and, with one thing or other, was very unsettled for some months.'[46] The same experience of long periods without a settled place must have been that of many servants. When, at her place in Staines, Mary gave warning to her mistress, she could find nothing else in the Staines area and had to pay her 'own expenses to London, and employment to seek afterwards'.[47]

On the other hand she was always prepared to speak of the generosity or kindness of her mistresses if they treated her well. At Hoxton she 'was well fed—living just the same as they did, and partaking of whatever they had'.[48] The fact she thinks this worth mentioning might suggest it was by no means always the case. When she went as housemaid to the clergyman's widow in Lambeth Terrace, she 'worked very hard, but my mistress, who was an excellent manager, regulated my work, so that I took no harm'.[49] Of another place she wrote how 'my mistress was kind to me beyond everything, and I had a most excellent place'.[50] Of the Epsom household she moved to in May 1812, she wrote that 'they were very pleasant people to live with, and I gave them great satisfaction and did their work with pleasure'.[51] 'They were kind people' she said of the Chelsea family she worked for, 'who did a great deal of good amongst the poor persons in the neighbourhood. I liked them very much indeed . . . When the year was up I had not the least inclination to leave'.[52] Even when she was dismissed in order to make way for a former servant who wished to return to her earlier employ, she goes out of her way to mention 'that my late mistress was, on all occasions, extremely kind to me'.[53]

Of what did her work as a domestic servant consist? In all her early places she seems to have been expected to turn her hand to whatever job needed doing—from nursing and looking after children to splitting firewood. Sometimes she acted as general skivvy doing a wide variety of tasks, including the pumping out of water from a cellar that flooded every winter. At the house of an old lady she went to she had to clean the entire house 'which was very dirty with her being so long alone'. All she had to do it with

[46] Ibid. 34.　[47] Ibid.　[48] Ibid. 23.　[49] Ibid. 35.　[50] Ibid. 39.
[51] Ibid. 45.　[52] Ibid. 52.　[53] Ibid. 63.

was cold water 'as I had so little fire'.[54] The same old lady not only had a lodger but a monkey, two dogs, a cat, and many birds—all of which Mary had to look after. One thing that made her mistress angry was that Mary always referred to the 'paws' of the monkey, 'the most vicious little beast that ever was' not to its 'hands'.[55] On one occasion she was hired as 'servant-of-all-work' and discovered this included all the cooking for the household.[56] It is an indication of how little significance had the labels given to servants in small households. She told her mistress she was unable to manage the cooking. Her mistress said she would instruct her, and did so, but six months after being hired Mary Ashford moved on. She had an offer of a place as a cook, but was afraid to take it 'as my knowledge of cooking was very limited at that time'.[57] A cheesemonger's wife told her 'she thought I might better myself'.[58] She started looking for a 'plain cook's place'.[59] On one occasion in 1817 when her master went abroad, her mistress and two of her sons with a friend, Mrs M., and her six children, a lady companion, two nurses, and a servant lad, went to Brighton for a holiday. The whole household numbered fifteen and Mary Ashford with the help of the lad was responsible for 'the whole of the domestic work'. As she later commented, 'very heavy work it was ... I was glad to get home again'.[60]

Later, having acquired more experience, she was employed as a cook. But despite being able to offer some degree of skill it was not always easy to find a place she liked. One one occasion when out of a place she 'went into many shops and heard of many cooks' places'. She 'went after nine or ten, but did not engage with any; there was either something that I did not suit them, or they did not suit me'.[61]

A Licensed Victualler's Daughter provides us with more than an account of the different places Mary Ashford occupied as a servant, the nature of the work involved, and the relationship she had with her employers. For it also tells us something of the way in which such a servant girl was courted, by whom, and her marriage chances and prospects. If Mary ever had advances made to her by her masters, she makes no mention of them. Her account of her life as a servant makes clear how rare were the occasions for meeting the opposite sex. When she was in a house which took

[54] *Life of a Licensed Victualler's Daughter*, 28.   [55] Ibid. 32.   [56] Ibid. 35.
[57] Ibid. 41.   [58] Ibid.   [59] Ibid. 42.   [60] Ibid. 54.   [61] Ibid. 49.

lodgers they seem to have treated her well. So in the household of the old lady who lived in the City Road, the lodger 'was always very civil to me'.[62] Once when she was out of a place she went to live with an old friend of her mother's. A young man, a jeweller, who visited them sent her an ardent love letter. He appealed to the people of the house to intercede on his behalf. They did so by assuring her of his good circumstances and the likelihood that his parents 'would yield to his wishes'. But Mary thought him 'effeminate' and when she told them he was 'only like a great girl, such as I was myself' they were 'highly offended' and she immediately decided to look for a permanent place rather than stay there.[63] In her Epsom place, when she was 24, the son of a market gardener started courting her. When he proposed to her he made it clear he did not expect her to leave her place. Indeed he wished her to remain there 'for some time afterwards'.[64] He thereupon published the banns and started spreading the rumour they were 'as good as married'.[65] But Mary Ashford was cautious. She remembered, she wrote later, she had once heard from a curate at Lambeth that the '"putting up of the banns" was often made the instrument of seduction'.[66] When she was taken out walking in a lonely wood and he started talking of the unfair execution of a man who had lately committed 'an outrage on a female' she insisted on hurrying home.[67] She had begun to notice his 'envious and covetous nature' and, aware that she had no property, started to wonder how he might treat her as his wife.[68] She wrote to him saying they were not suited to each other and breaking off their engagement. His response was to threaten to make her fulfil her promise to him by telling her mistress and master about it. She forestalled him by telling them herself and, luckily for her, they were entirely on her side. So the relationship ended.

Only when she was 30 and working at the school for soldiers' children did she finally marry. As with most servants it was a late marriage. Mary had just been told her employment was coming to an end. She was not dismissed by her mistress, but told that she should look for another place. It had been a terrible shock, for she had 'never had warning given to me before'.[69] What made it doubly hard was that this was a mistress and family she liked above all others and with whom she thought she had an excellent

[62] Ibid. 30. [63] Ibid. 34–5. [64] Ibid. 45. [65] Ibid. [66] Ibid.
[67] Ibid. 46. [68] Ibid. 47. [69] Ibid. 58.

relationship. The sergeant shoemaker she was to marry she had known for some few years. His first wife had died not long since; he had regularly made and mended her shoes. His courtship of Mary was brief. When she received a message that he wanted to speak to her she assumed it was to do some work for him, but she found him 'preparing his dinner' with 'a saucepan in one hand and pepper-box in the other'.[70] She made quite clear to him she was busy and had no time to waste and asked what he wanted. He explained stumblingly that it was not about work he had wanted to see her, but that 'if I had a mind to marry, and would have him, he would have me'.[71] He asked her for an answer as soon as possible. If she decided to marry him then there would be no point in her looking for another place and they would be married at once. What she told him she had decided to accept he was delighted, explaining that so nervous had he been the previous morning that he had put far too much pepper in his dinner and spoilt it. They put up the banns in Chelsea old church.

After her marriage to the shoemaker and the birth of her first child, Victoria, her husband's health began to decline. Several more children were born and she began to worry about what would happen to her family if her husband died. She would be left 'with his children to rear'.[72] She started to plan accordingly. Just after Victoria was born the Duke and Duchess of Kent had come to visit the institution where she worked. The Duchess had admired the baby and, on leaving, had issued her order that the baby be called Victoria Louisa Maria after the Queen. Mary obeyed. She went to visit the duchess regularly in the hope, she admits, that some day she might employ her daughter. 'I used to take Victoria to Kensington about once a year', she relates, 'merely that the Duchess should remember her; as I thought she might, at some future time, take her into her service, or put her forward, without putting herself out of the way'.[73] This the Duchess did not, but later she was to be generous to Mary when her husband died a few months after her sixth child was born. She had to leave the house in the place where her husband had worked and rent a small house. The only work she could find was looking after a kind of tuck shop in the boys' school. It was, she wrote, 'a humble occupation' and to accept it she 'had to crush all the pride' she had, 'which was very little'.[74]

[70] *Life of a Licensed Victualler's Daughter*, 57.   [71] Ibid. 58.
[72] Ibid. 70.   [73] Ibid.   [74] Ibid. 74.

Fifteen months after the death of her husband in June 1830, Mary Ashford married again. Her second husband was a sergeant-tailor of nearly 70 years of age who had been a friend to both Mary and her first husband for some years. She was still, she wrote, 'as badly off as ever as regarded my family'.[75] Having some difficulty in making ends meet, her daughter, 'who was always a good girl, said that she knew I was at a great expense . . . and if I would get her a place she would go to service'.[76] This her mother did. When Victoria later left her situation and came home she obtained a place as parlour maid with the wife of the commanding officer of the military institution at which her mother lived. Mary Ashford's experience as a domestic servant had not always been easy, she may earlier have entertained other hopes for her daughter, but in the difficult financial times she was to experience in married life, domestic service still provided an opening. It may well have been one of the few openings for girls of her daughter's age. In fact, Mary Ashford does not seem to have regarded it as anything but a suitable occupation for her daughter.

Her second husband was increasingly crippled by rheumatism in his arm and found difficulty in doing his work. He was told he must give up working. He applied for a superannuation allowance but heard nothing. Meanwhile he had become so crippled he was unable to do much for himself. Mary could not leave him for long, so she could not go out to work. The prospect was the rapid eating-up of her savings and poverty. In April 1836 they received notification that her husband's application had been turned down. She decided to petition Queen Adelaide, and three months later a superannuation allowance was granted.

The *Licensed Victualler's Daughter* comes within the category of working-class autobiography described by Regenia Gagnier as that of 'storytellers'. But Mary Ashford's story does not conform to Gagnier's description of the category as 'always nostalgic'.[77] There is no suggestion that she looked back on her seventeen years in service with anything approaching nostalgia nor is there support for the notion that such autobiography tends to romanticize the past. It is a straightforward unembellished account of her experiences. Her readers are addressed in a matter-of-fact tone: this is how my life was. Unlike Susan Hopley's story this one was true. 'The public will recognise', wrote George Acorn in 1911,

[75] Ibid. 79.   [76] Ibid.   [77] *Subjectivities*, 156.

'that experiences lived and written down however poorly are of more real value and interest than imaginary fictions beautifully disguised.'[78] It would be interesting to speculate about why Mary Ashford chose to call her autobiography *A Licensed Victualler's Daughter* rather than, say, *The Life of a Domestic Servant*. Was it her way of paying some sort of tribute to the memory of her father? Or was it, rather, aimed at her relations who scorned domestic service as a fitting employment for a licensed victualler's daughter who had been genteelly educated? Was it pride in her own achievement in writing her autobiography and a desire to attract the attention of those who had earlier despised her that made her choose such a title? We can never know.

Mary Ashford was, in many ways, unusual as a London domestic servant in that she had been born there and was not a migrant from the countryside. She was also unusual in having a brother close at hand whom she could visit occasionally, and friends like Mrs Bond to whom she could resort if she had difficulties. Sometimes her friends made her 'presents' to help her out while her wages were low. Remarkable and most exceptional were her relations with the Duke and Duchess of Kent which she had skilfully cultivated. Mary Ashford was also far from typical in the education she had received—first with a governess who had just started a day school (Mary and another girl were her first pupils) and then as a day scholar at a boarding-school. But her experience as a domestic servant must have been close to that of many others in London, both in the kind of households which employed her and in the variety of work they did. We should note that, although she chose to go into service, the range of choice open to her was severely restricted—namely, either to become an apprentice to a dressmaker or milliner or to be a domestic servant. If she chose the latter she seems to have had few illusions about what the occupation involved. It was work that was available, provided her with a roof over her head—of particular importance to a girl just orphaned—and a wage that perhaps in time might allow modest savings. In fact in thirteen years she accumulated savings of only £9—not a great sum to contribute towards her old age. For her, as for many female servants, marriage signalled the end of her life as a resident domestic servant although not the end

[78] As quoted by Gagnier, ibid. 145.

of her working life. Despite her relations' warning that once a servant she 'could not be introduced into society' she seems not to have had any social pretensions. There was never any mention by her of prospects or of social betterment. If marrying a shoemaker and then a tailor can be called bettering herself, materially she benefited little if at all from her marriages. There was little of ambition in her frequent changes of place. Often the work she had to do was extremely arduous, the hours long, and the free time minimal. If she had some mistresses who treated her kindly there were others who did not. In her account she remains very tolerant in her attitude to even the harshest of her mistresses. Frequently it is clear she felt extremely lonely and isolated in households where she was the only servant—and even sometimes the only occupant of the house. The lines with which she ends her autobiography suggest a life of continuous labour and of endurance:

> Let us, then, be up and doing,
> With a heart for any fate;
> Still achieving—still pursuing,
> Learn to labour and to wait.[79]

[79] *Life of a Licensed Victualler's Daughter*, 91.

11

Richardson's Pamela *and Domestic Service*

'The literary servant does not represent actual servants, or at most does so only tangentially'.

Bruce Robbins, *The Servant's Hand*, 11–12

'The most familiar literary portraits of servants—Richardson's Pamela, Jane Eyre, Becky Sharp—embodied the belief that domestic service offered an opportunity for upward mobility through marriage. The notion was calculated to appeal to the middle-class faith in individual achievement, but it also had a basis in fact'.

Theresa McBride, 'Social Mobility for the Lower Classes', 63

AT least one reason for the immense popularity of *Pamela* was the excitement generated by the story of a servant-maid who succeeded not only in bettering herself but in marrying her rich and aristocratic master. It must have given hope to thousands of parents—and indeed their daughters—young girls about to leave their homes to find places as domestic servants. For the hope of social betterment was undoubtedly one of the attractions of entering domestic service. It serves in part to explain the celebration at the village of Slough where the novel, which appeared in instalments, was read aloud to the whole village by the blacksmith. When Pamela finally succeeded in bringing Mr B. to the altar they were so delighted they rang the church bells.[1] If it could happen to Pamela it could also happen to their own daughters—or so it was assumed. So it was that Lady Mary Wortley Montagu

---

[1] J. D. Chambers, *Population, Economy and Society in Pre-Industrial England* (1972), 52–3.

saw Pamela's 'undeserved' success in bringing Mr B. to the altar as 'the joy of the chambermaids of all nations'.[2]

Marriages between widowers and their servants, particularly their housekeepers, motivated by the need to find a replacement as quickly as possible for their wives as household managers, were not uncommon. When Thomas Turner's wife died in 1761 he confessed he 'hardly knew which way to turn'. Four years later when he was contemplating remarrying a neighbour's servant, he gave his reasons for thinking she would make him a good wife. His house, he complained, was no longer 'at all regular'. He had no one, he said, he could 'trust the management of my affairs to that I can be assured in their management will be sustained no loss'.[3] But very few servants seem to have married their young bachelor masters. In October 1720 Sir John Rudd, a 16-year-old baronet, fell in love with the servant girl of a school friend and went through a clandestine marriage with her. When his parents discovered the truth they were horrified and shipped him off to Holland. Virtually abandoned, his wife—now Lady Rudd—was deliberately lured into a second marriage by rumours of the death of her husband, in order that the parents could provide grounds for the dissolution of the first.[4] It was exactly the kind of situation that Hardwicke's Marriage Act of 1753 was designed to avoid, although the Act was perhaps more aimed at preventing rich heiresses from being kidnapped and married off clandestinely— a very different case. So one must sympathize with Fielding's reaction to *Pamela* and his belief that 'Richardson insulted the intelligence of readers by asking them to believe that a servant could dissuade a man of Mr. B's position from having his way with her'. He could not imagine 'that a man of such station would so overvalue the virginity of a woman who was not particularly well-born'.[5] Mr B. unlike Sir John Rudd, was not a young boy or inexperienced. His behaviour towards Pamela does stretch credulity. Equally while Pamela's persistent repulsing of Mr B.'s advances and the ultimate triumph of virtue may be admirable, and

---

[2] Lady Mary Wortley Montagu, *Letters and Works*, ed. Lord Wharncliffe, 3rd edn., 2 vols., with additions and corrections derived from the original manuscripts, illustrative notes, and a new memoir by W. Moy Thomas (1891), ii. 200.

[3] *The Diary of Thomas Turner 1754–65*, ed. David Vaisey (1985), 233, 319.

[4] Lawrence Stone, *Uncertain Unions* (1992), 158–60.

[5] As quoted in Nancy Armstrong, *Desire and Domestic Fiction* (1987), 29.

explain in part the remarkable popularity of the novel, it is, as Nancy Armstrong has written, 'not very true to life'.[6]

A century later 'love affairs, even marriages, between Victorian gentlemen and maid servants or other "inferior" women, were by no means unknown' although still comparatively rare.[7] The love affair and eventual marriage between Arthur Munby and Hannah Cullwick, a maid-of-all-work, is one example. But even in sustaining this relationship there were enormous difficulties and obstacles—and one reason given for the long delay of the marriage was 'the class difference between them'.[8] The pressures brought to bear by a society that still considered the crossing of class frontiers unthinkable cannot be understimated. When Arthur Munby asked Hannah whether she understood what the word *mésalliance* meant, she answered 'Yes, Massa—you and me.'[9] When Mrs Hanbury of Scarborough discovered her 'very amorous' son had fallen in love with her 'extremely modest and honest' waiting-woman, her servant was instantly dismissed. The Duchess of Marlborough commented that she was not at all surprised 'that Mrs. Hanbury was frightened, for nobody would be pleased to marry their son to their woman'.[10] In 1862, after a lengthy courtship, the marriage took place between Lord Robert Montagu, the second son of the sixth Duke of Manchester, and his housemaid, Betsy Wade. It caused a considerable scandal. Society was aghast at 'the shocking degradation of poor Lord Robert, and of his hopeless exclusion from family and friends by reason of this inexplicable depravity'. Among the fellow servants and friends of Betsy Wade, the reaction was different. As Munby writes, 'there is envy among housemaids, there is increased yearning for the fortune-teller's promise to us, of being a "lady"; there is the conviction that we are as good as she is.' Munby discussed it with a Miss Williams, a society lady of his acquaintance. She had been outraged by the marriage. 'She refused to believe that any such woman could by possibility be refined in nature', Munby recorded, 'or be companionable for a man of education. She knew them by experience: their faces might be pretty and their manners

[6] As quoted in Nancy Armstrong, *Desire and Domestic Fiction* (1987), 49.
[7] Derek Hudson, *Munby: Man of Two Worlds: The Life and Diaries of Arthur J. Munby 1828–1910* (1972), 145.
[8] Michael Hiley, *Victorian Women: Portraits from Life* (1979), 29.
[9] Hudson, *Munby: Man of Two Worlds*, 429.
[10] Quoted from Dorothy Margaret Stuart, *The English Abigail* (1946), 89.

modest, but within they were full of baseness & vulgarity. And no man of refinement & gentlemanly feeling could ever degrade himself by such an union.' How different was the view of Mrs Davis, a nurse with whom Hannah Cullwick discussed the case. 'There is the proud patronising thought that she did well, as a champion of her class.' When told that Betsy Wade had had a sweetheart of her own rank, Mrs Davis retorted to Hannah: 'Sweethearts be blowed!... why if you had a chance to marry a gentleman, would you be such a fool as to let a sweetheart stop you?'[11]

Samuel Richardson always said the story of Pamela was based on fact. In a letter to Aaron Hill in 1741 he explained that twenty-five years earlier a close friend had stumbled across the story of the real Mr B. It was to be 'the foundation of Pamela's story'. Twelve years later he claimed *Pamela* 'had some slight Foundation in Truth'. It was published, he said, as 'a pseudo-biography' based on 'genuine letters'.[12] Nevertheless it must have been its very uniqueness which caught his attention.[13] Yet Diderot in his Eulogy of Richardson also emphasizes that Richardson's 'scenes are taken from the life; his personages are all real; his characters are found in the midst of society'.[14] But Diderot's knowledge of English society was limited.

One reason why Lady Mary Wortley Montagu did not approve of *Pamela* was because she did not like 'the heroes and heroines of the Age' being 'Cobblers and Kitchen Wenches'.[15] What made Richardson choose a servant-maid as his heroine? There was a precedent of course in Defoe's *Moll Flanders* which Defoe, like Richardson of *Pamela*, always insisted was a moral tale—'the history of a wicked life repented of'.[16] Moll, aged 14, becomes servant to a 'gentlewoman' with two sons, the eldest of which, on the pretext of having fallen in love with her, promises to marry her and, without any of his family having an inkling of his intentions,

[11] Hudson, *Munby: Man of Two Worlds*, 146, 167, 429.
[12] *Selected Letters of Samuel Richardson*, ed. John Carroll (1964), 39–40; Naomi Tadmor, ' "Family" and "Friend" in *Pamela*: A Case-study in the History of the Family in Eighteenth-century England', *Social History*, 14/3 (1989), 289–306.
[13] M. Kinkead-Weekes, 'Pamela', in John Carroll (ed.), *Samuel Richardson* (1969), 20–7 at p. 20.
[14] *Eulogy of Richardson*, trans. from the French of Diderot, from *The Works of Samuel Richardson*, ed. Edward Mangin, 19 vols. (1811), vol. i, pp. i–xxx.
[15] As quoted in Ann Buck, 'Pamela's Clothes', *Costume*, 26 (1992), 21–31 at p. 21.
[16] Daniel Defoe, *Moll Flanders*, Abbey Classics edn. (1924), p. xvi.

seduces her. Meanwhile his younger brother falls in love with her and with far less caution and secrecy than his brother proposes 'fairly and honourably' to marry her. The family become aware of the situation and the elder brother, by now anxious to be free of her, seeks to persuade her to marry his younger brother who, Moll tells us, 'I had not the least affection for'. The elder brother makes clear the alternatives facing her: 'to marry a gentleman of good family in good circumstances, and with the consent of the whole house' or 'to be sunk into the dark circumstances of a woman that has lost her reputation'. With the offer of a bribe of £500 'to make some amends for the freedoms I have taken with you' he persuades Moll that a husband 'of good family in good circumstances' was better than none and she marries the younger brother. Having 'been tricked once by that cheat called love' hers is not the decision Pamela would have made, but Moll is a pragmatist.[17] If Richardson read the novel one wonders whether he was so outraged by Moll's calculated rejection of his notion of sexual morality that he felt called on to write a different version of the tale.

Was *Pamela* intended by Richardson as a story to compensate 'for the monotonous drudgery and limited perspectives of ordinary domestic life'—particularly when experiencing it as a female servant?[18] A nineteenth-century editor of *Pamela* insists it 'was chiefly intended for the lower classes'.[19] We know that, with apprentices, domestic servants were foremost among those swelling the ranks of the reading public—and we now know that in the eighteenth century they were a sizeable group. Often they worked in houses with libraries. Frequently they seem to have been given access to books. Jane Eyre's introduction to *Pamela* comes from Bessie, the Reeds' servant. One source of 'the tales Bessie sometimes narrated' is '(as at a later period I discovered) ... the pages of *Pamela*'.[20] Q. D. Leavis has suggested it may well have been from 'the packmen' who 'took round *Pamela* in cheap parts it being so popular with the servants' that Charlotte Brontë first heard of the novel.[21] Whatever versions of *Pamela* domestic servants had access to, the story was known to many. About the

---

[17] Daniel Defoe, 20, 45, 43, 47.   [18] Ian Watt, *The Rise of the Novel* (1963), 212.
[19] *The Works of Samuel Richardson*, vol. i, p. xix.
[20] Charlotte Brontë, *Jane Eyre*, Penguin edn. (1953), 11.
[21] Bruce Robbins, *The Servant's Hand, English Fiction from Below* (1986), 105.

time *Pamela* was published, Mary Leapor, the kitchen maid–poet, was almost certainly free to make use of the well-stocked library of her mistress, Susannah Jennens, a widow entirely sympathetic to her employee's ambitions to write poetry.[22] As Pamela's former mistress 'used to say' Pamela 'lov'd Reading', and Mr B. tells her she 'may look into any of her Books, to improve' herself.[23] So Pamela has been seen as the 'culture-heroine of a very powerful sisterhood of literate and leisured waiting-maids'.[24] Indeed Pamela is as well read as her master. When Mr B.'s classical allusion to *Lucretia* is taken up by Pamela, he is annoyed at this proof of educational equality with him and tauntingly remarks 'you are well read I see'.[25]

While some servants married fellow servants, lesser tradesmen, or craftsmen, and enjoyed a modest standard of living, it was rare for them to leave their own class. The lives of the vast majority of female domestic servants were far less happy. Forbidden to marry until 21 many desperately sought by slow accumulation of their savings to amass a dowry sufficient to attract any young man. Many employers refused to allow their servants to marry. Employers in general were far from welcoming towards visiting suitors. Little wonder then that female domestic servants tended to marry late—if at all. So hopes of social betterment by female servants or their parents were largely frustrated. Pamela's marriage to Mr B. may have represented her 'only chance of escaping servitude until her majority'.[26]

Most servants in the eighteenth century were recruited from the countryside. Often it would seem their parents had difficulty in supporting them. One of the attractions from their point of view of their daughters entering domestic service was that it provided 'bed and board'. In this Pamela's background might be seen as representative. Her parents have 'enough to do to maintain' themselves without having the additional burden of Pamela to support. When she contemplates a return home she fears she will be 'a clog upon my dear parents' who 'are very poor, and find it hard enough to live'. Her father, we are told, is able to read and

---

[22] Richard Greene, *Mary Leapor* (1993), 10.
[23] *The Shakespeare Head Edition of the Novels of Samuel Richardson*, 18 vols. (1929), i. 3–4.
[24] Watt, *The Rise of the Novel*, 49. [25] *The Novels of Samuel Richardson*, i. 31.
[26] Watt, *The Rise of the Novel*, 149.

is 'well able to teach', but his attempt to set up a school has failed. Nevertheless, her parents try to reassure her that if she returns home they 'will live happily together', for with her father's 'diligent labour', her 'poor mother's spinning', and Pamela's needlework they will 'do better and better'.[27]

Many young girls started in domestic service at a young age. Pamela starts three years before her mistress's death when she 'was not twelve years old'.[28] At such a tender age it seems waiting-maids were not always eligible for wages. Writing of servants in husbandry, Ann Kussmaul suggests that very young servants might not receive any payment. The minimum age for which wages were specified was between 12 and 16 for a female. First they had to prove themselves worthy of payment. Even when wages were paid they were not adult wages until the servant was in her late teens or early twenties.[29] When preparing to leave Mr B.'s employ, Pamela consults Mrs Jervis on whether she should keep the four guineas that came out of her 'good lady's pocket, when she died', and which she had already sent home to her parents.[30] She tells Mrs Jervis she has received no wages in the previous three years, 'my lady having said she should do for me as I deserved'.[31] When Mr B. loads her mistress's fine clothes upon her, Pamela's first thought is to sell them and send the proceeds home, but she is prevented by the thought that it would be an 'Affront to him'.[32] Almost certainly, this sending of remittances of money or clothes to their parents was common among servants. It was certainly not unusual for personal maids, on the death of their mistresses, to receive their clothing as a bequest. In 1763 Lady Mary Wortley Montagu left her personal maid 'all my wearing apparel either made or not made and all my Linen either for the Bed, Table or my person'.[33] Mrs Delany left her servant all her 'wearing apparel and body linen that has not been washed and once worn'.[34] In an earlier chapter, I quoted the example of the Revd. William Cole's neighbour, Mrs Willis, who left her maid all her clothes.[35] Clothes given to servants would often be sold in the second-hand market and the money received passed on to their

---

[27] *The Novels of Samuel Richardson*, i. 1, 2, 5, 9, 39.   [28] Ibid. 21.
[29] *Servants in Husbandry in Early Modern England* (1981), 37–8.
[30] *The Novels of Samuel Richardson*, i. 104.   [31] Ibid. 2.   [32] Ibid. 11.
[33] Buck, 'Pamela's Clothes', 22.   [34] Ibid.
[35] *The Blecheley Diary of the Rev. William Cole 1765–7*, ed. Francis Griffin Stokes (1931), 221. See also above, p. 67.

parents. We know servants in husbandry, especially when very young, would send their wages to their parents.[36] It is difficult to find evidence of female domestic servants in the eighteenth century sending all or part of their wages home, although it seems likely that some of them did. Of those in Victorian Candleford, Flora Thompson has written how 'every month, when the girl received her wages, a shilling or more would be sent to "our Mum" and as the wages increased, the mother's portion grew larger'.[37]

The two households in which Pamela lives during the years covered by the novel are substantial. Both employ a number of servants. At his main residence in Bedfordshire, Mr B. keeps eleven servants: a steward who 'is reckoned worth a power of money', 'John, the footman', a 'Mr. Jonathan, our butler', who was 'a very grave good sort of old man', and three other male servants. Of the female servants, the housekeeper Mrs Jervis, is head, and responsible for keeping the household accounts. She is 'a gentlewoman born' but has had 'misfortunes'. There is also a cook, Jane, who is 'a little snappish and cross sometimes', 'our Rachel who is the house-maid', and two other female servants.[38] Similarly in Mr B.'s Lincolnshire estate there are at least eight servants: the housekeeper, Mrs Jewkes, a cook and house-maid, a coachman, a groom, a helper, and a footman, in addition to a gardener. The size of his households suggests Mr B. is a man of some considerable fortune. His two households are far from representative. Most country gentlemen, Hecht tells us, employed a staff of about seven.[39] Mr B. employs well over double that number in his two establishments. Why did Richardson choose to set his story in such an unrepresentative household? W. M. Sale has suggested Richardson's 'taste for aristocracy, like that of his heroines, is an index of his need to make common cause with a superior social class'.[40]

One aspect of the role played by female domestic servants that Richardson emphasizes in *Pamela* is the loss of their personal identity when they enter the household of their employers. Some-

[36] Kussmaul, *Servants in Husbandry in Early Modern England*, 76.
[37] Flora Thompson, *Lark Rise to Candleford* (1977), 165.
[38] *The Novels of Samuel Richardson*, i. 48, 56, 63, 65.
[39] J. Jean Hecht, *The Domestic Servant in Eighteenth-Century England* (1956), 6.
[40] William M. Sale Jr., From *Pamela* to *Clarissa*', in John Carroll (ed.), *Samuel Richardson* (1969), 39–48 at p. 43.

times they were even deprived of their real names—particularly if the mistress of the house thought them unsuitable for a servant. 'Servanthood', Cissie Fairchilds has written, 'often stripped them of many elements necessary to a sense of identity'.[41] Indeed, as she adds, it was often a quite deliberate ploy to establish control over them. This was particularly true of lady's maids who were closest to their mistresses. Pamela receives from her mistress an education which, she confesses, makes her 'qualify'd above' her degree.[42] But this was something required of lady's maids. As Anthony Heasel made plain in 1773, it was often impossible to occupy such a position so close to their mistresses 'unless their education has been something above the ordinary rank of other women'.[43] Mrs Hackman of Lymington took upon herself the education of Nancy Bere before she became her lady's maid.[44] 'Maids', Janet Todd has written, 'were often as educated as their mistresses; they frequently read the same novels and they probably spoke similarly.' And, as she adds, 'a female education delivered gentility'.[45]

In 1751 Dr John Hill, in recommending the establishment of a Registry Office for servants, explained that the 'happiness and prosperity of society depends in a great measure on each of its members being employed in a station suited to his capacity and his abilities'. Unfortunately this point had been 'left in a great degree to accident'. Hence the 'imperfect manner' in which it was performed.[46] Pamela's parents feared lest she might be 'brought to any thing dishonest or wicked, by being set so above' herself.[47] When contemplating returning home Pamela realizes she has 'nothing on my back, that will be fit for my condition'. She needs to get herself 'at once 'quipp'd in the dress that will become my condition'.[48] Handbooks aimed at servants were always reminding them that all the comforts and even luxury they enjoyed were temporary—'circumstances in your service and not given to you

---

[41] *Domestic Enemies: Servants and their Masters in Old Regime France* (1984), 101.
[42] *The Novels of Samuel Richardson*, i. 1.
[43] *The Servant's Book of Knowledge* (1773), 69.   [44] See Ch. 12.
[45] '*Pamela* or the Bliss of Servitude', in *Gender, Art and Death* (1993), 63–80, at p. 63.
[46] *The London Daily Advertiser* (31 Oct. 1751) as quoted in M. Dorothy George, 'The Early History of Registry Offices', *Economic History*, 1 (1926–9), 570–90 at p. 579.
[47] *The Novels of Samuel Richardson*, i. 4.   [48] Ibid. i. 49–50.

to last'. They were cautioned that their hearts should remain where their 'station is—among the poor; so that if you have to return to your old ways of living when your years of service are over you may not feel hurt or degraded but as if you were returning home'.[49] Pamela tells Mr B. that she has 'been in disguise, indeed, ever since my good lady your mother took me from my parents'. For her mistress had given her clothes 'supposing I was to wear them in her Service' and such clothes identified maid with mistress. The fine clothes of her mistress's that Mr B. gives Pamela, she laments, are 'too rich and too good' for her. Mrs Jervis interprets Mr B.'s intentions as those of fitting Pamela 'for a Waiting-maid's Place on Lady *Davers* own Person'.[50] Conscious of just how unsuitable is the style of her clothes for her servants, Richardson's Clarissa employs a mantua-maker to alter a gown she has given to a servant, explaining that 'the dress, and the robings and facings must be altered for your wear, being, I believe, above your station'.[51]

There were many complaints in the early eighteenth century that it was becoming impossible to tell servants from their mistresses. But among the upper classes having well-dressed servants was a mark of prestige. 'We are obliged to take the lowest of the people', wrote Soame Jenyns, 'and convert them by our own ingenuity into the genteel personages we think proper should attend us.'[52] As a story in the *Lady's Magazine* of 1785 recounted: 'My wife . . . prides herself on having the smartest servants in the neighbourhood. Mrs Becky, let me tell you, does some credit to her taste; who would think she was a servant of all work?'[53] Yet this did not prevent servants being accused of aping their betters. It was ladies' maids in particular who were constantly being criticized for 'appearing in a Habit above their Degree . . . For being cloathed above their Equals, they think themselves equal to their Superiors, and begin to act accordingly'.[54] Eliza Haywood warned servant-maids 'of imitating their betters'. Servants should aim in their dress at 'a decent Plain-

---

[49] *The Lady's Maid* (Houlston's Industrial Library), as quoted in E. S. Turner, *What the Butler Saw: 250 Years of the Servant Problem* (1962), 124.
[50] *The Novels of Samuel Richardson*, i. 11, 13, 49, 68, 71, 102.
[51] As quoted in Anne Buck, *Dress in Eighteenth-Century England* (1979), 115.
[52] *The Works of Soame Jenyns*, ed. C. N. Cole, 4 vols. (1790), ii. 116.
[53] As quoted in Hecht, *The Domestic Servant in Eighteenth-Century England*, 63.
[54] Anon, *The Servants Calling* (1725), 21.

ness'.[55] In order to return to her home Pamela makes herself 'a new and more suitable dress'—'more suitable to my Degree'.[56] It has been suggested that this 'disguise of herself as the country girl disrupts her identity', but it is questionable whether as a servant in Mr B.'s household she really had one. But Pamela, by donning rustic guise, is certainly 'making a claim for self-definition and self-representation' and by so doing 'the eighteenth-century fear that clothes were ceasing to function as a reliable guide to status . . . is . . . confronted through a reversal'.[57] As Jocelyn Harris has pointed out, Mr B. 'assumes the right to define her, calling her hussy, saucebox, gewgaw, speaking picture, artful young baggage'.[58] Certainly Pamela sees her country clothes as enabling her to reassume her original identity as the daughter of the rural poor which, since she entered her mistress's house, has been submerged. When Mr B. under the pretence of thinking her Pamela's sister, tries to kiss her, she cries out vehemently 'Indeed I am *Pamela, her own self!*'[59] She continues to wear her country clothes until just before her wedding, when Mr B. asks her to put on again the clothes she had worn as her mistress's maid. She looks at herself in the mirror and thinks herself 'a Gentlewoman once more' but now with the confidence of her new status. As she puts it, she is now 'able to put on this Dress with so much Comfort'.[60]

Richardson was not unaware of the dangers of a female servant losing her place. Nor is Pamela. When contemplating returning to her home she hopes Mr B. 'will let Mrs Jervis give' her 'a character for fear it should be thought that I was turn'd away for Dishonesty'.[61] Earlier she has been deterred from running away by the thought that it will 'be reported, I have stolen something, and so was forc'd to run away'. If a female servant was dismissed without a character it might well prove impossible for her to obtain another place. When Pamela rebukes Mrs Jewkes for calling her Madam, she reminds her that she is still a servant but 'a servant inferior to you and so much more, as I am turned out of a place'.[62]

Her kind mistress has taught her 'to write and cast accounts

[55] Eliza Haywood, *A Present for a Serving Maid* (1743), 24.
[56] *The Novels of Samuel Richardson*, i. 51, 71.
[57] Tassie Gwilliam, *Samuel Richardson's Fictions of Gender* (1993), 31, 32–3.
[58] Jocelyn Harris, *Samuel Richardson* (1987), 17.
[59] *The Novels of Samuel Richardson*, i. 70.   [60] Ibid. ii. 85.
[61] Ibid. i. 21, 38.   [62] Ibid. 21, 144–5.

and made me a little expert at my needle'. When Lady Davers congratulates Pamela on her letter-writing she is told that Pamela owes it all 'to my late excellent lady'.[63] Was this education and training of servants usual in such households? In the early eighteenth century it was almost certainly not uncommom. There was then far more paternalism in relations between employers and their servants than later when it became increasingly a contractual relationship. The educational needs of servants were not always heeded by their masters or mistresses, but sometimes they were. So John Baker, a lawyer, 'undertook to teach one of his maids himself' while Dr Claver Morris sent a maid in his service to the local dame school in order that she should learn to read.[64] In 1767 the Revd William Cole recorded in his diary 'spoke to the Schole Master, Mr Spain, for both my servants to learn of him'. He even had a 'Music Master from Buckingham . . . to instruct Tom', his man servant, on the German Flute.[65] With such accomplishments as she has acquired through her mistress, Pamela recognizes that it is 'not every family that could have found a place that your poor *Pamela* was fit for'. But what use are such accomplishments as singing, drawing, or working 'fine Work with my Needle' in the village to which she is returning? They would make her, she says, 'but ill company for my Milk-maid Companions that are to be', just as her fine clothes would 'bring all the little village upon my back'. What, Pamela asks, are all her fine accomplishments 'to the purpose'? She had far better 'have learned to wash and scour, and brew and bake, and such like'. And in a pathetic effort to prepare herself for hard labour she tells her parents that she 'tried when Rachel's back was turned, if I could scour a pewter plate she had begun. I see I could do't by degrees: it only blistered my hand in two places.' When Mr B. reverses his earlier decision and asks her to stay on he laments the need for her to 'return again to hard Work' as she must if she goes home. Indignantly Pamela answers him: 'I'd have you know, sir, that I can stoop to the ordinariest work of your scullions, for all these nasty soft hands.'[66]

'You are so pretty', Mr B. tells Pamela, 'that go where you will,

[63] Ibid. 1, 111, 57.
[64] Hecht, *The Domestic Servant in Eighteenth-Century England*, 99–100.
[65] *The Blecheley Diary of the Rev. William Cole*, 55, 300.
[66] *The Novels of Samuel Richardson*, i. 1, 97–8, 87–8.

you can never be free from the Designs of some or other of our Sex.' His sister, Lady Davers, we are told by Pamela, thought her 'too pretty to live in a Batchelor's House since no Lady he might marry would care to continue me with her'. When a number of 'fine ladies' come to catch a glimpse of Pamela it is Lady Towers who makes the same point when she says 'with a free air (for it seems she is called a wit), Well, Mrs *Pamela*, I can't say I like you so well as these Ladies do; for I should never care, if I had a Husband, and you were *my* Servant, to have *you* and your *master* in the same house together'.[67] Mrs Pepys would have agreed with the sentiments expressed by Lady Towers.

When, in February 1669, Pepys with some indignation recorded in his diary his wife's belief that he had been 'false to her with Jane', producing 'three or four silly circumstances of her not rising till I come out of my chamber, and her letting me thereby see her dressing herself, etc.', we remember, even if he has chosen to forget, his entry for the previous September. 'Dressing myself did begin para toker the breasts of my maid Jane, which elle did give way to more than usual here to fore so I have a design to try more when I can bring it to.' How common was it for the master of the household to dally with his maids? If Pepys is any guide it was very common. With another maid who returns to their employ after an absence he admitted he could 'hardly keep myself from having a mind to my wench' but sanctimoniously adds that he hopes he 'will not fall to such a shame'. Almost certainly he had already been to bed with her. Nell Payne had hardly arrived in the household before Pepys was regularly pursuing his 'dalliance' with her. Little wonder that Pepys's wife became 'mighty angry with Nell' and dismissed her.[68] 'Judging by the diary', as Peter Earle has pointed out, 'most of the girls seemed to regard Pepys's exploration of their person as just part of the job.'[69] How many mistresses dismissed female servants only because of the danger they presented to their husbands? But, as far as we know, although Pepys may have committed rape, unlike Mr B., he had no illegitimate children. But as Lady Davers is so anxious to convey

[67] *The Novels of Samuel Richardson*, 8, 64, 112.
[68] *The Diary of Samuel Pepys*, ed. Henry B. Wheatley, 3 vols. (1946), iii (vol. viii of diary) 207–9, 98, i (vol. ii of diary), 281, iii (vol. vii of diary), 54.
[69] *The Making of the English Middle Class* (1989), 224.

to Pamela, her brother 'never was a common Town Rake, and had always Dignity in his Roguery'.[70]

Pamela makes clear that the nature of Mr B.'s advances is anything but exceptional among the local gentry—with disastrous consequences for the women concerned. If female servants were in danger from their masters they were also in danger from fellow servants. 'There is Squire Martin in the Grove', Pamela relates, 'has had three Lyings-in, it seems, in his House, in three Months past; one by himself, and one by his Coachman, and one by his Woodman'. Such were the 'Hardships poor Maidens go thro' whose Lot it is to go out to service'.[71] Nor would the local gentry have seen anything wrong in such dalliance with servant-maids. 'Sexual favours of his female domestics', Sara Maza writes, 'were part of the privileges of a patriarch.' 'A master', she writes, 'had certain rights, amounting almost to property rights, over the bodies of his servants, analogous to the rights of a husband over the body of his wife and a father over the bodies of his children.'[72] On Mr Williams attempting to get some of Mr B.'s neighbours to help Pamela, one, Sir Simon, replies: 'Why, what is all this . . . but that our neighbour has a mind to his mother's waiting-maid! And if he takes care she wants for nothing, I don't see any great injury will be done her. He hurts no *family* by this.'[73] As Naomi Tadmor has emphasized, daughters of poor parents like Pamela were considered to have no family of their own although they could join a family by becoming servants.[74] Outside fiction Sir Simon's views were shared by many in the eighteenth century. Dr Johnson argued that a man 'does not do his wife a very material injury if, for instance, from mere wantonness of appetite he steals privately to her chambermaid' for the result was no 'confusion of progeny'.[75] But what is also revealed by Sir Simon's comment is the dilemma Mr B. finds himself in when 'he falls in love with the girl' whom by the standards set by society 'he should seduce'.[76] 'My Pride and Condition', he tells Pamela, 'made me both tempt

---

[70] *The Novels of Samuel Richardson*, iii. 41.   [71] Ibid. i. 89–90.
[72] *Servants and Masters in Eighteenth-Century France: The Uses of Loyalty* (1983), 138.   [73] *The Novels of Samuel Richardson*, i. 179.
[74] Tadmor, ' "Family" and "Friend" in *Pamela*', 297.
[75] G. B. Hill and L. F. Powell (eds), *Boswell's Life of Johnson*, 6 vols. (1934–50), ii. 55–6.
[76] John Carroll (ed.), *Samuel Richardson* (1969), 44.

and terrify you to other Terms [than marriage]'.[77] What has been called the 'eroticism of inequality' is certainly not absent from Mr B.'s advances.[78] He constantly reminds Pamela of his power over her.

Pamela as a servant-maid seems at times to be resisting if not actually challenging the whole notion of caste as an explanation of the differences between masters and servants. Lowly she certainly is, but, as she frequently makes clear to Mr B., not therefore lacking in such qualities as virtue. As Janet Todd has written, she 'beats Mr B. at his own game by accepting his social hierarchy and glorying in her lower rung'.[79] But as a servant she remains her own person. No one owns her. When Mr B. on being repulsed, accuses her of denying his property rights in her she responds 'how came I to be his property? What right has he in me but such as a Thief may plead to stolen Goods?'[80]

Before her marriage Pamela begins to learn her new role. In part she is instructed by Mr B. who, forced to act entirely out of character in order to win Pamela, on succeeding, very quickly makes clear that he remains master, and that his wife, like his maidservant, owes him entire obedience. 'In Mr B.'s required scheme, a wife is the extension of the maid.'[81] The first problem, Mr B. tells her, is what female company she will have when married given that his 'Station will not admit it to be with my Servants; and the Ladies will fly your Acquaintance; and still, though my Wife, will treat you as my Mother's Waiting-maid'. Pamela's response is that if he will give her leave, she 'will . . . look into such parts of the Family-Oeconomy, as may not be beneath the Rank to which I shall have the Favour of being exalted', adding cautiously 'if any such there can be.'[82] Lady Davers clearly thinks there are none. She too sets about educating Pamela to fill her new role which, she explains, does not require her to be 'quite a domestic Animal'. If she continues to employ 'herself in such Works as either must be a Reproach to herself or to them' no ladies will visit her. Her new duties are clearly outlined by Lady Davers. Above all else they consist of giving

---

[77] *The Novels of Samuel Richardson*, ii. 79.
[78] Maza, *Servants and Masters in Eighteenth-Century France*, 166.
[79] *Gender, Art and Death*, 66.   [80] *The Novels of Samuel Richardson*, i. 167–8.
[81] Todd, *Gender, Art and Death*, 68.
[82] *The Novels of Samuel Richardson*, ii. 27, 29.

'Orders'. She must take on the role of 'Task-mistress' and regard 'the common Herd of Female Servants, as so many Negroes directing themselves by your nod'.[83]

Once wife to Mr B. Pamela nevertheless remains a servant. Indeed Pamela passes easily between the two roles. If anything she is more servile as wife than she formerly was as waiting-maid. It becomes necessary, writes Nancy Armstrong, 'to distinguish the unnatural submission of a household servant to her master in an erotic adventure from the natural subordination of a female to male in an ideal marriage'.[84] Once married, Pamela 'has little freedom "to be her own self"'.[85] She 'blessed God ... for all his gracious Favours to his unworthy Handmaid!'. When Lady Jones expresses gracious approval of how Pamela has served her, Pamela replies that she hopes 'her good Master's Favour' will 'never make me forget, that it is my Duty to wait upon his Friends'. She writes to her parents that 'the dear, dear, good Gentleman ... has thus exalted his unworthy Servant'. And later, 'what is it for such a Worm as I to be exalted!' Just after the marriage she tells Mr B. that she will 'more and more shew' him 'that I have no Will but yours'.[86] And this, as an early eighteenth-century manual on service makes clear, was the essential characteristic of servant–master relations, 'that you diligently apply yourselves to know and do the Will of your Master'.[87] Mr B. becomes increasingly imperious as husband. As Lady Mary Chudleigh had written in 1703,

> Wife and servant are the same,
> But only differ in the name:
> For when that fatal knot is tied,
> Which nothing, nothing can divide,
> When she the word *Obey* has said,
> And man by law supreme has made,
> Then all that's kind is laid aside,
> And nothing left but state and pride.[88]

Leonore Davidoff has probed further this analogy between the subordination of servants and that of wives. The 'majority of

[83] Ibid. iii. 41.   [84] *Desire and Domestic Fiction*, 130.
[85] Harris, *Samuel Richardson*, 33.
[86] *The Novels of Samuel Richardson*, ii. 40, 60–1, 145, 153, 170, 200.
[87] Anon., *A Present for Servants*, 2nd edn. (1710), 14.
[88] *Eighteenth-Century Women Poets*, ed. Roger Lonsdale (1989), 3.

girls', she writes, 'moved from paternal control in their parents' home, into service and then into their husbands' home—thus experiencing a life time of personal subordination in private homes'. Pamela is only different in marrying into the aristocracy. 'The overwhelming fact is that the whole life of the servant and wife, from material support to human surroundings, depends on the household of which she happens to be a member.'[89] As wife to Mr B. Pamela takes on the role of 'upper servant'. Obedience to her husband replaces obedience to her master, but there is now an additional element in this relationship of subordination—that of total dependence. No longer is there the compensating knowledge of earning her keep and a wage. Earlier Pamela not only accepted her lowly place in the social hierarchy but from her pride in her family and background derived a certain autonomy defying the assumptions of status. After her marriage to Mr B. she appears totally to have accepted the role of female subordination in marriage. As servant she had angrily rejected the notion that she was her master's property. As wife she glories in his ownership of her.

Perhaps unwittingly, Richardson tells us a great deal about servants and their masters and mistresses in *Pamela*, but the story he unfolds is more fiction than fact. One can readily understand why it was so popular. It was a fairy story and many servant-maids must have read it 'as a Cinderella escape from their ashes to imaginary high life, or as advice on how to rise to the highest ranks of society'.[90] It may well have done something to propagate the myth of domestic service being the road to social betterment.

---

[89] 'Mastered for Life: Servant and Wife in Victorian and Edwardian England', in Pat Thane and Anthony Sutcliffe (eds.), *Essays in Social History*, ii (1986), 126–50 at pp. 129, 143.

[90] R. P. Utter and G. B. Needham, *Pamela's Daughters* (1936), 7–8.

12

Literate and Literary Servants in Eighteenth-century Fact and Fiction

> You laugh and think 'twill be a Jest,
> To see a Muse in LIVERY dress'd:
> But when I mount behind the Coach,
> And bear aloft a flaming Torch;
> Methinks on PEGASUS I fly,
> With Fire Poetick blazing thro' the Sky.
>
> from Robert Dodsley's *A Muse in Livery: or the Footman's Miscellany* (1732)

> When reason first adorn'd my infant mind,
> To books and poetry my heart inclin'd
> And as my years advanc'd, the passion grew,
> And fair ideas round my fancy flew.
> The Muses seem'd to court me for their friend,
> But fortune would not to their suit attend;
> She understood who proper subjects were,
> To hold a converse with those airy-fair,
> Must be possess'd at least of independence,
> That to the Muses they may give attendance,
> By books and study fructify the mind,
> And lead the genius where it was inclin'd.
>
> from Jane Cave's 'The Author's Plea', in *Poems on Various Subjects, Entertaining, Elegiac, and Religious* (1783), 1–2

IT has often been claimed that the overwhelming majority of servants in the early modern England were illiterate in the sense that they could neither read nor write. As illiterates they have been seen as essentially simple, often moronic, people with no interest in intellectual or cultural pursuits. There were contemporaries who would have agreed on the illiteracy of servants. 'Many', wrote Richard Mayo in 1693, 'by the Poverty and Carelessness of their Parents, and Friends, cannot so much as Read.'[1] Until very recently historians have tended to endorse such views. The ability of men and women to sign their names rather than make a mark on a marriage certificate has been assumed to be a reliable measure of literacy. More recent work has challenged such an assumption and forced us to think just how important complete literacy was to the occupations of men and women of the labouring classes. Earlier it was assumed anyone who could read could sign their name. We now know this to be false. Reading was always taught first in schools, writing came later. Many must have left school before anything but the rudiments of reading had been taught—if that. Even more had no schooling at all. Yet among the labouring poor there were those well able to read, and teach others to read, who were unable to sign their names. There were also those able to read and write who nevertheless chose to make a mark rather than sign their names. Such facts suggest some caution is needed before drawing conclusions from the use of the word 'illiterate' about servants.

Servants in England, claims D. A. Kent, 'were usually illiterate'.[2] 'The greatest illiteracy', writes Keith Thomas, 'was found at the bottom of the social scale, among the labourers and maidservants.'[3] In Scotland levels of illiteracy were close to those in England but 'female servants', R. A. Houston writes, 'were highly illiterate and much more so than males in the same occupation'.[4] French servants in the eighteenth century were also 'for the most part illiterate'.[5] As Houston has suggested of Scotland, there was an important distinction to be made between levels of literacy in men and women. 'Illiteracy', we are told, was always 'much more widespread among women than men.' Indeed a 'fully literate

---

[1] *A Present for Servants* (1693), 48.
[2] 'Ubiquitous but Invisible: Female Domestic Servants in Mid-Eighteenth-Century London', *History Workshop Journal*, 28 (autumn 1989), 111–28, at p. 111.
[3] 'The Meaning of Literacy in Early Modern England', in Gerd Baumann (ed.), *The Written Word: Literacy in Transition*, Wolfson College Lectures 1985 (1986), 97–131 at p. 121.
[4] *Scottish Literacy and the Scottish Identity* (1985), 34, 60.
[5] Sara C. Maza, *Servants and Masters in Eighteenth-Century France: The Uses of Loyalty* (1983), 52.

woman' in Tudor and Stuart times, it is claimed, was something of a rarity.[6] There were still 'three out of four women . . . illiterate in the early Hanoverian period'.[7] This proportion, it is argued, was reduced to two-thirds by 1760. Whether or not we agree with these figures literacy certainly improved in the eighteenth century—slowly at first and more rapidly from the middle of the century, but where servants were concerned even as late as the 1850s Henry Mayhew could lament that 'female servants . . . are badly educated'.[8] It was perhaps significant that the spread of literacy in the eighteenth century coincided with a general outcry about how education was ruining servants. The danger of too much education for the lower classes, it suggests, was already being experienced by some employers. As with the movement among employers for the abolition of vails, such opposition to educated servants may well indicate increasing tensions between employers and their servants—particularly male servants.

If servants, and in particular female servants, were among the most illiterate in the eighteenth century, it seems there were exceptions. So the literacy rate of female servants in London from the last decades of the seventeenth century was markedly higher than in country districts. Female migrants to London, Peter Earle has suggested, represented ' "the cream" of provincial girls'.[9] It was only the more literate, it is argued, who made the decision to migrate to London. By far the greatest concentration of domestic servants is found in London and most came from the country. In Scotland, while the majority of servants were illiterate, those 'who were servants to gentry and professionals had appreciably better literacy attainments than those working in craft or trade households or businesses'.[10] This was possibly because such employers were more likely to own books and to value education in their servants. In France in the eighteenth century 'servants may have been poor and vulnerable, but they also had a cultural headstart over unskilled workers in other occupations. In any town in

[6] David Cressy, 'Illiteracy in England 1530–1730', *The Historical Journal*, 20 (1977), 23, 9.
[7] David Cressy, *Literacy and the Social Order* (1980), 145.
[8] As quoted in E. S. Turner, *What the Butler Saw: 250 Years of the Servant Problem* (1962), 225.
[9] 'The Female Labour Market in London in the Late 17th and Early 18th Centuries' *Economic History Review*, 2nd ser., 42/3 (1989), 328–53 at p. 335.
[10] Houston, *Scottish Literacy and the Scottish Identity*, 60.

France, a male servant was more likely to know how to sign his name than was a gardener or a docker.' Domestic service in urban France, it is argued, attracted—and not merely to the larger households—'the more educated and probably the more resourceful among migrant workers'.[11]

Considering the obstacles and difficulties in the way of expanding the reading public—the absence of leisure, the lack of privacy in most houses, the cost of candles, the high price of books, the rarity until after 1740 of lending libraries, it would not be altogether surprising to find few literate servants. Yet the reading public certainly expanded, particularly in the second half of the century. Among those using the new circulating libraries, the lower orders, it was held, were a not insignificant number. In particular, it was 'servant-women of the better sort', it was argued, who were debauched by the 'slop-shops in literature'. Judging by the frequency of accusations of 'literary pretensions of the lower orders', and more especially against apprentices and domestic servants, the expansion of the reading public owed something to domestic servants.[12] It is difficult to come to any firm and quantifiable conclusions on servant literacy. What seems to have been true is that literacy levels varied enormously between servants like the cook, Susan, in Fielding's *Grub-Street Opera*, who tells another servant 'I can neither write nor read,—it was my parents fault, not mine, that gave me not a better education', to those like Mary Leadbeater's Mary Casey who is described as 'Not knowing how to write, though she could read', to those who were fully literate.[13] The same wide range in levels of literacy is found in male servants. It confirms the view of early modern society as a 'partially literate society' in which 'there coexisted people living at very different levels of intellectual sophistication'.[14] What is more difficult to understand is how a significant number of servants were not only literate but literary, writing poems, plays and novels, memoirs and autobiographies, of—what is now accepted as—a high standard.

What of contemporary opinion of the desirability of education

---

[11] Maza, *Servants and Masters in Eighteenth-Century France*, 49, 52.
[12] Ian Watt, *The Rise of the Novel* (1963), 44, 49.
[13] Henry Fielding, *A Grub-Street Opera* (1731), 27; Mary Leadbeater, *Cottage Biography* (1822), 38.
[14] Thomas, 'The Meaning of Literacy in Early Modern England', 103.

in servants? Bernard Mandeville expressed the view of many in the eighteenth century when he wrote that 'reading, writing, and arithmetic are ... very pernicious to the Poor'. 'Knowledge of the Working Poor', he added, 'should be confin'd within the Verge of their Occupations, and never extended ... beyond what relates to their calling'.[15] One of Johnson's *Idler* essays tells the story of a charity school girl, Betty Broom. The school had been maintained 'by the contributions of wealthy neighbours'. Suddenly one of the subscribers turned against the education of the children of the poor. It was, she claimed, 'little less than criminal to teach poor girls to read and write. They who are born to poverty ... are born to ignorance, and will work the harder the less they know.' Appealing to the mercenary side of the other subscribers, she declared herself resolved 'to spoil no more girls; those who were to live by their hands should neither read nor write out of her pocket'. The school was closed.[16] But if there were those who thought education was not for servants and that it was destructive of good servants, there were others who thought their education of the utmost importance. Richard Baxter in 1673 suggested to masters that 'if you have servants that cannot read let them learn yet (at spare hours) if they be of any capacity and willingness'.[17] Admittedly his end was that servants should, above all else, be able to read the Bible. Richard Mayo foresaw that not all masters were in a position to educate their servants. 'If any of you are not able to instruct them, be deeply humbled presently and get others to instruct them.'[18] 'I cannot help observing', wrote Jonas Hanway in 1760, 'what a gross impropriety it appears to me in receiving either Sex as *Domestic Servants*, without considering *reading* as a necessary qualification. What *can* they know of Religion; at least how *are they* to fill up the *many vacant hours*, which there must necessarily be in all great families, *if they cannot read?*'[19]

On the education required by a 'waiting woman', *The Compleat Servant-Maid* recommended that she should 'write well and legibly, know language and good English and have some skill in

---

[15] Bernard Mandeville, *The Fable of the Bees*, 2 vols. (1724), i. 328.
[16] *The Yale Edition of the Works of Samuel Johnson*, 16 vols. (1958–90), ii. 80–1.
[17] *Christian Directory* (1673), 4. [18] *A Present for Servants*, 46.
[19] *Eight Letters to his Grace Duke of——on the Custom of Vails-giving in England* (1760), 56.

arithmetic'.[20] The education of a lady's maid, Samuel and Sarah Adams argued in 1825, 'should be superior to that of the ordinary class of females'. If their mistresses expected such servants to read to them they were advised to 'practise reading aloud, from the best authors'.[21] Anthony Heasel in 1773 made it clear that a lady's maid or waiting-woman could never attain this position without some education and in particular that an essential qualification was 'an ability to read well aloud'.[22] In a place where the mistress was in favour of education in a servant, the demands of their role often extended that education. A waiting-maid, Molly Quick, in Johnson's *Idler* essays, explains to Johnson that 'when first I came to this lady, I had nothing like the learning that I have now, and I have much time to read'.[23] While the object of Hannah More's Sunday schools for the poor of the Mendips was to instil principles of willing submission and piety in the labouring class, she recognized that in order to achieve this they must be able to read. In one of her Repository Tracts she anticipated the sort of criticism which her project was to encounter. She has a Farmer Hoskins who insists that 'of all the foolish inventions, and new-fangled devices to ruin the country, that of teaching the poor to read is the very worst'. To which Hannah More, in the guise of Mrs Jones, replies: 'And I, farmer, think that to teach good principles to the lower classes is the most likely way to save the country. Now in order to this we must teach them to read.'[24] Hannah More's object was to train the labouring class to be good, obedient, loyal servants. Dr William Kitchiner in 1829 advised masters to 'Hire no servant who cannot read or write.'[25] By this time it was becoming more important that servants should be able to read and write. 'Notions about what a servant girl's education should be', writes Olwen Hufton, 'had become more sophisticated: a girl seeking a position in a substantial household who hoped to advance beyond basic kitchen drudgery must be minimally literate and

---

[20] As quoted in Violet A. Simpson, 'Servants and Service in Eighteenth-Century Town and Country', *Cornhill Magazine*, 14 (1903); 398–409 at p. 409.

[21] *The Complete Servant* (1825), 236, 238–9.

[22] *The Servant's Book of Knowledge* (1773), 69 as quoted in J. Jean Hecht, *The Domestic Servant in Eighteenth-Century England* (1956), 61.

[23] *The Yale Edition of the Works of Samuel Johnson*, ii. 144–5.

[24] As quoted in Donna Landry, *The Muses of Resistance* (1990), 123, from Hannah More, *Cheap Repository Tracts: The Sunday School* (n.d.), 10.

[25] As quoted in Turner, *What the Butler Saw*, 109.

nicely spoken.'[26] In 1870 a report for the Metropolitan School District on Eliza Lewis, a workhouse girl, explained that although she 'never gives a pert answer, at age 14 [she] cannot read or count change or tell the time so she will have to leave her place'.[27]

If there were literate servants in the eighteenth century, their literacy was either already acquired when they entered service, or was the result of education received in service from their fellow servants or their masters and mistresses. It was one thing to advise masters to educate their servants, but another for them to do so. How often did they take responsibility for the education of their servants? David Cressy suggests it was rare. 'Young people in service', he writes, 'were no more likely to acquire literacy than children at home unless they were unusually fortunate in their choice of master.' 'It is unlikely', he continues, that experience in service 'was any kind of substitute for going to school.'[28] Yet when John Macdonald, the footman who wrote his memoirs, was only 9 he 'had a great desire to read, and the servants gave me a lesson when time permitted'.[29] In *The History of Betty Barnes*, a novel about a maidservant ascribed to Sarah Fielding, it is the housekeeper who teaches her to read.[30] At the end of the seventeenth century Richard Mayo talked of some servants who had 'Masters that do purposely allow them time, and see they spend it in Reading, and other Duties'. But there were also 'rough and careless masters', as Mayo acknowledged, 'that hurry them to bed, that they may rise the sooner about their Work, and think all time lost when that is not in hand'.[31] William Fleetwood in 1716 hinted that sometimes the promise of 'instruction' was included in the contract with servants.[32] But the term 'instruction' is ambiguous and may here have been limited to vocational training. On the other hand, when Nancy Bere was taken from the local poorhouse to weed in the Hackman's garden at Lymington some time in the

---

[26] 'Women, Work and Family', in Natalie Zemon Davis and Arlette Farge (eds.), *A History of Women*, iii (1993); 15–45 at p. 21.
[27] As quoted in Leonore Davidoff and Ruth Hawthorn, *A Day in the Life of a Victorian Domestic Servant* (1976), 77.
[28] *Literacy and the Social Order*, 41.
[29] *Memoirs of an Eighteenth-Century Footman, John Macdonald*, ed. John Beresford (1927), 27.
[30] *The History of Betty Barnes*, 2 vols. (1753), i. 15.
[31] *A Present for Servants*, 70–1.
[32] *The Relative Duties of Parents and Children, Husbands and Wives, Masters and Servants*, 2nd edn. (1716), 314.

1770s or 1780s, graduating first to kitchen maid, and finally to lady's maid, Mrs Hackman 'had her carefully instructed in all the elementary branches of education'.[33]

There certainly were masters and mistresses throughout the eighteenth century who were concerned to educate their servants. When, later in life, John Macdonald entered the service of Lord Hamilton and Lady Anne, they 'were informed that I was desirous to learn to read'. They sent him to school where, he wrote, 'in the course of time I got reading, writing and arithmetic'.[34] Later he was to write a most articulate and readable account of his life as a servant. John Baker, the lawyer, took a personal interest in his servants' education, rewarding them when they did well. So Nanny Peters, in January 1775, was given a shilling 'for reading and prodigious attention and improvement'.[35] In 1828 John Skinner, the Somerset rector, recorded that his daughter Anne was 'engaged in teaching the servants to write and cypher'. Skinner was not at all sure he approved. He had begun, he recorded, 'to have... doubts about teaching the lower orders beyond reading'.[36]

What is surprising is that out of this so-called illiterate occupational group—both male and female servants—there should come some remarkable dramatists, novelists, and, perhaps above all, poets. How did they acquire an education that fitted them to write? Jane Holt (née Wiseman, fl. 1701–17) was both dramatist and poet. She came from very humble origins, but when in her young days she became a servant to the Recorder of Oxford, William Wright, she was given access to his library. As a servant she was particularly fortunate in 'having a pretty deal of leisure Time, which she spent in Reading Novels and Plays'.[37] It was in Wright's household she commenced the play *Antiochus the Great: Or, The Fatal Relapse. A tragedy*, the only play she wrote but one which was performed on the London stage in 1701 and again in 1711, 1712, and 1721. It was published in 1702. Mary Collier (1690?–c.1762), the washerwoman poet, was born near Midhurst,

---

[33] Richard Warner, *Literary Recollections*, 2 vols. (1830), i. 48–9.
[34] *Memoirs of an Eighteenth-Century Footman*.
[35] *The Diary of John Baker*, ed. Philip C. Yorke (1931), 52.
[36] *Journal of a Somerset Rector 1803–34*, ed. Howard and Peter Coombs (1930), 320.
[37] *Eighteenth-Century Women Poets*, ed. Roger Lonsdale, (1989), 72. I acknowledge a very special debt to Roger Lonsdale without whose anthology this chapter would not have been possible.

Sussex, of 'poor but honest parents', by whom she was 'taught to read when very Young'. She had taken 'great delight in it'. When her mother died, her education came to an abrupt halt. She never attended school but was 'set to such labour as the country afforded'. Some time after her father's death in 1720 she moved to Petersfield in Hampshire where, she tells us, 'my chief employment was Washing, Brewing and such labour, still devoting what leisure time I had to Books'.[38] She was later to acquire a patron—'a gentlewoman whom she nursed through an illness'.[39] Some time after Mary Collier had started to write poetry she confessed she 'had learn'd to write to assist my memory' which suggests—astounding although it is—that until that time all her poetry had been committed to memory.[40]

Another woman poet, Susanna Harrison (1752–94), whose family probably came from Ipswich, was one of a large family. When her father died Susanna was still a child. The family was left in straitened circumstances. At the age of 16 Susanna went into service. With no formal education, while in service, she tells us, she taught herself to read and write. Her favourite books were the Bible and Watts's hymns. She was to become a hymn-writer herself and her *Songs in the Night* (1780) included many hymns. She says nothing of help from her employers, but the existence of books about the house may well have contributed to her efforts.[41] The servant, Betty Broom, in one of Johnson's essays tells him that 'his first essay . . . was sent down into the kitchen, with a great bundle of gazettes and useless papers'.[42]

The poet, Mary Leapor (1722–46) was the daughter of a gardener, who at the time of her birth worked on the estate of Sir John Blencowe at Marston St Lawrence in Northamptonshire. Whether she had any formal education is uncertain. It is possible that she attended the Free School in Brackley run by Magdalen College School at a time when the schoolmaster was a Richard Cooper who, with some success, did his best to improve standards at the school. Remarkably, Latin was taught to children of

---

[38] Mary Collier, *Poems on Several Occasions* (1762), p. iii.
[39] Stephen Duck, *The Thresher's Labour*, Mary Collier, *The Woman's Labour*, published in one vol. with an introduction by E. P. Thompson (1989), p. x.
[40] As quoted in *Eighteenth-Century Women Poets*, 171.
[41] *A Dictionary of British and American Women Writers 1660–1800*, ed. Janet Todd (1984), 153.
[42] *The Yale Edition of the Works of Samuel Johnson*, ii. 80.

the poor. The Leapor family's resources were scant. According to Mary's father 'she was always fond of reading every thing that came in her way, as soon as she was capable of it'. She particularly liked poetry 'but had few opportunities of procuring any Books of that kind'. She could 'write tolerably' by the time she was 10 or 11, when her first verses were written.[43] In many ways she was remarkably fortunate both in the mistress of a household where she went into service as kitchen maid when still an adolescent, and, later, in her patron, Bridget Freemantle. Susanna Jennens, the daughter of Sir John Blencowe, who had employed Mary Leapor's father, was a widow who lived alone at Weston Hall, Northamptonshire. She was probably Mary Leapor's first employer. Coming from a literary family, she was something of a poet herself and, according to Sir George Sitwell, devoted time to reading. It seems more than likely that 'she gave attention to her kitchen-maid and that she encouraged her to read and write poetry'.[44] She certainly 'corrected Leapor's verses', and criticized them.[45] Later, when Mary Leapor had left a place with the Chauncy family at Edgcote House and returned to her father's house and was housekeeping for him, she met Bridget Freemantle. Two or three years before getting to know the author, after reading Leapor's poems, Freemantle wrote that she found them 'extraordinary Performances for a girl of her Age, and one that had so little Advantage (or rather none at all) either from Books or Conversation'.[46] Freemantle was an almost perfect patron: encouraging, a willing audience, and a great promoter of Leapor's poetry. She was also an educated woman, well read, and must have had a profound influence over Leapor, but it was only to last fourteen months before Leapor died. It is possible that, had Leapor lived longer, the relations with her patron might have soured, but in their short acquaintance Freemantle's influence was entirely beneficial. In answer to a query to the *Gentleman's Magazine* asking who Molly Leapor was, a letter appeared in 1784 in which she was described as 'some time cook-maid in a gentleman's family'. Whether this was Edgcote House we do not know, but clearly her 'scribbling' was not entirely welcomed. 'Her fond-

---

[43] As quoted in Richard Greene, *Mary Leapor* (1993), 8. In all I say of Mary Leapor I must acknowledge my debt to Richard Greene's work.
[44] Ibid. 13.   [45] Ibid. 14.
[46] Mary Leapor, *Poems upon Several Occasions*, 2 vols. (1748–51), pp. xviii–xix.

ness for writing verses there', we are told 'displayed itself by her sometimes taking up her pen while the jack was standing still, and the meat scorching.'[47]

Mary Leapor was unusually fortunate. In her account for Johnson of the various places she has occupied in service, Betty Broom talks of the brief period when her mistress 'spent her time with books, and was pleased to find a maid who could partake her amusement'. It was 'the only happy part' of her life.[48] Also fortunate was Clara Reeve (1729–1807), the novelist and critic, who was the daughter of a cleric at St Nicholas, Ipswich. He had a large family. Such education as she acquired was from her father's encouragement. From an early age she was made to read parliamentary debates, Greek and Roman histories, Rapin's *History of England*, and Plutarch's *Lives*.[49] In her novel *The Two Mentors* she gives an account of two former servants. Hecht commented that she had 'herself lived as a domestic, and knew service intimately as an occupation'.[50]

The poems of Janet Little (1759–1813), the milkmaid poet of Nether Bogside in Dumfries, were published in 1792. Her parents 'were not in circumstances to afford her more than a common education'. She became servant to a clergyman. Then she applied to be chambermaid or nurse to Mrs Frances Dunlop of Dunlop House, Ayrshire, who, recognizing her talents, became her patron, attempting to win the support of Burns for the publication of her poetry. Later she was put in charge of the dairy at Loudoun Castle rented by the daughter of Frances Dunlop.[51] From the poems of Elizabeth Hands (fl. 1789) we learn that before her marriage she too was a domestic servant. She described herself in 1789 as 'born in obscurity and, and never emerging beyond the lower stations of life'.[52] She expressed thanks to patrons, among whom was Philip Bracebridge Homer, a minor poet who taught at Rugby School, and who actively promoted a subscription for the publication of her main poem *The Death of Amnon*. He was not altogether convinced that the poem would be received well. It dealt in five cantos with the subject of incestuous rape—hardly, it

---

[47] *Gentleman's Magazine*, 54 (1784), 807.
[48] *The Yale Edition of the Works of Samuel Johnson*, ii. 90.
[49] *A Dictionary of British and American Writers*, 266.
[50] *The Domestic Servant in Eighteenth-Century England*, 223.
[51] *Eighteenth-Century Women Poets*, 453.   [52] Ibid. 422.

was thought, a suitable subject for a woman. Of how she had acquired her education we remain ignorant. It was the brother of Ann Yearsley (1752–1806), the milkwoman poet and novelist, who taught her to read, and, according to Hannah More, to write. She had never attended a school. But according to a correspondent in the *Gentleman's Magazine* of 1784, Yearsley told him that 'her mother was not only a woman of sense, but delighted in books, and from thence that passion arose in *her*'. When asked how her mother had obtained books she answered 'She applied to *her betters* who kindly lent them to her.'[53] By the time her collection of poems was published in 1792 Ellen Taylor (fl. 1792) was no longer a domestic servant, but earlier she had been 'a servant in a Gentleman's Family'. She was 'the daughter of an indigent cottager... who had barely the ability to afford common sustenance to her and a numerous family during his lifetime'. Her education had included only 'the most common rudiments of reading and writing'. She described herself as 'in a state of the most retired obscurity'. One of her poems is addressed 'To a Gentleman who had lent her some books'. They included Milton, Thomson, and Young. In the copy of her poems in the Bodleian Library in handwriting there is a suggestion that the gentleman was a 'Mr Dowdall with whom she afterwards was at service'.[54]

[53] *Gentleman's Magazine*, 54 (1784), 897. Mary Waldron's recent work on Yearsley ('Ann Yearsley and the Clifton Records', in Paul J. Korshin (ed.), *The Age of Johnson*, iii (1990), 301–29) has suggested that she was not strictly speaking a servant at all but, as a milkwoman, was self-employed. It is a fair argument but one that could be used of eighteenth-century charwomen and washerwomen although both were embraced by the term 'servant'—loosely used as it was. But Yearsley is also described as a milkmaid. Hannah More referred to her as 'a milker of cows, and a feeder of Hogs' which suggests she did the work of a farm-servant. Joseph Cottle wrote of her as a milkmaid. She was also described by J. C. Squire in 1921 as 'the Bristol charwoman', which may refer to her work at an earlier period of her life. The social pretensions Yearsley may have had from her husband's 'estate of near six pounds a year' at the time of their marriage and which was entirely lost before her meeting Hannah More, can hardly have been furthered by the work of a milkwoman. It was work that was regarded as that of the very lowest social group of women workers. It was the occupation that the poorest Irish women immigrants moved into on their arrival in England. If Waldron is right in claiming that Yearsley saw herself as middle-class and therefore as apart from 'the feckless labouring masses', by the time Hannah More became her patron any basis for such pretensions had long gone and she differed little from the rest of the labouring poor. As far as More was concerned Yearsley unquestionably belonged to the labouring class.

[54] *Eighteenth-Century Women Poets*, 455; *Poems by Ellen Taylor, the Irish Cottager* (1792), 6–7.

Robert Dodsley, the poet and dramatist, was born at Mansfield, Nottinghamshire, in 1703. 'The humble situation and circumstances of his parents', his biographer tells us, 'precluded him from the advantages of a liberal education'.[55] He started out as apprentice to a stocking-weaver, but ran away when he was 'starved and ill-treated' and entered service.[56] It was while footman to the Hon. Mrs Lowther that he wrote many of his poems. John Lamb (1725?–1799), who published *Poetical Pieces on Several Occasions* in 1777, was the father of Charles and was 'descended from rural folk of small means'. He had but minimal schooling before he left home to find work. He first became a footman in Bath before moving to London, where he was employed by Samuel Salt, who owned an extensive library. It was the source of his education, but it also provided accessible books to both Charles and Mary, his children.[57] Joseph Mayett, a farm servant in Buckinghamshire who wrote an autobiography, was 'taught to read by his mother, from her godmother's gift first of a Bible and then of the little illustrated chapbook, *The Reading made Easy*'. His mother was able to read but could not write. At the age of 11 he was loaned *Pilgrim's Progress*—we are not told by whom. But 'once acquired, his literacy was nurtured at times by the farmers who employed him as servant'.[58] The father of John Jones, the Catterick butler who with the help of Southey published his poems in 1831, had been a gardener. His mother kept a small village shop in which he helped from the age of 7; this put an end to his school education, brief though it had been. His teacher was 'an old woman, with whom I learnt my letters and spelling, but I believe I made but little progress in reading'. For two winters he went to 'an old man, by trade a stone-cutter', who gave lessons when he returned from work in the evenings. At the age of 10 he had read only 'the Psalter and Testament, and sometimes a chapter in the Bible'. But with the little money he now earned he 'purchased songs—the Mournful Lady's Garland, and such stories as are generally hawked about in a pedlar's basket'. When

[55] 'The Life of Dodsley', in *A Complete Edition of the Poets of Great Britain*, ed. Robert Anderson, xi (1795); 77–114 at p. 77.
[56] From the 'Dedication to Subscribers', in Robert Dodsley, *A Muse in Livery: or, the Footman's Miscellany* (1732).
[57] Winifred F. Courtney, *Young Charles Lamb 1775–1802* (1982), 4, 8.
[58] Ann Kussmaul, *The Autobiography of Joseph Mayett of Quainton (1783–1839)*, Buckinghamshire Record Society, xxiii (1986), pp. x–xi.

he was 17 he obtained a place as a footboy. He worked under a French butler who often went out all day until dinner leaving John Jones to lay the cloth. In the dining-room was a bookcase 'which was left open'. As a result he read all of Shakespeare's plays.[59] William Tayler, the footman who wrote a journal in 1837, came of 'a large family of a yeoman farmer' at Grafton in Oxfordshire. He went into service first locally and then in London. His journal was begun because, as he admitted, he was 'a wretched bad writer' and was long encouraged by his friends to practise more.[60]

Why were so many of these literary domestic servants poets? The answer might be that the leisure a servant had for writing was liable to be interrupted at any point, their train of thought broken. Or was it that poetry 'offered the existence of a richer, more rewarding world' in sharp contrast to the drudgery of service?[61] Jane Cave (c.1754–1813) whose *Poems on Various Subjects, Entertaining, Elegiac, and Religious* were published in 1783, supported herself, it is thought, either as 'a servant or teacher'.[62] In her poems she describes the difficulties facing poets like herself when duty intervened and inspiration was lost:

> So when the Muses come on anxious wing
> Some pleasing subject to my fancy bring

she encourages them to enter.

> But ere, perhaps the conversation's o'er
> Duty commands that we converse no more.
> Now Duty's call, I never must refuse,
> I rise, and with a blush myself excuse,
> Tell them I must withdraw a while, and when
> Duty admits, I will return again.
> Sometimes till I return, they deign to stay,
> Sometimes they take offence, and fly away.

No wonder then that

> what the Author to the World presents,
> Appears through numberless impediments.[63]

---

[59] Robert Southey, *The Lives and Works of the Uneducated Poets* (1831), 1, 171–3.
[60] *Useful Toil: Autobiographies of Working People from the 1820s to the 1920s*, ed. John Burnett, 2nd edn. (1994), 172.
[61] Martha Vicinus, *The Industrial Muse* (1974), 147.
[62] *Eighteenth-Century Women Poets*, 373.
[63] Jane Cave, *Poems on Various Subjects, Entertaining, Elegiac, and Religious* (1783), from the poem 'The Author's Plea', 1–5.

The Muses were no more tolerant of Janet Little. 'I cannot boast of any favours', she wrote, 'they have deigned to confer upon me as yet; my situation in life has been very much against me as to that.' One of her poems, 'To a Lady who sent the Author some paper with a reading of Sillar's poems', regrets that

> the Muses are fled far away,
> They deem it disgrace with a milkmaid to stay.

She now dreads their approach and, rather than be dismissed like those

> whose pretensions to fame
> Are slight as the bubble that bursts on the stream.

she will abandon writing for ever.[64]

When Ellen Taylor is sent down to the banks of the Barrow to wash linen she is visited by the Muses:

> But servitude, with brow austere,
> Commands me straight away.

She is even brought to envy the lot of fellow servants with no pretensions to education:

> Thrice happy she, condemned to move
> Beneath the servile weight,
> Whose thoughts ne'er soar one inch above
> The standard of her fate.[65]

Ann Yearsley wrote of her own poems that they were written 'in the short intervals of a life of labour'.[66] In his Dedication to Subscribers in *A Muse in Livery*, Robert Dodsley wrote that few in his station were 'able to find Leisure for Employments of this Nature'. He begged his readers 'to consider the very many Disadvantages the Author labours under' but what could be expected from a mere footman who lacked 'Friends, Fortune, and all the Advantages of a liberal Education?'[67] When, in 1827, the butler John Jones, aged 54 and a servant all his life, sent his poems to Southey, he described himself as 'a poor, humble, uneducated

---

[64] *A Dictionary of British and American Women Writers*, 199; *The Poetical Works of Janet Little, the Scotch Milkmaid* (1792), 206–7.
[65] *Eighteenth-Century Women Poets*, 456.
[66] *Poems on Various Subjects* (1787), dedication.
[67] *A Muse in Livery: or, the Footman's Miscellany*.

domestic'. Living in a family with fourteen children, he wrote apologetically of his poems that he had 'devoted but little time to their construction, they having been chiefly composed when in the exercise of my domestic duties, and frequently borne on my memory for two or three weeks before I had the leisure to ease it of its burden'. 'I have seldom sat down to study anything', he confessed, 'for in many instances when I have done so a ring at the bell, or a knock at the door, or something or other, would disturb me—and not wishing to be seen, I frequently used to either crumple my paper up in my pocket, or take the trouble to lock it up, and before I could arrange it again, I was often ... again disturbed.'[68] But poetry may have seemed to lend itself better than other writing to the conditions of service. Poems were much shorter than novels or plays. They could be thought out while working, committed to memory (something it is far easier to do with verse than with prose), and written down quickly when the opportunity arose.

We might pause to consider what the existence of such literary talent among domestic servants from consistently poor backgrounds means. It might suggest that schooling was far from a necessary preliminary to literacy. Parents and more particularly mothers certainly played an important role in teaching their sons and daughters to read. Servants often taught each other. Masters and mistresses would sometimes arrange for the education of their servants or make books accessible to them. But in many cases it was these servants' own determination to read and write that made their achievement possible. What is interesting in all these examples of literate and literary domestic servants—more particularly women—is the kind of reaction their writing provoked. The neighbours of Mary Leapor, when as a child 'she always chose to spend her leisure Hours in Writing and Reading, rather than in those Diversions which young People generally chuse', were concerned that she 'should overstudy herself, and be mopish'.[69] Not always were parents sympathetic to their daughters' reading books or 'scribbling'. Of Mary Leapor's parents Bridget Freemantle wrote how, when as a child of 10 or 11 she started writing verse, 'her mother was at first pleas'd ... But

---

[68] 'John Jones, An old Servant: An Account written by himself', from Southey, *The Lives and Works of the Uneducated Poets*, 172.

[69] Leapor, *Poems upon Several Occasions*, vol. ii, p. xxx.

finding this Humour increase upon her as she grew up, when she thought her capable of more profitable Employment, she endeavour'd to break her of it'. Her father 'having no Taste for Poetry, and not imagining it could ever be any Advantage to her, join'd in the same Design'.[70] In the preface to her *Poems on Several Occasions* of 1733, Mary Masters wrote that 'her Genius to Poetry was always brow-beat and discountenanc'd by her Parents'. It was a familiar parental reaction. 'From my earliest Infancy', wrote Laetitia Pilkington, poet and autobiographer, 'I had a strong Disposition to Letters'. Her mother did not encourage her to indulge it, 'regarding more the Beauty of my Face, than the Improvement of my mind'.[71]

As with so many women writers in the eighteenth century, these literary domestic servants were often accused of plagiarism. It was considered impossible that a mere servant could write novels and plays let alone poetry. Female servants suffered a double disadvantage—as servants and as women. As Jane Wiseman commented on her critics, 'the language they are unwilling to believe my own'. The prologue and epilogue of *Antiochus* were in fact 'writ by a friend'. But her critics 'have chose one of our best Poets for my Assistant, one I had not the happiness to know, 'till after the Play was finished'.[72] Some of these women poets wrote poems in answer to those who questioned their authorship. So Mary Masters managed, in her answer to a gentleman who doubted her authorship of a collection of poems, to suggest it was a defect in his own judgement which prevented him seeing that she was the poet. And, she wittily implies, such are his assumptions, that if he admitted her authorship, he would find defects in the poems.

> Search but these Strains, you think so much excel,
> Scan every Verse, and try the Numbers well:
> You'll plainly see, in almost ev'ry Line,
> Distinguishing Defects to prove them Mine.[73]

Mary Collier must also have come in for the same criticism, for the third edition of *The Woman's Labour* carried a statement dated 21

[70] Ibid., pp. xxix–xxx.
[71] Laetitia Pilkington, *Memoirs of Mrs. Laetitia Pilkington (1749–54)*, 3 vols. (1770), i. 13.
[72] *A Dictionary of British and American Writers*, 329.
[73] Masters, *Poems on Several Occasions*, 45.

September 1739 and signed by nine residents of Petersfield vouching for the authenticity of her poem. As her friends made clear in the advertisement to the first edition of *The Woman's Labour*, 'the Novelty of a *Washer-Woman* turning poetess, will procure her some Readers'.[74]

Ann Yearsley was described by Joseph Cottle as 'a very extraordinary individual'. She had, he insisted, 'an unusually sound masculine understanding'. After reading her novel *The Royal Captives*, he wrote that there was 'a vigour in her style, which scarcely appears compatible with a wholly uneducated woman'. However, when she is compared to Hannah More, her patron, she is described by Cottle as 'a strong-minded illiterate woman' ('illiterate' here may well signify her particular ignorance of Latin and Greek as well as her lack of an education). More, on the other hand, possessed 'a refined mind, delicately alive to the least approximation to indecorum'.[75] Hannah More told Elizabeth Montagu that she had been shown some verses 'said to be written by a poor illiterate woman ... who sells milk from door to door'. She was, she told Montagu, 'destitute of all the elegancies of literature' and was unaware of 'a single rule of Grammar'. She had 'never *seen* a Dictionary'.[76] The suspicion is that class played a role in defining literacy. The labouring classes were expected to be illiterate. 'It enabled the upper classes to despise their inferiors as "illiterate clowns"'.[77] So in the plays and novels of the time servants become comic characters prone to dropping or inserting aitches.

It was thought there was something inherently subversive about servants who 'scribbled'. After the French Revolution it was said that 'many candid and enlightened men' apprehend 'danger from a *general* diffusion even of the elementary knowledge of reading and writing'.[78] In her *A Poem, On the Supposition of an Advertisement appearing in a Morning Paper, of the Publication of a Volume of Poems, by a Servant-Maid*, Elizabeth Hands imagines its reception among those of quality:

> 'What ideas can such low-bred creatures conceive?'
> Says Mrs Noworthy, and laughed in her sleeve.

[74] Collier, *The Woman's Labour*, advert. preceding the poems.
[75] Joseph Cottle, *Early Recollections*, 2 vols. (1837), 69–70, 75.
[76] Yearsley, *Poems on Various Subjects*, pp. viii, xi.
[77] Thomas, 'The Meaning of Literacy in Early Modern England', 117.
[78] Thomas Bernard, *The Barrington School* (1812).

> Says old Miss Prudella, 'If servants can tell
> How to write to their mothers, to say they are well,
> And read of a Sunday *The Duty of Man*,
> Which is more I believe than one half of them can;
> I think 'tis much *properer* they should rest there,
> Than be reaching at things so much out of their sphere.'[79]

It was on the whole agreed that servants were more useful to their employers if they could read, but there was no purpose in extending their education beyond that point. Much of the criticism of these servant–poets was that their lack of education led to serious defects in their poetry. It was a criticism much resented by Robert Dodsley:

> Methinks I would not have it said,
> As all my Praise, when I am read,
> *The Lines, considering whence they came,*
> *Are well enough, nor merit Blame*[80]

In *A Poem, on the Supposition of the Book having been Published and Read*, Hands captures the reaction of a local cleric:

> The Rector reclined himself back in his chair,
> And opened his snuff-box with indolent air:
> 'This book', says he (snift, snift), has, in the beginning,
> (The ladies give audience to hear his opinion),
> 'Some pieces, I think, that are pretty correct:
> A style elevated you cannot expect;
> To some of her equals they may be a treasure,
> And country lasses may read 'em with pleasure.'[81]

Other women poets, although never domestic servants, made some of the same points. Jane West, both poet and novelist, for example, who was always very conscious of her 'confined education' (she was largely self-educated), wrote a poem on the reaction of the fashionable world to a woman, and a mere farmer's wife at that, writing poetry:

> A man of rank grew warm, and swore
> The times were bad enough before.
> He offered to bet ten to one
> The nation would be soon undone:

---

[79] *Eighteenth-Century Women Poets*, 426.
[80] From a poem 'The Guardian Angel', in Dodsley, *A Muse in Livery*, 132.
[81] *Eighteenth-Century Women Poets*, 429.

> For honour, spirit, courage, worth,
> Were all appendages on birth;
> And if the rustics grew refined,
> Who would the humble duties mind?[82]

And, indeed, he had a point. If the lower orders started having literary aspirations who was going to do the dirty work?

Some of these poets talked of the drudgery of their working lives. Mary Collier, for instance, described a day's work at the 'House'. It began very early in the morning and involved washing a great variety of fabrics all of which required the 'utmost skill and Care'. The mistress comes to check what work has been done:

> Lays her Commands upon us, that we mind
> Her Linen well, nor *leave the dirt behind.*
> Not this alone, but also to take care
> We don't her Cambricks or her Ruffles tear,
> And these most strictly does of us require:
> To save her Soap, and sparing be of Fire;
> Tells us her Charge is great, nay, furthermore,
> Her Cloaths are fewer than the time before.

The work is so hard that

> Not only sweat but Blood runs trickling down
> Our wrists and fingers; still our Work demands
> The constant action of our lab'ring Hands.

The washing is finally finished but 'to make complete our Slavery' they are given the task of cleaning all the pewter. Then when finally preparing to end their working day the beer of the house begins to run low and the mistress asks them to prepare for brewing. The final lines of 'A Woman's Labour' are an indictment not only of the life of a charwoman but of the whole class basis of service:

> So the industrious Bees do hourly strive
> To bring their Loads of Honey to the Hive;
> Their sordid Owners always reap the Gains,
> And poorly recompense their Toil and Pains.[83]

Robert Dodsley, in his poem 'The Footman', outlines the way in which he occupies his working day in London. It starts—even

---

[82] *Eighteenth-Century Women Poets*, 383–4, from the poem 'To the Hon. Mrs C[ockayn]e'.

[83] Mary Collier, *The Woman's Labour: An Epistle to Mr Stephen Duck; in Answer to his late Poem, called 'The Thresher's Labour'* (1739).

before he is dressed—with cleaning 'Glasses, Knives and Plate'. Directly his mistress appears he is sent on messages:

> The Charge receiv'd, away run I,
> And here, and there, and yonder fly,
> With Services, and How-d'ye-does,
> Then Home return full fraught with News.

Next he lays the table for dinner, brings in the ale and beer and decants the wine. After serving the company he stands waiting for instructions. It is this time in the whole of his day he likes most. It is

> the only pleasant Hour
> Which I have in the Twenty-four;

For while he strives to appear

> to understand no more
> Than just what's called for

he listens to the conversation, noting every witticism and 'fine expression'. In the evening the whole process of visiting takes up his entire time. But while he waits for his mistress to emerge he goes into the servants' hall where other servants are waiting on their employers. The main topic of conversation, he admits, is their employers:

> But here amongst us the chief Trade is
> To rail against our Lords and Ladies;
> To aggravate their smallest Failings,
> T'expose their Faults with saucy Railings.[84]

The whole evening of visits he finds tedious, his day is a long one, but when compared to Mary Collier's daily drudgery it can hardly be called hard work.

Much the same daily routine of a footman is described by John Lamb, the father of Charles, in a poem entitled 'The Lady's Footman', except that he emphasizes the constant complaints of his mistress about her servants.

> When Dinners serv'd she then begins,
> Sure thus I'm teazed for my Sins;
> The Mutton's raw and Turnips cold,

[84] Dodsley, 'The Footman', in *A Muse in Livery*, 26–8, 30.

> Indeed, my Dear, I've Cause to scold:
> The heedless Slut's in Love I think,
> Or else it is the Effects of Drink.
> That Fellow too I'll part with soon,
> For drunk he mostly is ere Noon;
> Then Glass and China goes to pot,
> I cannot bear a drunken Sot.[85]

Masters and mistresses did not always react with sympathy to discovering their servants were sometimes better educated than themselves. One remembers Richardson's Pamela, who reveals in conversation with her master Mr B. that she well understands his literary allusions. Mr B. is taken aback at this equality of understanding in his servant-maid.[86] When Jenny Jones becomes servant to a schoolmaster in Fielding's *Tom Jones*, she is taught Latin by him until she becomes 'a better scholar than her master'. When his wife dismisses Jenny the schoolmaster expresses his satisfaction, 'saying she was grown of little use as a servant, spending all her time in reading and was become, moreover, very pert and saucy'. As Fielding tells us 'she and her master had lately had frequent disputes in literature, in which ... she was become greatly his superior'.[87] When, in Johnson's *Idler* essays, the servant-maid Betty Broom is discovered reading a book, she is told 'that wenches like me might spend their time better; that she never knew any of the readers had good designs in their heads', and dismissed. As Betty Broom comments, it is the 'first time that I found it thought criminal or dangerous to know how to read'.[88]

Not always was a servant who could read and write and who indulged her talents popular with other servants. When Betty Broom is hired by the housekeeper of 'a splendid family' she is given the task of 'buying necessaries for the house'. But when it is found her account of daily expenses fails to tally with the housekeeper's she is told by her 'that there should be no pen and ink in the kitchen but her own'. In another place she is welcomed by a novel-loving lady's maid 'who could not bear the vulgar girls',

---

[85] John Lamb, *Poetical Pieces on Several Occasions* (1777), 38.
[86] *The Shakespeare Head Edition of the Novels of Samuel Richardson*, 18 vols. (1929), i. 31.
[87] *The Wesleyan Edition of the Works of Henry Fielding*, 9 vols. (1972–88), *The History of Tom Jones*, 2 vols. (1974), i. 81, 85.
[88] *The Yale Edition of the Works of Samuel Johnson*, ii. 90.

until, growing jealous of Broom's popularity with the other servants, she is forced to leave.[89]

Some time after Mary Leapor had left Weston Hall she became kitchen maid to the Chauncy family of Edgcote House. From this, her last place, she was dismissed. Exactly what was the cause of her dismissal we are not told, although there are hints in her poetry, where, under the guise of Crumble Hall and Sophronia, both Edgcote House and Mrs Chauncy are discussed. In the character of Sophronia we meet a mistress—or possibly a housekeeper—with little sympathy for the servant–poet who was always 'scribbling' when she should have been working. Why was she dismissed? 'It may be', writes Richard Greene, 'that the spectacle of an intellectually ambitious kitchen-maid unnerved her employers, and that she posed a threat to their view of a proper social order.'[90]

In 'An Epistle to Artemisia. On Fame' Leapor describes her relations with either her mistress or the housekeeper, Sophronia:

> Then comes *Sophronia*, like a barb'rous *Turk*:
> 'You thoughtless Baggage, when d'ye mind your Work?
> Still o'er a Table leans your bending Neck:
> Your Head will grow preposterous, like a Peck.
> Go, ply your Needle: you might earn your Bread;
> Or who must feed you when your Father's dead?'
> She sobbing answers, 'Sure I need not come
> To you for Lectures, I have store at Home.
> What can I do?'
>   '—Not scribble.'
>   '—But I will'
> 'Then get thee packing—and be aukward still.'[91]

This fear of 'scribbling' servants getting above themselves was perhaps what lay behind the explosive relationship that developed between Ann Yearsley and her patron Hannah More. Although More admired her verse, was prepared to help her with her grammar and spelling, and to edit and find subscribers for her poetry, she was also strongly opposed to anything which would remove Yearsley from her own class or indeed make her independent of her patrons. More certainly never entertained the idea that Yearsley might be freed from her labours as milkwoman in

---

[89] Ibid. 90, 91.   [90] *Mary Leapor*, 91.
[91] *Eighteenth-Century Women Poets*, 206.

order to devote her whole time to writing poetry. 'It is not intended to place her in such a state of independence', More wrote to Elizabeth Montagu of her protégée, 'as might seduce her to devote her time to the idleness of Poetry'.[92] 'What at last is to be done for her is not positively resolved', wrote a correspondent to the *Gentleman's Magazine*, 'but it is likely to end in settling her in a school, where her talents may be exerted, her instructions become of service, her life be softened, and her own little family be brought forward.'[93] More was in fact planning to open a school for Yearsley to run, but events intervened. The patron–poet relationship is, perhaps, just as complex and difficult as that of master–servant. The cause of the rupture was the control and disposal of the money raised by the sale of her poems. More, and her fellow patron, Elizabeth Montagu, had invested the money in stocks in their joint names as trustees for Yearsley, who received only the annual interest, and even that was to be laid out as More 'thought proper'.[94]

Trying to see the case for both sides, Joseph Cottle explained that 'from the constitution of the human mind, it was hardly possible for one who had greatly obliged another (and the recipient, in a subordinate station) to experience the least opposition, in an arrangement, deemed by the principal, expedient, without experiencing, at least an uncomfortable feeling'. Cottle imagined the thoughts passing through Hannah More's mind at the time. 'Ann Yearsley, you are at present decently apparelled, but without my patronage, you would be serving hogs, or be weighed down with a milk pail, and do you oppose any disposition I and Mrs Montagu may think proper to make!'[95] There is the remarkable story of More's anger soon after her confrontation with her protégée, at finding that Yearsley was buying 'the hog-wash of her kitchen' from the cook. As she wrote to a friend 'this *wretch* is arraigning my conduct, she is fetching the wash every day from my house'.[96] What seems to have annoyed More was not only that it revealed Yearsley as having a connection with the household quite independently of its head, but that her cook was receiving

---

[92] Yearsley, *Poems on Various Subjects*, pp. xii–xiii.
[93] *Gentleman's Magazine*, 54 (1784), 897.
[94] *Poems on Various Subjects*, xvi.   [95] *Early Recollections*, i. 74–5.
[96] Yearsley, *Poems upon Several Occasions*, p. xxi n.; *Poems on Various Subjects*, 4th edn. (1786), pp. xviii–xix.

money from Yearsley. What More wanted from her protégée was 'deference and conciliation', but at the same time she wanted her to become more genteel and civilized.[97] The relationship between poet and patron was only a particular example of the complex and paradoxical relationship between servants and their employers. At one and the same time they wanted them to be in close contact, often carrying out the most intimate of services for them, and, in their dress and behaviour, for their servants to reflect their own high status. But on the other hand they wanted to distance themselves from their servants and make clear the class gulf that separated them.

In reviewing Southey's *The Lives and Works of the Uneducated Poets* in 1831, the *Edinburgh Review* described the attractions of patronage. 'The scribblings of peasants have been seized upon by those who have desired to be known as patrons of literature, and by those who have felt the necessity of assuring themselves of their own virtue'. It talked of 'the misery which has been brought about by blind and selfish patronage'.[98] Hannah More, it has been said, 'very much enjoyed the prospect of patronage'.[99]

At their final interview after the rift between them More called Yearsley 'a savage'.[100] She had 'a reprobate mind and was a bad woman'. There was no doubt in More's mind from the start of their relationship that Yearsley was to remain one of the labouring class but to become, perhaps, a little more polished and tamed member of that class. It was a role Yearsley firmly rejected. As she told her patron, 'she had rendered obligation insupportable'.[101] 'Commonly a poet was dropped', writes Martha Vicinus, 'when he showed signs of overstepping his station in life'.[102] More's attitude to Yearsley was no different from that towards the women in the schools of the Mendips she ran with her sisters. In the hard winter of 1801 she told them their lot would have been much worse had it not been for their receiving 'the benefits flowing from the distinction of rank and fortune', which had 'enabled the *high* so liberally to assist the low'. She trusted that the poor, 'especially those that are well instructed, have received what has been done for them as a matter of *favour, not of right*'. By the end

---

[97] Cottle, *Early Recollections*, i. 75.   [98] *Edinburgh Review*, 54 (1831), 72.
[99] Waldron, 'Ann Yearsley and the Clifton Records', 309.
[100] Yearsley, *Poems upon Several Occasions*, p. xx.   [101] Ibid.
[102] *The Industrial Muse*, 177.

of the century, perhaps in part as a result of her experience with Yearsley, Hannah More was arguing against teaching the poor to write. 'They learn of weekdays', she wrote, 'such coarse works as may fit them for servants. I allow of no writing.'[103] She thought they had no need of it. Others, like Priscilla Wakefield, would have limited servants' instruction in writing to just enough to 'enable them to set down the articles of their expenditure, or to write a receipt'.[104]

To be a servant–poet cannot have been easy. Quite apart from the obstacles to their acquiring sufficient education to write at all and their lack of access to books, there was the disapproval of many employers and, often, the discouragement of the literary élite. In a poem 'To my Aunty', Janet Little wrote of a dream she had which was all about the response of critics to her poetry.

> Voratious critics by the way
> Like eagles watching for their prey,

who made no allowances for her lack of education.[105] 'That a man of defective education, and living in a menial capacity, should write anything that can be dignified with the name of poetry', wrote the *Edinburgh Review*, 'is a strong presumption of the existence of poetical talent'.[106] But few would have endorsed such a view. To get their poems published often required a patron, with all the problems that so often brought. When John Jones first started to write he wrote a play and sent it off to the Haymarket Theatre. After a long interval it finally replied that 'it would not do for representation' and advised Jones 'not to spend . . . time in such difficult undertakings'.[107] The rescuing of these domestic servant–poets from obscurity has revealed not merely that many of them can compete on equal terms with poets of the literary canon but that if they accepted the poetic forms of contemporary male poets, they often used those forms to say very different things.

---

[103] *Mendip Annals: or, A Narrative of the Charitable Labours of Hannah and Martha More*, ed. Arthur Roberts, 2nd edn. (1859), 6, 243–4.

[104] *Reflections on the Present Condition of the Female Sex with Suggestions for its Improvement*, 2nd edn. (1817), 138–9.

[105] *The Poetical Works of Janet Little, the Scotch Milkmaid*, 165.

[106] *Edinburgh Review*, 54 (1831), 72.

[107] Southey, *The Lives and Works of the Uneducated Poets*, 174.

13

Conclusion

'As I stood in my lonely bedroom at the hotel, trying to tie my white tie myself, it struck me for the first time that there must be whole squads of chappies in the world who had to get along without a man to look after them. I'd always thought of Jeeves as a kind of natural phenomenon; but, by Jove! of course, when you come to think of it, there must be quite a lot of fellows who have to press their own clothes themselves, and haven't got anybody to bring them tea in the morning, and so on. It was rather a solemn thought . . .'

P. G. Wodehouse, *Jeeves Omnibus*, 243

'The hard reality is, surely for the likes of you and I, there is little choice other than to leave our fate, ultimately, in the hands of those great gentlemen at the hub of this world who employ our services'.

Mr Stevens, the butler, in Kazuo Ishiguro, *The Remains of the Day*, 244

'The kind of society I want is one in which my cook and I can eat in the diningroom together.'

G. D. H. Cole, cited in Robbins, *The Servant's Hand*, 205

THROUGHOUT the early modern period and well into the eighteenth century the term 'servant' was loosely used. It covered very different people, both men and women, in very different occupations. But even the term 'domestic servant' is vague and indistinct. It is not precise enough to say that domestic servants were resident in households, for this still leaves room for an immense range of people performing quite distinct tasks in households of different sizes as well as in taverns, inns, and coaching-stations. Nor does it really help to add that domestic servants were mainly concerned with domestic work in the house. For many this was simply not true. The frequency with which domestic servants throughout the eighteenth century vacillated between tasks in the house and other tasks outside in the fields or garden makes the distinction between domestic servants and farm servants anything but clear. Then many so-called domestic servants, as we have seen, worked as shop assistants, or sometimes in small workshops, and relatively little, if any, of their work was domestic. To rely on the labels attached to servants to define their work would be extremely rash. For a great many servants in single-servant households, the range of tasks they were called on to do, whatever their label, did not always necessarily have much to do with what is now understood as domestic work. This is why any attempt to define an 'average domestic servant' is fraught with difficulties. Talking of the problems of nineteenth-century censuses in dealing with domestic servants and more particularly of the problem posed by the failure of censuses to identify kin acting as housekeepers and other servants, Edward Higgs has suggested that domestic service was an 'umbrella category' covering not one occupation but many.[1] He has a point. On the other hand, diverse as they were in the households that employed them and in the work they were called on to perform, they shared the duty of complete and unquestioning obedience to their masters and mistresses, the subsuming of their own background, social identity, and personality in that of their employers. In this sense servants did form a homogeneous body. And while it is important to identify the basic differences between apprenticeship, service in husbandry, daily hired labour, and resident domestic service we should be under no illusions about their work necessarily being separate and distinct. All too often their work roles coincide.

If in general grander and richer households kept more servants than more modest and humble households we have learnt to be wary of making any assumptions about the number of servants kept by a household of a certain size and income. Other factors—the nature and age of household members, the particular and changing needs of the household, the way of life of the family—were as important as the household's wealth and size. If we now know that the servant hierarchy as it appeared in some large and wealthy households was exceptional and far from representative,

[1] 'Women, Occupations and Work in the Nineteenth-Century Censuses', *History Workshop Journal*, 23 (spring 1987), 59–80 at p. 68.

with what notion of service are we to replace it? We can say that by far the greater number of domestic servants in the eighteenth and early nineteenth centuries in London and provincial towns were employed in small households of families of moderate or even humble circumstances. An investigation of the Westminster parish of St Martin-in-the-Fields in the eighteenth century revealed 'bricklayers, clear starchers, hatters, milliners, plasterers, silk dyers' among those accustomed to employ a single servant. Even milk-sellers, the occupational group to which the poorest Irish immigrants gravitated, could employ servants.[2] Most of these 'single servants' were women. 'Tradesmen', writes Olwen Hufton, 'might employ a girl both to work in the shop and to run errands delivering and picking up work; tavern keepers employed girls as barmaids, waitresses, and washers up; busy housewives helping in family businesses such as cookshops and bakeries employed girls to do anything from turning a hand in commercial food production to taking the family's washing to the washplace, carrying or pumping water, or lighting and maintaining ovens or fires.'[3] We might add that they were usually referred to as 'general' servants, or 'skivvies', although even this is far from defining their work role. But apart from confirming the existence of such single servants in humble households what do we know of their working lives and of their relations with their masters and mistresses? Unfortunately very little.

An intriguing question but not one I have addressed here is the reason for the fascination of the upstairs/downstairs model of servant life. It has had and continues to have a powerful hold on the public imagination. Is it a sentimentalizing of class as it was once thought to have been? This is certainly how many understand domestic service. And how are we to explain the gradual metamorphosis of the servant in literature from the simple, but nearly always dishonest, menial—an object of humour—to the immaculate and infinitely discreet butler of Sir James Barrie's *The Admirable Crichton*, who was the fount of all wisdom and managed his masters' affairs with great intelligence and skill? It is

[2] D. A. Kent, 'Ubiquitous but Invisible: Female Domestic Servants in Mid-Eighteenth Century London', *History Workshop Journal*, 28 (autumn 1989), 111–28 at pp. 119–20.
[3] 'Women, Work and Family', in Natalie Zemon Davis and Arlette Farge (eds.) *A History of Women*, iii (1993), 15–45 at p. 20.

perhaps significant of the confused class consciousness of such servants that Crichton's only criticism of his master is that he is 'not sufficiently contemptuous of his inferiors'.[4] And what of the servant who assumes total mastery over his employer with the roles of servant and master reversed? We might note that such modern 'heroes' of domestic service are consistently male and mostly butlers or gentlemen's gentlemen—the élite of male servants.

In what direction might future research go? There are areas into which I have made only the most preliminary skirmishes which deserve much greater study. Following the work of Jessica Gerard we need to pose the question of just how far in the countryside in the eighteenth century the domestic servant needs of small and moderate-sized households were met by local casual labour.[5] How far were large households constantly supplementing their needs by the employment of local hired labour, both male and female? Was this a universal phenomenon in rural England? The ease with which such labour seems to have been available suggests there was a vast body of unemployed or partially unemployed labour in rural areas. And, considering the ease with which charwomen and washerwomen could be hired in London and other towns, how far was something similar to be found in urban life? Gerard has suggested that such casual labour was better paid than regular service, but it was also more flexible and responsive to employers' needs, giving them access to servants if and when they needed them. Employers hired labour to do quite specific tasks when the occasion arose. It would be interesting to know more of relations between such local casual labour and resident servants. Was the hired labour seen as inferior because it was supplied by an outsider who did not really belong to the household?

The attractions of obtaining domestic servants at little or no expense were clearly great—and not just confined to the small, low-income households. Despite her unsatisfactory nature, Pepys was delighted at the thought of obtaining Pall so cheaply. It almost persuaded him later to re-engage her. There is far more

---

[4] E. S. Turner, *What the Butler Saw: 250 Years of the Servant Problem* (1962), 251.

[5] Jessica A. Gerard, 'Invisible Servants: The Country House and the Local Community', *Bulletin of the Institute of Historical Research*, 57/136 (Nov. 1984), 178–88.

work to be done on what seems to have been an extensive use of kin as servants, on the conditions under which they worked, and the distinctions between them and ordinary servants. Similarly, the impression one has of eighteenth-century charity schools is of institutions turning out an endless supply of mainly female servants—more or less trained. Yet these were only one of several sources of children of the labouring poor destined for domestic service who could be employed at a minimal—or no—wage. Parish records of settlement of pauper and orphaned children, it is suggested, could 'give numerous examples of migration of females into domestic service'.[6] Female domestic servants, as we have seen, often remain invisible, but pauper servants are even more difficult to distinguish. One suspects that those who had them in their households were not too anxious to advertise the fact and hoped they would be regarded as ordinary servants. In the same category of cheap servants comes the endless stream of young boy servants—'yard boys' or 'livery boys' as they were sometimes called—who performed a host of errands and tasks—for their clothes and often no wage at all or, at best, pocket-money. We need to know more of the households into which they went. Some, as we have seen, moved on into adult roles in service, but others left. What sort of occupation did their experience as boy servants fit them for? One comes across them frequently in middle- and upper-class households, but one suspects that many humble households may have seen a boy as a readily available, cheap servant—the nearest thing to the female skivvy. And what of the young female servant who for the first years of her employment earned no wages at all? Richardson's Pamela is a case in point—but it was not confined to fiction. This use of cheap child labour in domestic service is an area which needs much more investigation.

We tend to assume that the very isolation of servants' lives dictated against their organization or any expression of protest. But there has been little or no serious investigation of this, not merely the organized protest of eighteenth-century footmen and their resistance to attempts to abolish vails and perquisites, which certainly deserves study, but of the kind of subtle protest made by servants against what they increasingly saw as the unreasonable

---

[6] John Patten, *Rural–Urban Migration in Pre-Industrial England* (1973), 12–13.

demands of their employers. There was resistance to the obligation on servants to attend church. The newly engaged cook of the Revd, John Skinner, when told her master insisted on all servants attending church, answered that 'she could not stay beyond the month'. She left, but Skinner may have regretted her going when he heard that before she left the locality she 'took this opportunity of saying everything to my disadvantage'.[7] Much of the insolence in servants so complained of by employers was almost certainly one form of protest. Changing places was frequently a servant's only answer to bad treatment, or to mean or exploiting employers. As we have seen, if employers of 'scribbling' servants had bothered to read their poetry they might have learnt something about how their servants regarded them and what their employees thought of their servile relationship with masters and mistresses.

Sources tapped by recent research have varied. Historians of the nineteenth century have concentrated on the analysis of the occupational census statistics for local areas. This, despite the acknowledged shortcomings of census statistics, particularly where domestic servants are concerned, has produced some valuable results on the size and standing of servant-holding households in individual towns and localities. But the nature of the information yielded about servants is mainly quantitative; the number of servants in any locality, and within that locality the size and nature of servant-employing households. There are, however, a host of other non-quantitative questions about servants which the census does not address. But before the nineteenth-century occupational censuses there is no such comparable regular source.

Peter Earle has focused on the structure of London households, relying on the series of assessments used for the tax on burials, births, and marriages of 1695. It has produced valuable findings about the size of households and the relationship of their members to the head of the house. Of the middle-class households analysed, Earle found 'virtually all the families had servants'.[8] But there are some problems with this source, not least that it fails to distinguish between servants and apprentices. Others have

[7] *The Journal of a Somerset Rector 1803–34*, ed. Howard and Peter Coombs (1930), 353, 378.
[8] *The Making of the English Middle Class* (1989), 213.

looked at Ecclesiastical Court records—a valuable source on servants as migrants. The London Consistory Court depositions have been used by Tim Meldrum for the period 1660–1750. But by the eighteenth century the cases that came before such courts were mainly matrimonial or defamation cases. They were brought, as Meldrum readily acknowledges, by 'servant-employing Londoners of the "middling sort" or their social superiors'.[9] They are unlikely to provide information about servants in humbler households. However honest a servant-witness might be, he or she was supporting the case of one of the contestants at the expense of the other. If it had not been so they would have been useless as witnesses. Very often, one suspects, money had been passed to persuade a servant to be a reliable witness. As Lawrence Stone has emphasized, 'the large and growing disparity between the income of the litigants and those of the witnesses—servants, neighbours, and professional oath-takers for money—made bribed testimony and perjury almost an inevitability, despite every effort by the court to curb it'.[10] Such witnesses for the cause of either masters or mistresses were unlikely to present their work anything but favourably, and if their testimony throws light on relations with employers it is hardly likely to be a balanced view. If for instance they were asked by the clerk of the court to disclose their worth in front of their masters and mistresses were they likely to give a strictly accurate answer?

Some historians of domestic service have concentrated on Settlement Examinations where, under a 1692 extension of the Act of 1662, a person could obtain a settlement in a parish if he or she had been hired as a servant, and remained hired for a whole year. We do now know that yearly hirings were by no means representative. In his work on London domestic servants in the period 1650–1750 Peter Earle has shown that nearly 40 per cent of a sample of female servants stayed six months or less in one place.[11] Settlement Examinations do often provide evidence of the name, address, and occupation of employers of servants, how long servants spent in one employment and the wages they received. But we rarely learn how large the household was, whether or not there were other servants, or of what their work consisted. Nor do

---

[9] 'Ubiquity and Visibility: Domestic Service in London, 1660–1750', paper given at the Economic History Society Conference (Apr. 1993), 1.
[10] *Broken Lives* (1993), 7–8.   [11] *A City Full of People* (1994), 129, Table 4.7.

we usually learn about what other places they occupied before or since the claimed annual hiring. It is rarely possible to get an idea of the working life of a domestic servant from the time they left home.

There is a great deal still to be learnt of domestic servants from the mining of local and national newspapers, a slow but often fruitful exercise. In the advertisements for servants, the reporting of cases where servants and their employers are in dispute about failure to pay wages, alleged theft, or claimed sexual harassment or ill-treatment by employers, there is valuable material. But on the whole what is recorded is the exceptional and scandalous.

Many historians have treated domestic service as an interesting historical phenomenon of the past. They have claimed that domestic service as it existed in early modern England and in the eighteenth and nineteenth centuries has ended. It is, of course, much easier to romanticize service if it is seen as a feature of a bygone age. But has domestic service no modern equivalent in this country? It is true that resident domestic servants are now rare, but a recent survey revealed that 37 per cent of professional women now have cleaners or nannies. 'There's been a massive expansion in the bottom end of female service sector jobs, in the very homes of those women who are the success stories of women's employment in the eighties and nineties.'[12] Without such service labour the careers of many such women would be threatened. Much of this service remains invisible and unknown. There are reasons for this. Not least, it is because many women do feel a moral unease about their own careers and liberation depending on what in comparison with their own salaries is cheap female labour. Their independence depends on the exploitation of women whose circumstances dictate casual, part-time employment of a flexible nature. Then there are the thousands of au pair girls quite outside any regulation who are employed by working mothers, often on their own terms and conditions. For all these workers hours remain long. They are often as isolated and vulnerable as domestic servants in the eighteenth and nineteenth centuries, and for many there is no insurance against old age, sickness, or unemployment. The reasons why there are always women and young girls readily available for such work are not so

[12] Lynn Hanna, 'Paid to do the dirty work', *Guardian*, 18 Aug. 1992.

different from why there were recruits to domestic service in the past—the absence of alternatives for the untrained. Casual part-time employment is the only option for those unable to afford child-minders or crèches to release them for full-time employment, or those who need to supplement inadequate pensions or social security.

If it is thought that such service is quite distinct from the resident domestic service of the past we have only to look at many areas of the Third World to find something remarkably similar to our own experience of service. Work done on rural–urban migration in England has shown that in the course of the eighteenth and nineteenth centuries women increasingly predominated in the migratory flow towards towns. In the far greater flood of rural–urban migrants that has taken place in many Third World countries in the last fifty years, there is the same trend towards an increasing number of women. Today, by far the greater number of migrants to the cities of Latin America, West Africa, Kenya, and many other parts of the Third World are women—and many of them on reaching the towns enter domestic service. It poses interesting questions for the historian of domestic service in the First World. As a counter to recent ideas of service as 'sufficiently attractive for some women to choose it as a way of life rather than simply a stage in their life-cycle', it is instructive to see service in much of the Third World as merging into the so-called 'informal economy' alongside of street hawkers, beer brewers and sellers, petty traders—and prostitutes.[13] The reasons for these female migrants leaving their villages are almost always economic and their main reason for entering domestic service is that no other work is available to them. For some, as in England in the eighteenth century, it may be an escape route from the oppressive patriarchal society of their villages. In an article of 1974 Eric Richards wrote that the trends development economists had noted in women's participation in the economic life of many Third World countries 'might also have some bearing on the working role of women in Britain for the last two and a half centuries'. He saw Victorian domestic service as 'a form a disguised under-employment'.[14] Domestic service and the rest of the

[13] Kent, 'Ubiquitous but Invisible', 112.
[14] 'Women in the British Economy since about 1700: An Interpretation, *History*, 59/197 (1974), 341.

informal economy is the Third World's answer to such underemployment. Twenty-five years ago Esther Boserup wrote of domestic service in many areas of the Third World as 'a characteristic feature of countries at an intermediate stage of economic development'. 'In general', she argued, 'the whole domestic service sector grows with economic development and, at the same time, tends to become more exclusively "feminine".'[15]

This recent experience of domestic service raises a host of questions about service in the eighteenth and nineteenth centuries: we still know far too little about rural migrants to London and other towns. Peter Earle has suggested that for many of those making their way to the capital 'arrival in London was cushioned . . . by the fact they had relatives in the metropolis with whom they could stay while they found their first place'. When Dorothy Catharell arrived in London from Chester, she 'lived with her unckle' for a year before getting a place in service.[16] Earlier many female migrants appear to have had kin in London with whom they stayed and 'whose responsibility it was to assist the young women to establish themselves and especially to find a suitable husband in the large metropolis'.[17] Peter Clark has found evidence in the seventeenth century 'for close and distant kinfolk providing temporary accommodation, food, assistance with finding a job, loans and other help'.[18] We know very little as yet of such kin networks in the eighteenth century and of how they cushioned the arrival in London of some young women looking for places. Daniel Roche has discovered evidence of such kin networks among immigrants in eighteenth-century Paris. Once settled they would send for their relatives and friends.[19] Such kin networks are frequently found today in areas of West Africa and in Latin America. In stressing the role played by alehouses as 'reception houses for lower-class migrants' Peter Clark has drawn

[15] *Women's Role in Economic Development* (1970); 2nd edn., 103.
[16] Peter Earle, 'The Female Labour Market in London in the Late 17th and Early 18th Centuries', *Economic History Review*, 2nd ser. 42/3 (1989), 328–53 at p. 344; id., *A City Full of People*, 53.
[17] Ilana Krausman Ben-Amos, *Adolescence and Youth in Early Modern England* (1994), 166.
[18] Peter Clark 'Migrants to the City: The Process of Social Adaptation in English Towns 1500–1899', in Peter Clark and David Souden (eds.), *Migration and Society* (1987), 267–91 at pp. 271–2.
[19] Daniel Roche, *Paris and her People*, trans. Marie Evans in association with Gwynne Lewis (1981), 25.

attention to the parallel function of the beer house in Nairobi. What has been called 'semi-prostitution' is common amongst domestic servants in the Third World. They are usually migrants from the countryside without support of family or friends. For most, prostitution is a temporary expedient resorted to when they are out of a place. It was almost certainly as common among eighteenth- and early nineteenth-century servants in England, but we know all too little about eighteenth-century prostitution and its link with domestic service.

For those convinced that the very nature of the work of domestic service dictates that it is women's work and that this has always been the case there is the situation of Shona women in colonial Southern Rhodesia. European women and the 'missions intent on making model Christian housewives of them' were agreed in opposing African women becoming domestic servants. Their true role, they argued, was in their own homes as wives and mothers. The missions feared the 'immorality of urban life'.[20] European wives feared the effect on their husbands of what was seen as the rampant sexuality of African women. The result was that African men dominated the domestic labour force and, despite some recent increase in women entering domestic service, continue to dominate it right up to the present day.

The experience as domestic servants of a vast number of the population in eighteenth- and nineteenth-century England is now being repeated in many areas of the world. Those interested in discovering more about domestic service in our past might find stimulation in the Third World experience. If nothing more, it might suggest new questions that need to be asked of our own history.

[20] Elizabeth Schmidt, *Peasants, Traders, and Wives: Shona Women in the History of Zimbabwe, 1870–1939* (1992), 13, 155.

Bibliography

Contemporary Writings

ADAMS, SAMUEL and SARAH, *The Complete Servant* (1825).
ALCOCK, THOMAS, *Observations on the Defects of the Poor Laws and on the Causes and Consequences of the Great Increase and Burden of the Poor* (1752).
ANON., *An Account of the Charity Schools lately erected* (1708).
ANON., *The Complete Servant Maid* (1677).
ANON., *Domestic Management, or the Art of Conducting a Family* (c.1800).
ANON., *Family Manual and Servants' Guide* (1856).
ANON., *Friendly Advice from a Minister to the Servants of his Parish* (1793).
ANON., *Friendly Hints to Family Servants* (1814).
ANON., *The Laws relating to Masters and Servants* (1755).
ANON., *A Present for Servants* (1st pub. 1693; 2nd edn. 1710, 3rd edn. 1726, 4th edn. 1768).
ANON., *A Present for Servants*, Religious Tract Society (1799).
ANON., *The Servants Calling* (1725).
ANON., *The Servant's Friend* (c.1780).
BAILEY, WILLIAM, *Treatise on the Better Employment and more Comfortable Support of the Poor in Workhouses* (1758).
BAINES, M. A., *Domestic Servants as they are, and as they ought to be* (1859).
BARKER, ANNE, *The Complete Servant Maid* (c.1770).
BROUGHTON, THOMAS, *Serious Advice and Warning to Servants* (1746).
CAPPE, CATHARINE, *An Account of Two Charity Schools* (1800).
—— *Observations on Charity Schools* (1805).
CHANCE, W., *Children under the Poor Law* (1897).
COLQUHOUN, PATRICK, *A Treatise on the Police in the Metropolis*, 3rd edn. (1796).
—— *A New and Appropriate System of Education for the Labouring People* (1806).
—— *A Treatise on Indigence* (1806).
COTTLE, JOSEPH, *Early Recollections*, 2 vols. (1837).
DEFOE, DANIEL, *The Behaviour of Servants* (1725).
—— *Everybody's Business is Nobody's Business* (1725).
DODSLEY, ROBERT, *The Footman's Friendly Advice to his Brethren of the Livery* (1731).
—— *A Muse in Livery: or, the Footman's Miscellany* (1732).
FIELDING, JOHN, *A Plan of the Universal Register Office* (1752).

FIELDING, JOHN, *The Universal Mentor* (1763).
——*Extracts from the Penal Laws as particularly relate to the Peace and Good Order of the Metropolis* (1762).
FIRMIN, THOMAS, *Some Proposals for the Imployment of the Poor* (1681).
FLEETWOOD, WILLIAM, *The Relative Duties of Parents and Children, Husbands and Wives, Masters and Servants*, 2nd edn. (1716).
GLASS, HANNAH, *The Servant's Directory* (1761).
HANWAY, JONAS *Eight Letters to his Grace Duke of——on the Custom of Vails-giving in England* (1760).
——*The Sentiments and Advice of Thomas Trueman* (1760).
——*An Earnest Appeal for Mercy to the Children of the Poor* (1766).
——*Letters on the Importance of Preserving the Rising Generation of the Labouring Part of our Fellow Subjects*, 2 vols. (1767).
——*Virtue in Humble Life*, 2 vols. (1777).
HAYWOOD, ELIZA, *A Present for a Serving Maid* (1743).
HEASEL, ANTHONY, *The Servant's Book of Knowledge* (1773).
HENDERSON, WILLIAM Augustus, *The Housekeeper's Instructor or Universal Family Cook* (1793).
HENDLEY, W., *A Defence of the Charity Schools* (1725).
HUNTINGFORD, J., *The Laws of Masters and Servants Considered* (1790).
LEADBEATER, MARY, *Cottage Dialogues*, 2 vols. (1811, 1813).
——*Cottage Biography* (1822).
MANDEVILLE, BERNARD, *The Fable of the Bees*, 2 vols. (1724).
MAYO, RICHARD, *A Present for Servants* (1693).
MUNBY, ARTHUR J. (ed.), *Faithful Servants: Epitaphs and Obituaries* (1891).
SMITH, JOHN THOMAS, *Nollekens and his Times*, 2 vols. (1828).
SOUTHEY, ROBERT, *The Lives and Works of the Uneducated Poets* (1831).
STEWART, J. A., *The Young Woman's Companion, or Female Instructor* (1814).
SWIFT, JONATHAN, *Directions to Servants in General and in particular to . . .* (1745).
TOWNLEY, JAMES, *High Life below Stairs* (1759).
TRIMMER, SARAH, *The Oeconomy of Charity; or an Address to the Ladies Concerning Sunday Schools etc.* (1787).
——*Reflections upon the Education of Children in Charity Schools* (1792).
——*The Servant's Friend* (1824).
——*Family Manual and Servants Guide* (1835).
TRUSLER, J., *The Way to be Rich and Respectable* (1775).
——*The London Adviser and Guide* (1786).
——*Trusler's Domestic Management* (1819).
WALSH, J. H., *A Manual of Domestic Economy*, 2nd edn. (1873).
WARNER, RICHARD, *Literary Recollections*, 2 vols. (1830).
WOLLEY, HANNAH, *The Compleat Servant-maid, or the Young Maiden's Tutor*, 4th edn. (1685; 1st pub. 1677).

Bibliography

Autobiographies, Diaries, Letters, Journals, etc.

J. Aitken (ed.), *English Diaries of the 16th, 17th and 18th Centuries* (1941).
The Diary of John Baker, ed. Philip C. Yorke (1931).
The Great Diurnal of Nicholas Blundell of Little Crosby, Lancashire, ed. J. J. Bagley, Record Society of Lancashire and Cheshire, cx (1968), cxii (1970), cxiv (1972).
Blundell's Diary and Letter Book, 1702–28, ed. Margaret Blundell (1952).
The Diary of Nicholas Brown 1722–27, in *Six North Country Diaries*, Surtees Society, cxviii (1910), 230–323.
The Journal of Timothy Burrell, Esq., Barrister at Law 1683–1700, Sussex Archaeological Collections, iii (1850), 117–72.
Memorandum Book of Sir Walter Calverley, Surtees Society, lxxix, *Yorkshire Diaries and Autobiographies*, 2 vols., ii (1886), 43–148.
Extracts from the Diary and Letters of Mrs. Mary Cobb (1805).
The Blecheley Diary of the Rev. William Cole 1765–7, ed. Francis Griffin Stokes (1931).
The Diaries of Hannah Cullwick: Victorian Maidservant, ed. Liz Stanley (1984).
Pamela Horn, *A Georgian Parson and His Village: The Story of David Davies (1742–1819)* (1981).
A Family History, Begun by James Fretwell, Surtees Society, lxv (1877); 164–244.
The Diary of Julius Hardy (1788–1793) button-maker of Birmingham, Birmingham Reference Library, 669002 (BRL MS 218), transcribed and annotated by A. M. Banks (Apr. 1973).
Mary Hardy's Diary, with an introduction by B. Cozens-Hardy, Norfolk Record Society, xxxvii (1968).
Letter Books of John Hervey, First Earl of Bristol, 1651–1750, iii, Suffolk Green Book, 1 (1894).
The Journal of Mr. John Hobson, Surtees Society, lxv, *Yorkshire Diaries and Autobiographies*, 2 vols., i (1877), 245–329.
The Diary of the Rev. William Jones, 1777–1821, ed. O. F. Christie (1929).
Life of A Licensed Victualler's Daughter, Written by Herself (1844).
Memoirs of an Eighteenth-Century Footman, John Macdonald, ed. John Beresford (1927).
The Marchant Diary, ed. Edward Turner, Sussex Archaeological Collections, xxv (1873), 163–99.
Kussmaul, Ann, *The Autobiography of Joseph Mayett of Quainton (1783–1839)*, Buckinghamshire Record Society, xxiii (1986).
The Diary of Samuel Pepys, ed. Henry B. Wheatley, 3 vols. (1946).

Laetitia Pilkington, *Memoirs of Mrs. Laetitia Pilkington (1749–54)*, 3 vols. (1770).
The Autobiography of Francis Place (1771–1854), ed. Mary Thale (1972).
Passages from the Diaries of Mrs. Philip Lybbe Powys of Hardwick House, Oxon. 1756–1806, ed. Emily J. Climenson (1899).
A Kentish Parson: Selections from the Private Papers of the Revd. Joseph Price Vicar of Brabourne, 1767–1786, ed. G. M. Ditchfield and Bryan Keith-Lucas (1991).
The Purefoy Letters 1735–53, ed. G. Eland, 2 vols. (1931).
The Diary of Benjamin Rogers, Rector of Carlton 1720–71, ed. C. D. Linnell, Bedfordshire, Historical Record Society, xxx (1950).
The Diary of Dudley Ryder 1715–16, ed. William Matthews (1939).
The Family Records of Benjamin Shaw, Mechanic of Dent, Dolphinholme and Preston 1772–1841, ed. Alan G. Crosby, Record Society of Lancashire and Cheshire, cxxx (1991).
Betsy Sheridan's Journal, ed. William Lefanu (1960).
The Memoirs of Susan Sibbald (1783–1812), ed. Francis Paget Hett (1926).
The Journal of a Somerset Rector 1803–34, ed. Howard and Peter Coombs (1930).
On the Domestic Habits and Mode of Life of a Sussex Gentleman, ed. Edward Turner, Sussex Archaeological Collections, xxiii (1871), 36–72.
The Journal of John Gabriel Stedman 1744–97, ed. Stanbury Thompson (1962).
The Autobiography of William Stout of Lancaster 1665–1752, ed. J. D. Marshall (1967).
Strother's Journal, Written by a Tradesman of York and Hull 1784–5, ed. Caesar Caine (1912).
The Diary of the Rev. John Thomlinson, in *Six North Country Diaries*, Surtees Society, cxviii (1910), 64–167.
The Torrington Diaries, ed. Bryn Andrews and Fanny Andrews (1934).
The Diary of Thomas Turner 1754–1765, ed. David Vaisey (1985).
Useful Toil: Autobiographies of Working People from the 1820s to the 1920s, ed. John Burnett (1st pub. 1974; 2nd edn. 1994).
The Diary of a West Country Physician 1684–1726, ed. Edmund Hobhouse (1934).
The Housekeeping Book of Susanna Whatman 1776–1800, ed. Thomas Balston (1956).
The Diary of a Country Parson: The Reverend James Woodforde, 1758–1813, ed. John Beresford, 5 vols. (1924–31).
A Parson in the Vale of White Horse: George Woodward's Letters from East Hendred 1753–61, ed. Donald Gibson (1982).
The Autobiography of Thomas Wright of Birkenshaw in the County of York 1736–97, ed. Thomas Wright (1864).

Foreign Travellers' Journals, etc.

DE LA ROCHEFOUCAULD, FRANÇOIS, *A Frenchman in England, 1784*, ed. Jean Marchand, trans. with notes by S. C. Roberts (1933).
DE SAUSSURE, CESAR, *A Foreign View of England in the Reign of George I and George II*, trans. and ed. Mme von Muyden, (1902).
GROSLEY, PIERRE JEAN, *A Tour of London...1771*, trans. from the French by T. Nugent (1772).
KALM, PEHR, *Account of his visit to England...in 1748*, trans. and ed. J. Lucas (1892).
KIELMANSEGGE, COUNT FREDERICK, *Diary of a Journey to England in the Years 1761–2*, trans. Countess Kielmansegge (1902).
MISSON, HENRI, *M. Misson's Memoirs and Observations on his Travels in England*, trans. John Ozell (1719).
Travels of Carl Philip Moritz in England in 1782, English trans. 1795, ed. P. E. Matheson (1924).
VON ARCHENHOLZ, J. W., *A Picture of England...1787*, trans. (1797).

Newspapers

Annual Register
The Edinburgh Review
The Gazette
The Gentleman's Magazine
Ipswich Journal
Jackson's Oxford Journal
The London Chronicle
London Daily Advertiser
The London Magazine
Morning Post
Oxford Magazine
Public Advertiser

Recent Studies: Books

ANDERSON, MICHAEL, *Family Structure in Nineteenth-Century Lancashire* (1971).
ARMSTRONG, A., *Stability and Change in an English Country Town* (1974).
ARMSTRONG, NANCY, *Desire and Domestic Fiction* (1987).
BAKER, D., *The Inhabitants of Cardington in 1782*, Publications of the Bedfordshire Historical Record Society, lii (1973).
BANKS, J. A., *Prosperity and Parenthood* (1954).
BEN-AMOS, ILANA KRAUSMAN, *Adolescence and Youth in Early Modern England* (1994).

BRANCA, PATRICIA, *The Silent Sisterhood: Middle Class Women in the Victorian Home* (1975).
—— *Women in Europe since 1750* (1978).
BUCK, ANNE, *Dress in Eighteenth-Century England* (1979).
CARROLL, JOHN (ed.), *Samuel Richardson* (1969).
COCKBURN, J. S., *Crime in England 1550–1800* (1977).
CRESSY, DAVID, *Literacy and the Social Order* (1980).
CUNNINGTON, PHYLLIS, *Costume of Household Servants* (1974).
LEONORE, DAVIDOFF, and HALL, CATHERINE, *Family Fortunes: Men and Women of the English Middle Classes, 1780–1850* (1987).
—— and HAWTHORN, RUTH, *A Day in the Life of a Victorian Domestic Servant* (1976).
DAVISON, LEE, HITCHCOCK, TIM, KEIRN, TIM, and SHOEMACKER, ROBERT B. (eds.), *Stilling the Grumbling Hive* (1992).
DAWES, FRANK VICTOR, *Not in Front of the Servants* (1984).
DOUGHTY, KATHERINE, *The Betts of Wortham in Suffolk* (1912).
DUNLOP, O. JOCELYN, and DENMAN, R. D., *English Apprenticeship and Child Labour: A History* (1912).
EARLE, PETER, *The Making of the English Middle Class* (1989).
—— *A City Full of People* (1994).
EBERY, M., and PRESTON, B., *Domestic Service in Late Victorian and Edwardian England 1871–1914* (1976).
FAIRCHILDS, CISSIE, *Domestic Enemies: Servants and their Masters in Old Regime France* (1984).
FIRTH, VIOLET M., *The Psychology of the Servant Problem* (1925).
FITTON, R. S., and WADSWORTH, A. P., *The Strutts and the Arkwrights 1758–1830* (1958).
GEORGE, DOROTHY M., *London Life in the Eighteenth Century* (1st pub. 1925; repr. 1965).
GILLIS, JOHN, *For Better for Worse* (1985).
GOODER, EILEEN, *The Squire of Arbury: Sir Richard Newdigate (1644–1710)*, Coventry Branch of The Historical Association (1990).
GOUGH, RICHARD, *The History of Myddle (1701–1706)* (1979).
GWILLIAM, TASSIE, *Samuel Richardson's Fictions of Gender* (1993).
HARRIS, JOCELYN, *Samuel Richardson* (1987).
HARRISON, R., *Rose: My Life in Service*, (1975).
HECHT, JEAN J., *The Domestic Servant in Eighteenth-Century England* (1st pub. 1956; repr. 1980).
HILEY, MICHAEL, *Victorian Women: Portraits from Life* (1979).
HILL, BRIDGET, *Women, Work and Sexual Politics in Eighteenth-Century England* (1989).
HOLE, CHRISTINA, *English Home Life 1500–1800* (1947).
HORN, PAMELA, *The Rise and Fall of the Victorian Servant* (1975).

Bibliography

HOUSTON, R. A., *Scottish Literacy and the Scottish Identity* (1985).
HUDSON, DEREK, *Munby: Man of Two Worlds: The Life and Diaries of Arthur J. Munby 1828–1910* (1972).
HUGHES, E., *North Country Life in the Eighteenth Century*, 2 vols. (1965).
JONES, M. G., *The Charity School Movement* (1st pub. 1938; edn. 1964).
KATZMAN, DAVID M., *Seven Days a Week: Women and Domestic Service in Industrialising America* (1978).
KUSSMAUL, ANN, *Servants in Husbandry in Early Modern England* (1981).
LANDRY, DONNA, *The Muses of Resistance* (1990).
LASLETT, PETER, and WALL, RICHARD (eds.), *Household and Family in Past Time* (1972).
Eighteenth-Century Women Poets, ed. Roger Lonsdale (1989).
MCBRIDE, THERESA, *The Domestic Revolution* (1976).
MARCUS, STEVEN, *The Other Victorians: A Study of Sexuality and Pornography in Mid-Nineteenth-Century England* (1966).
MARSHALL, DOROTHY, *The English Poor in the Eighteenth Century* (1926).
—— *The English Domestic Servant in History* (1949).
MAZA, SARA C., *Servants and Masters in Eighteenth-Century France: The Uses of Loyalty* (1983).
OXLEY, GEOFFREY W., *Poor Relief in England and Wales 1601–1834* (1974).
ROBBINS, BRUCE, *The Servant's Hand: English Fiction from Below* (1986).
ROCHE, DANIEL, *Paris and her People*, trans. Marie Evans in association with Gwynne Lewis (1981).
—— *The Culture of Clothing*, trans. Jean Birrell (1994).
RULE, JOHN, *The Labouring Class in Early Industrial England* (1986).
SHARPE, J. A., *Crime in Early Modern England 1550–1750* (1984).
SITWELL, GEORGE R., *The Hurts of Haldworth* (1930).
SPECK, W. A., *Society and Literature in England 1700–1760* (1983).
STONE, LAWRENCE, *The Family, Sex and Marriage* (1977).
STUART, D. M., *The English Abigail* (1946).
THOMSON, GLADYS SCOTT, *The Russells in Bloomsbury 1669–1771* (1940).
TODD, JANET, '*Pamela* or the Bliss of Servitude', in id., *Gender, Art and Death* (1993), 63–80.
TURNER, E. S., *What the Butler Saw: 250 Years of the Servant Problem* (1962).
UTTER, R. P., and NEEDHAM, G. B., *Pamela's Daughters* (1936).
VERNON, ANNE, *Three Generations: The Fortunes of a Yorkshire Family* (1966).
VICINUS, MARTHA, *The Industrial Muse* (1974).
WATERSON, MERLIN, *The Servants' Hall: A Domestic History of Erddig* (1980).
WATT, IAN, *The Rise of the Novel*, (1963).
WILLIAMS, E. N., *Life in Georgian England* (1962).

Recent Studies: Articles

BEATTIE, J. M., 'The Criminality of Women in Eighteenth-Century England', *Journal of Social History*, 8 (summer 1975), 80–116.

BROOM, L., and SMITH, J. H., 'Bridging Occupations', *British Journal of Sociology*, 14 (Dec. 1963), 321–4.

BUCK, ANNE, 'The Dress of Domestic Servants in the Eighteenth Century', *Strata of Society, Costume of Society* (1974), 88–9.

—— 'Pamela's Clothes', *Costume*, 26 (1992), 21–31.

BYTHELL, DUNCAN, 'Women in the Work Force', in Patrick O'Brien and Roland Quinault (eds.), *The Industrial Revolution and British Society* (1993), 31–53.

CLARK, PETER, 'Migrants to the City: The Process of Social Adaptation in English Towns 1500–1899', in Peter Clark and David Souden (eds.), *Migration and Society* (1987), 267–91.

CRESSY, DAVID, 'Illiteracy in England 1530–1730', *Historical Journal*, 20 (1977), 1–23.

DAVIDOFF, LEONORE, 'Above and Below Stairs', *New Society*, 26 (Apr. 1973), 181–3.

—— 'Domestic Service and the Working-Class Life Cycle', *Society for the Study of Labour History*, 26 (spring 1973), 10–13.

—— 'The Rationalization of Housework', in Diane Leonard Barker and Sheila Allen (eds.), *Exploitation in Work and Marriage* (1976), 125–51.

—— 'Class and Gender in Victorian England: The Diaries of Arthur J. Munby and Hannah Cullwick', *Feminist Studies*, 5/1 (spring 1979), 86–141.

—— 'Mastered for Life: Servant and Wife in Victorian and Edwardian England', in Pat Thane and Anthony Sutcliffe (eds.), *Essays in Social History*, ii (1986), 126–50.

DEPAUW, JACQUES, 'Illicit Sexual Activity in Society in Eighteenth-Century Nantes', in Robert Forster and Orest A. Ranum (eds.), *Family and Society* (1976), 145–91.

EARLE, PETER, 'The Female Labour Market in London in the Late 17th and Early 18th Centuries', *Economic History Review*, 2nd ser., 42/3 (1989), 328–53.

FAIRCHILDS, CISSIE, 'Female Sexual Attitudes and the Rise of Illegitimacy: A Case Study', *Journal of Interdisciplinary History*, 8/14 (spring 1978), 627–67.

—— 'Masters and Servants in Eighteenth-Century Toulouse', *Journal of Social History*, 12 (1979), 367–93.

GEORGE, DOROTHY M., 'The Early History of Registry Offices', *Economic History*, 1 (1926–9), 570–90.

GERARD, JESSICA A., 'Invisible Servants: The Country House and the

Local Community', *Bulletin of the Institute of Historical Research*, 57/136, (Nov. 1984), 178–88.

GILLIS, JOHN, 'Servants, Sexual Relations and the Risks of Illegitimacy in London 1801–1900', *Feminist Studies*, 5 (Feb. 1979), 142–73.

GREEN, J. A. S., 'A Survey of Domestic Service', *Lincolnshire History and Archaeology*, 17 (1982), 65–9.

HARRIS, OLIVIA, 'Households and their Boundaries', *History Workshop Journal*, 13 (1982), 143–52.

HIGGS, EDWARD, 'The Tabulation of Occupations in the Nineteenth-Century Census, with Special Reference to Domestic Servants', *Local Population Studies*, 29 (1982), 58–66.

—— 'Domestic Servants and Households in Victorian England', *Social History*, 8/2 (May 1983), 201–10.

—— 'Domestic Service and Household Production', in Angela V. John (ed.), *Unequal Opportunities: Women's Employment in England 1800–1918* (1986), 125–50.

—— 'Women, Occupations and Work in the Nineteenth-Century Censuses', *History Workshop Journal*, 23 (spring 1987), 59–80.

HUFTON, OLWEN, 'Women in Eighteenth-Century France', in R. B. Outhwaite (ed.), *Marriage and Society: Studies in the Social History of Marriage* (1981), 186–203.

—— 'Women, Work and Family', in Natalie Zemon Davis and Arlette Farge (eds.), *A History of Women*, iii (1993), 15–45.

KENT, D. A., 'Ubiquitous but Invisible: Female Domestic Servants in Mid-Eighteenth-Century London', *History Workshop Journal*, 28 (autumn 1989), 111–28.

KUSSMAUL, ANN, 'The Ambiguous Mobility of Farm Servants', *Economic History Review*, 34/2 (May 1981), 222–35.

MCBRIDE, THERESA, 'Social Mobility for the Lower Classes: Domestic Servants in France', *Journal of Social History* (autumn 1974), 63–78.

MARSHALL, DOROTHY, 'Domestic Servants of the Eighteenth Century', *Economica*, 9 (1929), 15–40.

MENDELS, F., 'Family Forms in Historic Europe: A Review Article', *Social History*, 11 (1986), 81–7.

POLLOCK, LINDA, 'Living on the Stage of the World: The Concept of Privacy among the Élite of Early Modern England', in Adrian Wilson (ed.), *Rethinking Social History* (1993), 78–96.

PROCHASKA, F. K., 'Female Philanthropy and Domestic Service in Victorian England', *Bulletin of the Institute of Historical Research*, 54 (1981), 78–85.

RICHARDS, E., 'Women in the British Economy since about 1700: An Interpretation', *History*, 59/197 (1974), 341.

RICHETTI, JOHN, 'Representing an Under Class: Servants and Proletarians in Fielding and Smollett', in Felicity Nussbaum and Laura Brown (eds.), *The New Eighteenth Century* (1987), 94–8.

ROBERTS, MICHAEL, '"Words they are Women and Deeds they are Men": Images of Work and Gender in Early Modern England', in L. Charles and L. Duffin (eds.), *Women and Work in Pre-Industrial England* (1985), 122–80.

—— '"Waiting Upon Chance": English Hiring Fairs and their Meanings from the 14th to the 20th Century', *Journal of Historical Sociology*, 1/2 (June 1988), 122–80.

SELESKI, PATTY, 'Women, Work and Cultural Change in Eighteenth and Early Nineteenth Century London', in T. Harris (ed.), *Popular Culture in England c.1500–1850* (1995).

SIMON, DAPHNE, 'Master and Servant', in John Saville (ed.), *Democracy and the Labour Movement* (1954), 160–200.

SIMPSON, VIOLET, 'Servants and Service in Eighteenth-Century Town and Country', *Cornhill Magazine*, 14 (1903), 398–409.

TADMOR, NAOMI, '"Family" and "Friend" in *Pamela*: A Case-study in the History of the Family in Eighteenth-century England', *Social History*, 14/3 (1989), 289–306.

THOMAS, KEITH, 'The Meaning of Literacy in Early Modern England', in Gerd Bauman (ed.), *The Written Word: Literacy in Transition* Wolfson College Lectures 1985 (1986), 97–131.

WRIGLEY, JULIA, 'Feminists and Domestic Workers', *Feminist Studies,*, 17/2 (1991), 317–29.

Unpublished Theses and Papers

BURNETT, M. T., 'Masters and Servants in Literature', D.Phil. thesis, Oxford, 1989.

HIGGS, EDWARD, 'Domestic Servants and Households in Rochdale 1851–71', D.Phil. thesis, Oxford, 1979.

MELDRUM, TIM, 'Ubiquity and Visibility: Domestic Service in London, 1660–1750', paper given at the Economic History Society Conference (Apr. 1993).

—— 'Domestic Service in London, 1660–1750: Training for Life or Simply "Getting a Living"', paper given at a conference on Women's Initiatives in Early Modern England, 1500–1750 (4 June 1994).

Index

Aberdeen 86
Acorn, George 205
Acton, William 100
Adams, Samuel and Sarah 25–6, 230
Adelaide, Queen 205
Addison, Joseph 13
Alcock, Thomas 67, 70, 72, 135
Anderson, Michael 16, 70, 115
Andrew, Donna 136
apprentices and apprenticeship 12, 129–34, 139, 141–3, 145, 148–9, 191, 212
Armstrong, Alan 15
Armstrong, Nancy 210, 223
Ashford, Mary 18, 75, 106–7, Ch. 10 *passim*
Ashford, Joseph 191
au pairs 9, 258

Bailey, William 132
Baines, M. A. 128
Baker, John 28, 85, 118–19, 219, 232
Bakewell, Robert of Dishley 117
Barrie, Sir James, *The Admirable Crichton* 253–4
Bath 74, 81–2, 117, 179
Baxter, Richard 229
Bedford and Bedfordshire 16, 215
Bedford, household of the Duke of 27
Bennett, Charles 114
Berkshire 130
Birmingham 11, 60, 118
Blundell, Fanny, daughter of Nicholas 169–70
Blundell, Frances, wife of Nicholas 81, 152–3, 155–7, 159–69
Blundell, Mally, daughter of Nicholas 163, 169–70
Blundell, Margaret 159
Blundell, Nicholas 14, 20, 28, 81, 183, Ch. 8 *passim*
Booth-Ainsley Classification 15
Boserup, Esther 260
Boswell, James 24
Branca, Patricia 29

Breton, Revd Moyle 70, 72
Brighton 14, 197, 202
Brontë, Charlotte 212; *Jane Eyre* 125, 212
Buckingham and Buckinghamshire 16, 113, 219
Burnett, John 23, 94, 105
Burns, Robert 235
Burrell, Timothy 102
Bythell, Duncan 16

Calverley, Sir Walter 76
Cappe, Catharine 31, 131, 134, 145–6, 149
Carpenter, Judith, Case of 123–4
Carpenter, William her brother 123–4
Cartwright, Major John 85
catholics as employers of servants 153–4, 160
Cave, Jane, poet 225, 238
charity schools 74, 129, 131, 136–9, 144–5, 147, 173, 255
charwomen 12, 73, 178
Chelsea 194, 201
Chelsea Royal Hospital 194
Chester and Cheshire 16, 260
christmas boxes servants received from tradesmen 89
Chudleigh, Lady Mary 223
Church Court Depositions 113
Churchill, Sarah 122
Clark, Peter 260
clergy, servants and the 26, 29, 53, 55–6, 65, 69–70, 70, 72, 94–5, 97–8, 121, 135, 143, Ch. 9 *passim*, 198, 201, 219, 232, 256
Cole, G. D. H. 251
Cole, Revd William of Blecheley 29, 65, 67, 175–7, 179–83, 185–9, 214, 219
Collier, Mary, the washerwoman poet 96, 232–3, 241–2, 244–5
Colquhoun, Patrick 6, 37, 42, 98–9, 137

Compleat Serving-Maid, The (1697) 92, 229
Corfield, P. J. 4
Cottle, Joseph 242, 248
Court of Requests, The 197
Cressy, David 231
Crosby Hall, home of the Blundell family 151, 153, 155–8, 160, 162, 164–7
Crowe, Catherine, author of *The Adventures of Susan Hopley* 192–3
Cullwick, Hannah, 44, 57, 107–8, 110, 119, 210–11
Cunnington, Phyllis 18, 30

D'Aeth, Revd Francis of Godmersham 29, 188
Davies, Revd David of Barkham in Berkshire 29, 188
Davidoff, Leonore, 13–15, 17, 31, 37–9, 51, 109–11, 223
Davis, Natalie Zemon 18
Day Schools of industry 138
Defoe, Daniel 2, 111, 121, 127, 129, 165–6, 168, 172
Moll Flanders 190–1, 231–2, 370–1
Delany, Mrs Mary 214
De Quincey, Thomas 111
Derby 16, 159, 162
Devonshire, Duke of 96
Diderot 211
Dodsley, Robert, the footman poet 66, 101, 225, 237, 239, 243–4
Dowton, Samuel 11
Dumfries 235
Dunlop, Mrs Frances 235
Durham 16

Earle, Peter 9, 12, 17, 26, 38, 41–2, 93, 109, 151, 220, 227, 256–7, 260
Ecclesiastical Court Records 257
Edinburgh 59, 86
Edinburgh Review 249–50
Erddig 65
'eroticism of inequality' 50–1, 107–8, 222
Exeter 14

Fairchilds, Cissie 6, 32, 39, 48, 51, 62, 117, 216
Fielding, Henry 46, 209; *Amelia* 113; *Grub Street Opera* 73, 228; *Tom Jones* 51–2, 246

Fielding, Sir John, 69, 98–9, 101
Fielding, Sarah, author of *The Adventures of David Simple* 124; *The History of Betty Barnes* 133, 231
Filmer, Frank 71
Firmin, Thomas 138
Fleetwood, William 101, 231
'followers' 54–5, 62
footmen 84–7, 105, 110, 134–5, 171, 238–9, 244–5, 255
France and the French 7, 13, 17–18, 24–6, 31, 44, 47–8, 60, 62, 84, 104–5, 107, 112, 117, 126, 226–8, 238
Freemantle, Bridget, patron to Mary Leapor 234, 240–1
Fretwell, James 116–17

Gagnier, Regenia 193, 205
The Gazette 83
Gentleman's Magazine 64, 73, 77, 234, 236, 248
George, Dorothy 7, 77, 86, 129–30
Gerard, Jessica, 311–12
Germany 86
Gillis, John 58
Glamorgan 16
Glasgow 87
Gloucester 139, 173
Goodwin, Mr of Tankersley 56, 187
Gough, Richard 116
Graves, Richard 53
Greene, Richard 247

Hall, Catherine 14–15, 17, 37
Hamilton, Duchess of 105
Hampshire 233
Hands, Elizabeth 235, 242–3
Hanway, Jonas 1, 4, 16–17, 27, 66, 77–9, 96, 98–9, 110, 130, 142, 229
Hardwicke's Marriage Act 209
Hardy, Julius 12, 60, 118
Harrington, Lord 75
Harris, Jocelyn 218
Harrison, Rosina 53, 93, 103, 112
Harrison, Susanna 233
Hawthorn, Ruth 31, 110
Haywood, Eliza 217
Heasel, Anthony 216, 230
Hecht, J. Jean 6–7, 9–10, 12, 24, 64–6, 86, 105, 112–13, 146, 151, 215, 235
Hendley, W. 174
Herbert, George 108, 172

Index

Hertford 16
Higgs, Edward 4, 13, 15, 106, 115, 119, 121, 129, 173
Hill, Aaron 211
Hill, Dr, John 216
History of Lavinia Rawlins, The, an anonymous novel 117–18
Hobsbawm, Eric 93
Hogarth, William 85; *Heads of Six Servants* 3; *A Harlot's Progress* 99
Holland 209
Holt, Jane 232
Homer, Philip Bracebridge 235
Houston, R. A. 226
Hufton, Olwen 7, 39, 44, 98, 106, 146, 230, 253
Huntingford, J *The Laws of Masters and Servants Considered* (1790) 73
Hutton, William 11, 125

India 4
'informal economy', the 259
Ipswich Journal, The 23
Ireland and the Irish 18, 139, 253
Ishiguro, Kazuo 251

Jennens, Susanna, Mary Leapor's employer 234
Jenyns, Soame 217
Johnson, Dr. Samuel 221; *Idler* essays 229–30, 233, 235, 246–7
Jones, John, the Catterick butler and poet 83, 237–40
Jones, Revd William, Vicar of Broxbourne 144, 188

Kent, D. A. 47, 103, 107, 226
Kent, Duke and Duchess of 204, 206
Kenya 259
King, Gregory 41–2
kin networks 261–2
Kitchiner, D. W. 230
Knatchbull, Sir Edward 28
Kussmaul, Ann 8, 13, 36, 116, 214

Lady's Magazine, The 217
Lamb, John 237, 245–6, 250
Lamb, Charles, his son 237, 245
Lamb, Mary, his daughter 237
Lancashire 15–16
Lancaster 147
Laslett, Peter 6, 26, 115
Latin America 4, 259–60

Leadbeater, Mary 58, 109, 228
Leapor, Mary or Molly, the kitchen-maid poet 117, 213, 233–5, 247, 240–1
Leavis, Q. D. 212
Leicester 16
Lichfield, Consistory Court of 50
Lincolnshire 16, 36, 215
Little, Janet, poet 235, 239, 250
Liverpool 20, 151–2, 162
London 1, 5, 6, 9, 14, 22, 24, 42, 60, 64–6, 101–2, 116, 133, 140–1, 160, 167–70, 180, 205, 226–7, 232, 236, 238, 240, 242, 246, 321, 335, 353, 362, 425, 449, 453, 458
London Adviser 118
London Chronicle 117, 120, 123, 125, 128–9, 140, 142, 161, 169, 173
London Consistory Court Depositions 452
London Foundling Hospital 225–8, 230, 237, 242–6
London Magazine 126
Lyons 107

McBride, Theresa 30, 37–8, 97, 103, 106–7, 113, 208
McClure, Ruth 142
Macdonald, John, footman 45–6, 52–3, 58–60, 69, 104–5, 171, 231–2
Magdalen Hospital, the 140, 143
Malcolm, J. P., American engraver and topographer 62
Mandeville, Bernard 2, 51, 64, 83, 85, 229
Marcus, Steven 47
marriage 5, 57, 108–9, 116, 143, 147, 174, 178, 202–5, 209–13
Marsh, Revd William 174
Marshall, Dorothy 10, 134
Masters, Mary 241
Mayett, Joseph 237
Mayhew, Henry 73, 75, 171, 173, 227
Mayhew, Augustus 173
Mayo, Richard 12, 111, 226, 229, 231
Maza, Sara 31, 47, 104, 112, 221
Meldrum, Tim 41, 99, 109, 111, 257
Meller, John of Erddig 65
Mendels, Franklin 1, 3, 6, 8

Mendips 137, 140, 230, 249
middle class, changing lifestyle of, and the employment of servants 39–41, 90–1, 147
Middle East 4
midwives 37
Moir, John 44
Montagu, Elizabeth 242, 248
Montagu, Lord Robert 210
More, Hannah 137, 140, 144, 230, 236, 242, 247–50
Morning Post, The 54
Morris, Claver 54, 56, 79, 81, 219
Munby, A. J. 57, 62–3, 96, 112, 210
Munby, Hannah, *see* Cullwick, Hannah
Myddle 11, 50, 107–8, 116, 148, 174

Nairobi 261
Nantes 47, 58
Newdigate, Sir Richard 13, 25, 28, 68, 76, 101, 179–80
Newport 180
New York 4
Nollekens, Joseph 67, 71, 85
Nollekens, Mrs 71
Norfolk 85, 179
Northampton 16, 233–4
North's, Lord, Servant Tax 37–8, 135
Nottingham 15–16, 237
Norwich 175, 180, 182, 186; Consistory Court of 212

Osborn, Lady 120
Oxford 179, 232, 238

Pakistani 4
Paris 32, 99, 107, 266
Pawson, Eric 103
Pennant, Thomas 151
Pepys, Samuel 9, 18, 45–6, 52, 68, 122–3, 127, 134, 151, 220, 254
Pepys, Elizabeth, his wife 45, 52, 122, 151, 220
Pepys, Pall 122–3, 127, 254
Pettingal, Dr Prebendary of Lincoln 187
philanthropy 136, 143–4, 147
Pilkington, Laetitia 241
Pinchbeck, Ivy 7
Pitt's tax on servants 38
Place, Francis 10, 55, 57
Pollock, Linda 91

Portsmouth 89
Powys, Mrs Philip 67
Preston 16, 151
Price, Revd Joseph 28, 70, 122, 187
privacy and the work of servants 40, 45, 90–1
Prochaska, F. K. 128–9
prostitution 51, 99–100, 143, 259, 261
Purefoy, Elizabeth 14, 52, 57, 68–9, 73, 96, 170, 173
Purefoy, Henry 28, 173

Raikes, Robert 139
Reeve, Clara, *The School for Widows* 133, 235; *The Two Mentors* 235
registry offices 216
Richards, Eric 259
Richardson, Samuel, *Pamela* 2, 18, 51, 67, 98, Ch. 11 *passim*, 246, 255
Rickman, John 106
Robbins, Bruce 2, 90–1, 208
Roberts, Michael 113–14
Roche, Daniel 26, 32, 260
Rochdale, Lancs 15–16, 115, 119
Rochefoucault 25, 27, 30
Rogers, Benjamin, rector of Carlton 188–9
Rudd, Sir John 209
Russell family, the 209
Rutlandshire 115
Ryder, Dudley 46, 48, 62

Sale, W. M. 215
San Francisco 4
Scotland and the Scots 16, 18, 85–7, 139, 191, 226–7
Scott, Sarah, *Millenium Hall* 52, 126, 144

SERVANTS:
    allowances: board wages 70–2; clothing 66–8; tea 70; washing 65–6
    categories of: boy servants 33, 68, 101, 174–6, 179–81, 184; casual labour and 'fill-in' servants 12, 35, 158–60, 177–8, 254; farm servants or servants in husbandry 8, 11, 14, 36, 90, 252; kin as servants 20, 34, Ch. 6 *passim*; pauper servants 20, Ch. 7 *passim*; servants employed in inns,

Index

taverns and coffee houses 13, 46, 86, 251; old servants 96–7, 155, 161, 178–9, 199
'characters': 98–9, 168, 218
clothing: allowances 66–8; cast-offs 66–7; employers gifts of 87–9; livery 3, 30, 68–70, 168, 179; *see also under* allowances
conditions: accommodation 44–5; recruitment 11, 23–4, 160–3, 183–4; wages 17, 24–7, 31, 33–4, 65, 75–9, 86–90, 92, 96–8, 148–9, 151, 162–4, 168, 170, 174, 179–80, 185, 197–8, 206, 214–15, 254–5, 257; *see also under* allowances
class implications of: class and service 5–6, 31, 112–14, 146, 195–7, 207; the hierarchy of service 10, 22–3, 151, 156, 170–1, 252–3; identity of servants and its loss 112, 215–18; servility 196; stigma of service 112–13, 196–7, 206–7
crimes and 'misdemeanours': crime 166–7, 185–7; illegitimate births among servants 57–9; infanticide 61; pregnancies 19, 48–51, 57, 59–61, 100, 187; punishment of 78, 101, 105, 131–2, 148; theft among 72–4, 166–7
definition of 11–13, 22, 251–2: 'upstairs-downstairs' model of service 10, 22–3, 253
dismissal of 12, 33–4, 48, 51, 53, 59–60, 94–5, 98–9, 101–3, 165–8, 203, 218; 'a month's wages or a month's warning' 101–3; *see also under* crimes and 'misdemeanours'
education of 195, 206, 212–13, 216, 218–19, 227–40, 242–3, 246–7, 250; by their employers 119, 121, 212–13, 216, 218–19, 229, 231–2, 234–7; servant literacy 20, Ch. 12 *passim*
in the first Occupational Censuses 7, 14, 23, 42, 115–16
images of service: in literature 2, 20–1, Ch. 11 *passim*, 253–4; visual depictions of servants 2–3
in large households 9–10, 15–17, 20, 23, 25–31, 103, 151, 170–1, 178, 195, 215
men and women as 4–5, 8–10, 15–19, Ch. 2 *passim*; differentiation in wages 20, 24–6, 35–6; feminization of service 19, 31–2, 35–9, 41–3; flexibility of function 154–8, 170–1; sexual division of labour 22–4, 26–7
numbers in England and Wales 6–7
numbers in London 6–7, 16
in one-servant households 9–10, 16–17, 23, 32–5, 41, 45, 104–5, 151, 171, 193–4, 197–9
prospects: effects of illness and disease 95–7; 'out of a place' 94–5, 97–104, 196–7, 200–1, 218; possibility of social betterment 105–6, 207–8, 224; provision for old age 96–7, 206; savings 97, 198, 205–6; sending savings home 98, 215; security of service 93–4
relations with employer: ill-treatment of servants 74–6, 101, 105, 131–2, 142, 149, 198–200, 207 *see also under* crimes and misdemeanours; between masters and servants 2, 6, 10, 17–18, 23, 35, 38, 47, 53–6, 64–5, 88–92, 190, 219–24, 227; relations between mistresses and servants 5–6, 17, 33–4, 38, 51–3, 64–5, 218–20
resistance and revolt of: riots involving servants 86–7; signs of resistance 1, 25, 38–9, 64, 77–8, 82–9; threat to footmen as occupants of theatre galleries 1, 84
sexual relations: servants and prostitution 51, 99–100, 143, 259, 261; sexual frustration of servants 19, 62–3; vulnerability of female servants Ch. 3 *passim*, threats from masters to female servants 19, 44, 47–51, 56, 132, 187, 202, 209, 220–2
work: housework and household technology 8–9, 39–41; range of work 1–2, 10–11, 14, 17, 33–4, 40–1, 46–7, 170–1, 179–82, 198, 201–2; service as unproductive work 8

Settlement Examinations 125, 255, 257
Sharpe, J. A. 61

Shaw, Benjamin 147
Shenstone, William 111
shona women of Southern Rhodesia 261
shopkeepers as employers of servants 16, 32
Shropshire 119, 174
Sitwell, Sir George 234
Skinner, Revd John, the Somerset rector 29, 47–8, 50, 55–6, 61, 74, 97, 121, 135, 174, 177, 232, 256
Smith, Revd Sydney 26
Smollett, Tobias, *Humphry Clinker* 66, 73
Society for Promoting Christian Knowledge 144
Southern Rhodesia, servants in pre-colonial 261
Southey, Robert 237, 239, 249
Stapley, Anthony, of Hickstead Hall 69, 75
Stedman, John Gabriel 54, 56, 70, 73, 95, 101
Steele, Sir Richard 171
Stone, Lawrence 6, 103, 257
Stout, Elin, sister to William 120
Stout, Josias, brother to William 120
Stout, Leonard, brother to William 120
Stout, William, of Lancaster 120–1
Strutt, Eliza 68
Strutt, Jerediah, the Derbyshire hosier 68
Stuart, D. M. 22, 122
Sunday schools 129, 137, 139–40, 144, 173–4, 230
Sunday School Society 140

Tadmor, Naomi 221
Taxes on servants 37–8, 135 & n. 29
Tayler, William, footman 238
Taylor, Ellen, poet 236, 239
Thicknesse, Philip 57–8
'Third World', the 4, 8, 259–61
Thomas, Sir Keith 226
Thomlinson, Revd John 54, 116
Thompson, Edward 65
Thompson, Flora 215
Thompson, Gladys Scott 86
Todd, Janet 216, 222
Townley, James, *High Life below Stairs* 84

Trimmer, Sarah 74, 136–7, 146
Trusler, Revd J. 29, 70, 74, 101, 172, 179
Turner, Revd Edward 85
Turner, E. S. 128
Turner, Thomas, of East Hoathly 33, 48–9, 59, 80, 119, 123, 209

United States, the 8

Veil, Colonel de 84–5
Vicinus, Martha 249

Wakefield, Priscilla 146, 250
Waldron, Mary 236 n. 54
Wales and the Welsh 16, 18, 42, 139–40
Walkowitz, Judith 100
Wall, Richard 115
Walsh, J. H. 23
washerwomen 12, 61, 70, 177–8, 195, 232–3, 239, 242, 253
Wedgwood, Josiah 12
West, Jane, poet and novelist 243
West Africa 259–60
West Riding 16
Whatman, Susanna 28, 46, 65, 71–2
Wiseman, Jane, poet and playwright 241
Wodehouse, P. G. 251
Wollstonecraft, Mary 126
Woodforde, Revd James 29, 50, 53, 56, 65, 69–70, 80–2, 94–5, 97–8, 135, 174–6, 179–89
Woodforde, Nancy 175, 184
Woodward, Revd George of East Hendred 29, 116, 175, 177–8, 181–4, 188–90
Workhouse Schools 130, 135, 138, 146
Wortley Montagu, Lady Mary 208, 211, 214
Wright, Sue 17
Wright, Thomas, of Birkenshaw 125
Wright, William, Recorder of Oxford 232
Wrigley, Julia 8

Yearsley, Ann, the milkwoman poet 236, 239, 242, 247–50
York and Yorkshire 15–16, 28, 98, 140
York Grey Coats School 131, 145–7
Young, Arthur 36